The Dialogic Classroom

The Dialogic Classroom

Teachers Integrating Computer Technology, Pedagogy, and Research

Edited by

Jeffrey R. Galin
California State University, San Bernardino

Joan Latchaw
University of Nebraska at Omaha

National Council of Teachers of English
1111 W. Kenyon Road, Urbana, Illinois 61801-1096

Manuscript Editor: Bonny Graham

Production Editor: Kurt Austin

Interior Design: Tom Kovacs for TGK Design

Cover Design: Loren Kirkwood

NCTE Stock Number: 11459-3050

Library of Congress Cataloging-in-Publication Data

The dialogic classroom: teachers integrating computer technology, pedagogy, and research/edited by Jeffrey R. Galin and Joan Latchaw.
      p.   cm.
    Includes bibliographical references and index.
    ISBN 0-8141-1145-9 (pbk.)
    1. English philology—Study and teaching (Higher)—Technological innovations. 2. English philology—Study and teaching (Higher)—Data processing. 3. English philology—Study and teaching (Higher)—Research. 4. Information technology. I. Galin, Jeffrey R., 1961– .
II. Latchaw, Joan, 1944– . III. National Council of Teachers of English.
PE66.D53 1998
428'.007—dc21   98-41102
                                            . CIP

Contents

III Writing as a Social Act

IV Reflecting Dialogically

Foreword

Gail E. Hawisher
University of Illinois at Urbana-Champaign

Cynthia L. Selfe
Michigan Technological University

We consider this book an important contribution to the profession of English studies because it helps teachers identify strategies for acting productively in the face of social changes that are so rapid and far-reaching that they threaten to paralyze us with fear and inaction. As the twentieth century draws to a close, we find ourselves very much in need of such advice. Our own classrooms—and those of most of our colleagues— seem to be populated by students who see little connection between traditional literacy education and the world problems that they currently face—the continuing destruction of global ecosystems, the epidemic spread of AIDS and other diseases, terrorism, war, racism, homophobia, the impotence of political leaders and the irrelevance of political parties.

Faced with these challenges and with others of equal magnitude, many faculty teaching in English studies programs find themselves scrambling to rethink and redesign educational efforts within expanded ethical contexts that recognize vastly different global perspectives, learning how to function with an increasing sense of responsibility in new and taxing economic parameters, and acknowledging and then addressing the need to learn a range of rapidly changing technologies that allows for an expanded network of communication and intellectual exchange.

But these projects are complicated endeavors. And they do not promise easy success. Moreover, we often find ourselves, as teachers of English, ill-prepared to take on many of the tasks involved in these efforts. Most teachers of English, for example, have come of age in a print generation, and our thinking has both been shaped and limited by this fact. Few of us are equipped to function effectively and comfortably in virtual literacy environments. Indeed, like many citizens, English teachers are just beginning to learn what it means to function effectively within a society that is dependent on computer technology for literacy activities. We are only beginning to identify, for example, the complexity of the challenges posed by such a society, including the challenge of adapting to an increasingly rapid pace of change. Nor do we necessarily have the lived experiences that allow us to deal productively with this climate of change.

As a result, we often find ourselves trying to educate students for a world with which we, ourselves, are unfamiliar and about which we remain uncertain. In her 1970 book *Culture and Commitment*, Margaret Mead describes the unsettling sense of functioning within such a cultural milieu. In this work, she calls cultures of this kind "prefigurative." The prefigurative learning culture occurs in a society in which change is so rapid that adults are trying to prepare children for experiences the adults themselves have never had. The prefigurative cultural style, Mead argues, prevails in a world in which the "past, the culture that had shaped [young adults'] understanding—their thoughts, their feelings, and their conceptions of the world—was no sure guide to the present. And the elders among them, bound to the past, [can] provide no models for the future" (70).

Mead traces these broad patterns of cultural change particularly in terms of American culture, all the while setting her analysis within a global context. She claims that the prefigurative culture characteristic of the United States in the 1970s—and, we maintain, in the '80s and '90s— is symptomatic of a world changing so fast that it exists "without models and without precedent," a culture in which "neither parents nor teachers, lawyers, doctors, skilled workers, inventors, preachers, or prophets" (xx) can teach children what they need to know about the world. Mead notes that the immediate and dramatic needs our prefigurative culture faces—fueled by increasing world hunger, the continuing population explosion, the rapid explosion of technological knowledge, the threat of continued war, and global communication—demand a new kind of social and educational response that privileges participatory input, ecological sensitivity, an appreciation for cultural diversity, and the intelligent use of technology, among other themes.

In the prefigurative society, Mead notes, students must—at least to some extent—learn important lessons from each other, helping each other find their way through an unfamiliar thicket of issues and situations about which the elder members of the society are uncertain. As teachers in such a culture, our education contributions must take a dramatic turn. Unlike previous generations of teachers, we cannot promise to provide students with a stable and unchanging body of knowledge—especially in connection with technology use. Indeed, we cannot even provide ourselves with such intellectual comforts.

What we can do, as Galin and Latchaw point out so insightfully in this volume, is to model for students one possible way of approaching the unknown—a dialogic strategy for teaching and learning that we and they can apply productively not only to technology-rich problems but also to a range of situations. The tenets of this approach, as Galin and Latchaw describe it, are based on the work of Mikhail Bakhtin, who understood language itself as a field of creative choices, conflicts, and struggles.

In committing to a dialogic vision of education, the two editors note, teachers and students dedicate themselves to reseeing their situations by "disbanding their habitual orientations" and learning to "restructure and reexamine" conflicting sets of "perception and understanding." Dialogic teaching and learning involve, in part, an openness to the unknown and a rejection of stale or habitual approaches to education, especially within contexts that involve technology. These strategies, based on "small scale, interactive project-based teaching," reject the automatic gesture of turning to teaching and learning methods received from past situations. Instead, dialogic education seeks to instill, in both teachers and students, the habits of rethinking educational goals, critically examining generalizations and received wisdom, remaining open to taking risk and to embracing the challenges presented by uncertainty, and reflecting critically on students' responses to learning within the context of the social needs they identify and the literacy experiences they value.

The dialogic classroom, then, involves teachers and students in a collaborative effort to try and then to evaluate various approaches to teaching and learning, to make sense of the increasingly technological world and the contexts within which humans live and work. To succeed in establishing this kind of classroom, at least three things must happen. First, teachers must learn to become increasingly astute observers of students, and, second, students must learn to participate more actively and responsibly in their own education. Finally, all parties have to learn the importance of reflecting critically not only on their educational efforts in general but also on their uses of technology and the educational ends this use is designed to accomplish.

The teachers and authors contributing to this volume add voice and substance to this philosophical approach; they demonstrate the value of seeking understanding in unfamiliar places and learning in new ways, especially when using technology—of continuing to take risks even when those risks produce results that are unsatisfactory in some way. Given that we ourselves are uncertain of the directions that education will take in the coming century, we commend this approach—and this collection— as a productive and thoughtful one from which other teachers and learners are sure to benefit.

Work Cited

Mead, Margaret. *Culture and Commitment: The New Relationships between the Generations in the 1970s*. New York: Doubleday, 1970.

Acknowledgments

As University of Pittsburgh graduate students, we began our ten-year collaboration, meeting on a weekly basis to discuss assignments within a course sequence that Joan Latchaw developed. We continued this collaboration with a computer application called The Borges Quest, which provided us opportunities to develop our personal and professional relationships further by presenting at conferences and developing this collection. The inspiration guiding our quests over these years can be attributed to the strong philosophical and pedagogical directions we developed at the University of Pittsburgh. It is no accident that Dr. William L. Smith served on both our dissertation committees; in fact, his quintessential question—"What can computers do that can't be done in other ways?"—has inspired and informed our work in computers and composition over the last decade.

Many Pitt voices "let us hear" a critique of our own assumptions and confronted us with alternative positions. We are indebted to David Bartholomae, whose presence in the English Department and in the field of composition has profoundly shaped our professional lives. With his encouragement and support, we have developed course sequences for all levels of writing. Like Bartholomae, we are "continually impressed by the patience and goodwill of our students" (See "Inventing the University" in *When a Writer Can't Write*, edited by Mike Rose. New York: Guilford Press, 1985.). Some of them, like Ron in Chapter 3, are collegial voices that challenge our ways of thinking. We also thank William E. Coles Jr. for his expertise in sequencing, reflected in *The Plural I, Composing and Revising*, and *What Makes Writing Good?* Our assignments, classroom activities, and technological innovations engage students in term-long projects that support reflective and critical pedagogy. The experimentation necessary for creating suitable environments for this work involves courage and risk. The Pitt program allowed us the luxury of occasional failure along with the successes.

We thank our contributors for their courage in risking the technological and pedagogical failures always inherent in experimental projects and for discussing the accompanying benefits and liabilities honestly and openly. We hope our readers will use the experience and knowledge in these pages to begin their own quests.

Our vision for this book began years ago in a hotel room when Joan visited Joan Huntley to discuss a computers and writing workshop that Latchaw and Galin were co-organizing. After some discussion, Huntley came up with a prospective book title, based on the collected experiences of our workshop presenters. This discussion became the impetus for this volume. Nearly two years later, Dawn Rodrigues would suggest an alternative title that enabled us to clarify our vision by emphasizing the dialogical nature of integrating technology into teaching.

This vision was further strengthened by the gentle intellectual prodding of our editor, Michael Greer. Collaborating with an academic publisher has been a rare and fruitful experience. Michael's belief in the theory, contributors, and readership of *The Dialogic Classroom* has inspired us to explore relentlessly the Bakhtinian framework. Our colleague Ron West generously pushed our struggle forward by challenging us verbally and graphically throughout the dialogical process. Thanks for reading and collaborating on numerous drafts. R. S. Krishnan and Richard Bovard, Joan's colleagues at North Dakota State University, helped us resolve the struggle by reading and commenting on numerous drafts of the introduction and by discussing Bakhtin's notion of dialogism. Wade King, one of Joan's graduate students, was another willing colleague who spent days editing many chapters and constructing the glossary. Thanks also to Sharon Cogdill for helping us speak to a diverse audience.

Our appreciation extends to the entire computers and writing community both online and face to face. Many listservs such as ACW, Rhetnet, and MBU have provided a wonderful forum for intellectual exchange, friendship, and collegiality. In fact, neither the workshop that gave rise to this collection nor the book itself could have succeeded had it not been for the generosity and encouragement of a range of experts in the field who were willing to support the work of two unknown graduate students.

Finally, we would like to thank our families individually for their untiring support and encouragement. Thanks to Karen Galin for her love, support, and patience with Jeff as he worked to finish his dissertation, this book, and a range of other projects.

Thanks to Joan's sister, Sharon Garber, who guided her through the conception and design of The Borges Quest and to her brother-in-law, Bill Garber, for warmly accepting her into the household throughout the project. Thanks to her son, Greg Latchaw, for his many hours working on The Borges Quest in its beginning stages and for providing computer assistance when needed. Andy Latchaw gave his mom wisdom when he advised, "Mom, you shouldn't separate your life from your work." Ron West's loving support sustained me throughout this process. Last, but not least, thanks to Joan's own mother, Geraldine Fineberg, whose devotion, loyalty, love, and confidence in her daughter's abilities have remained unswerving.

I Framing the Dialogue

1 Introduction

Jeffrey R. Galin
California State University, San Bernardino

Joan Latchaw
University of Nebraska at Omaha

Like all editors, our aim is to bring together a set of texts that speak to a group of people with overlapping goals and interests. Our group, committed to integrating computer technology into writing classrooms, considers itself part of a "computers and writing" community. Within the confines of this printed text, this community also includes a diversity of voices and perspectives; some chapters are more theoretical, some highly pedagogical or methodological, and others more technical. In performing this editorial function, we do not expect adherence to or acceptance of all our principles. In fact, we invite readers, outside the confines of the text, to extend, challenge, and/or support the ideas presented here through their own philosophies, languages, and teaching practices. This book exists to strengthen our community—of high school teachers, community college instructors, technical writing professors, university academics, basic writing faculty, ESL faculty, and so on. Some of us have considerable experience with computer technology, some have very little, some are intrigued but skeptical, and some are die-hard enthusiasts.

This volume addresses those teachers who are interested in integrating computer technology into their classrooms but who may not have institutional support for computer software development, knowledge of available hardware and software to fulfill their specific classroom needs, or sufficient experience with the technology. Many teachers are not fully aware of what programs have been developed, how they are used, or why instructors use them. Others who are more familiar with technology are faced with a plethora of educational software that may suit their academic needs, but don't know which to choose. Given these restrictions, few teachers have had the opportunity to develop software for their classrooms or have even conceived of the possibility. The contributors to this volume offer a range of approaches for and address concerns of teachers who either want to develop programs for their classes—despite the limitations that may exist—or learn what others have done with commercially available software. The essays we have solicited for this volume reflect our belief that computer programs used in college and high school courses should serve pedagogical purposes, not just teach a technical skill or decrease the teacher's workload. We offer this book and its corresponding World Wide Web homepages (http://www.ncte.org/dialogic) as both resource and forum—to learn, think, and talk about the role of computer technology in various writing class-rooms.

The concept of dialogism that Bakhtin articulated in "Discourse in the Novel" undergirds the print and electronic forms of our text in two important ways. Dialogism is essentially social, and it operates through discourse that is comprised of various languages. Language (according to Bakhtin's theory of stylistics in the novel) is stratified (multivocal) into its "social dialects, characteristic group behavior, professional jargons, generic languages, languages of generations and age groups, tendentious languages, languages of authorities, . . . languages that serve the specific sociopolitical purposes of the day" (262–63). Each of these languages is spoken by different groups of people, each with their own ideologies, philosophies, and agendas. Bakhtin argues that various languages spoken by characters (and the narrator) in certain novels enrich the text, especially as they intersect, challenge, or even overthrow each other (291). Although Bakhtin uses dialogism to redefine stylistics in the novel—by breaking down diverse speech types into social dialects, group behavior, professional jargon, tendentious languages (263)—we use dialogism to explore "links and interrelationships" among teachers, students, researchers, technologists, computer enthusiasts, and computer phobics.

Borrowing Bakhtin's theory of discourse, we argue that individuals and subgroups in our computers and writing community have varying pedagogies, teaching styles, learning styles, jargon, and strategies informing and influencing their language. Each has its own sociopolitical agenda and various degrees of interest in and knowledge of computer technology. Some "speak" the language of research, some speak in "techie" jargon, and some use teacherly language. Others represent the voice of administrators or the student body. These various—and often conflicting—discourses can rub against each other, revealing underlying ideological assumptions. They may intersect within a single individual or between different people in a conversation (dialogue); as Bakhtin explains, "Dialogue may be external (between two different people) or internal (between an earlier and a later self)" (427). For instance, a student–teacher interaction (external dialogue), demonstrating a failure or success, might lead to an internal dialogue that calls into question certain elements of a teacher's pedagogy, which might in turn lead that teacher to undertake further research. Such dialogues result in critical inquiry on the part of teachers—which may mean rethinking the very fabric of the course. What is the nature of the course? Why is the technology being introduced? What can the computer do that cannot be done in other ways? What implications, consequences, and results might be expected in the computer-facilitated course?

Stratification into these various languages and positions is an ongoing *process* whose purpose is, according to Bakhtin, to "challenge fixed definitions" (433). As editors, one of our roles is to "coordinate these stratifying impulses" across the volume while highlighting their boundaries when we can. Contributors serve a similar role within each of their chapters as they offer a unifying narrative of their experiences and call attention to these separate "impulses" at the same time. By merging the discourse of teacher and critic, contributors examine both successes and failures of technology, which should enable them to revise and refine their pedagogy and practice. Your role as readers, in dialogue with us and our contributors, is to "find, reject, redefine a stratum of [your] own" (433).

In fact, at the end of this chapter we perform a dialogic reading of the essays in this book, whereby we find both unifying and disunifying trends—what Bakhtin calls centrifugal and centripetal forces (272). As we discovered common patterns and principles within the following chapters, we also set the chapters against each other, evaluating opposing views and questioning the validity of our own claims. We invite *all* readers to engage our text dialogically, whether supporting and extending or challenging and disrupting the theory and practice of integrating computer technology into writing classrooms—as we understand that process. We hope that the resulting discourses will intersect with each other in interesting ways as they appear on the Web site. Thus, like Bakhtin, we celebrate the social nature of discourse. We continually remind ourselves that technology is about people, specifically those in education. As our title suggests, teachers begin with a context (the classroom) and become agents in the act of integrating technology into the classroom.

The essays in this collection reflect our belief that computer technology should be integral to the primary work of a course. Because teachers have different goals and purposes, we discourage importing programs, assignments, and technologies under discussion into another classroom or adopting another teacher's approach. Rather, we offer detailed examples as resources for educators concerned about the issues and problems they might face in integrating technologies into their classes. Our aim is to encourage teachers to improve computer-facilitated education as a mode of learning by building on cognitive issues in their fields and making computers extensions of their classrooms. By cognitive issues, we mean the theoretical and pedagogical imperatives driving the course, such as collaborative learning, critical inquiry, disciplinary assumptions, and research methods. When computers extend and even transform the classroom, they help students progress in the primary work of the course.

The development of Litigation Strategies is a case in point. Many newly practicing attorneys criticize their education, which has traditionally focused on theory and research. One researcher noted a serious gap in the education of lawyers, a majority of whom complain that the study of law has little to do with the practice of law. Notwithstanding moot court, learning how to deal with living, breathing clients happens as a kind of apprenticeship—on the job. Although this failure is common knowledge among attorneys, who have obviously discussed the problem, their language has not "intersected" with that of administrators and law educators. Tradition has held firm. In the last decade, however, some law professors have responded by asking critical questions of their programs.

To develop more effective practitioners, a team of experts from Harvard Law School and the Harvard Graduate School of Education collaborated with the Rochester Institute of Technology to develop Litigation Strategies, a computer simulation program in videodisc technology.[1] The program (referred to as a "strategy game"), which exploits a cognitive style of learning, was designed as a highly interactive hypermedia program. In using sound, video, still frames, and text (at the bottom of the screen), this program represents Bakhtin's "professional stratification of language" (289). According to Bakhtin, "Literary language—both spoken and written—although it is unitary . . . is itself stratified and heteroglot in its aspect as an expressive system, that is, in the forms that carry its meanings" (288). These forms in the program— the textual (memos, cases, complaints, a database of information) and the visual–aural (the client's facial expressions, the legal assistant's tone of voice, the witnesses' body language)—"knit together with specific objects and with the belief systems . . . and points of view" (289). By interacting with the program's "system," the first-year law students became novice practitioners who were able to integrate, "knit together," prior classroom knowledge with experiential knowledge—professional points of view, belief systems, and language features.

The developer of Litigation Strategies explained in an interview that students, working in pairs, learn through interactive case studies, interviewing techniques, problem-solving strategies, and courtroom procedures how to relate to clients, develop a case, and file a complaint in court. The students loved playing this strategy game and sometimes had to be pried from their workstations so others could participate. Thus, in the case of law school, the gap between theory and practice is slowly being narrowed by curricular reform. Litigation Strategies has served a vital function in the education of prospective lawyers both because it has been adopted by other schools (i.e., Duke University) and because it is a model for radically new pedagogies. For instance, Harvard Law School has dived headlong into multimedia, developing eleven new programs. Development of the prototype, Litigation Strategies, was possible because (1) there was a vital need for it in the curriculum, (2) nothing like it existed on the market, and (3) the necessary design team was available. As this case demonstrates, integrating computers into curricula sometimes provides unique opportunities for students who might otherwise lack experience in their chosen fields.

However, most teachers will not be provided with design teams, substantial financial support, or sufficient time to develop a program like Litigation Strategies. In order to help teachers develop their own programs with minimal support or take advantage of preexisting software, the contributors to this book explain and demonstrate different user-friendly authoring and communications systems—specifically HyperCard, Storyspace, Netscape, Netnews, Confer, Daedalus, CommonSpace, MOOs, and other forms of Internet technologies and computer-mediated communications (CMCs). It is important to realize that these teachers-developers might never have conceived of their work without the availability of such authoring and communications software.

These technologies and their applications offer attractive and exciting opportunities to revitalize student learning. However, adopting them without the critical reflection of internal dialogism can be counterproductive. Without a sound pedagogy, adopting software might prove less efficient than traditional techniques. One of Latchaw's composition students had used Grammatik,[2] a computer program designed to help users identify and correct grammar and error problems, to work through one of his essays. When he then sat down with Latchaw, they spent over an hour focusing on every potential problem the program highlighted even though she was only concerned with his use of comma splices. There was no pedagogical reason for this student to be testing his entire essay for grammatical integrity. In fact, his use of Grammatik was counterproductive because he spent so much time on every issue Grammatik identified. Furthermore, he still did not understand what comma splices were or how to correct them. Latchaw had to teach him to identify them, and once she did, he could find and correct them on his own.

Grammatik's design operates on the assumption that the user understands the reasoning behind his or her own patterns of error. The developers have somehow ignored or been unaware of what composition theory has taught us about the existence and remediation of error. Mina Shaughnessey and David Bartholomae, in their groundbreaking work on error, have demonstrated that recognizing patterns of error and understanding their underlying logic are essential for writers because the surface of the text cannot recapture the intended meaning. Unless students understand the underlying logic of their own sentence structures, they are unable to "see" what the teacher sees or understand the concept behind a rule of syntax.[3] This example demonstrates that computer technology might prove inefficient and labor-intensive.[4] For this reason, we argue that the language of the teacher should be in dialogue with the language of the researcher. The sociopolitical agenda of software marketers often eclipses these other languages that address learning styles, learning theories, and teaching strategies.

The problems with Grammatik can occur even with theoretically informed and well-designed software, especially if it is not well integrated into the work of the course and does not encourage users to re-envision their practices. When they ask the questions we posed earlier, teachers activate the dialogical process in which goals, purposes, and expectations may undergo a radical shift:

What is the nature of the course?

Why is the technology being introduced?

What can the computer do that cannot be done in other ways?

What implications, consequences, and results might be expected in the computer-facilitated course?

In asking why technology is being introduced, teachers might discover that their methods (like many computer programs) are overly prescriptive, conflicting with process models of composing. Such a discovery might in turn lead to a critical inquiry that opens the door to risk and change. Over the past decade, for instance, many computer advocates have extolled the virtues of electronic mail (e-mail) and conferencing exchanges, which they have used across disciplines in numerous ways. From a social-construction point of view, this technology is theoretically sound. In computer-networked composition classrooms,

> the students . . . are supposed to write directly to each other regarding topics and material under discussion. In such an environment

> there are no isolated authors, no privileged texts, only actively en-
> gaged co-equal readers and writers. In this regard, the networked
> classroom . . . represent[s] a new form of social interaction . . .
> (Tuman 84).

Proponents of networked classrooms argue that such environments promote decentered classes, help nonverbal students express themselves,
and encourage collaborative work. Such claims have encouraged teachers to experiment in exciting ways with e-mail, conferencing and synchronous chat software, and virtual-reality environments available on
the Internet.

However, like the Grammatik example, bringing the technology into
the classroom is not necessarily a productive use of time and resources
for either students or teachers. For instance, we have seen pages and
pages of student-generated "conversation" from online logs that is gos-
sip or idle chatter rather than serious discussion on class topics and issues. Although there might be several interesting points embedded in
these sessions worth exploring for discussion, are they worth the time
and resources necessary to cull them out? Teachers and researchers have
been discussing these dilemmas and finding ways to revise their courses
so that the outcomes more nearly match the kind of computer-facilitated learning we advocate. To make computer conversations more effective, some teachers have asked students to print out class or group
transcripts and look for productive moments. Students extract threads
running through the dialogue, which they then outline, analyze, and
eventually critique. These higher-order activities keep students on track
and increase their critical-thinking abilities.

Teachers using the technology to increase critical thinking are less
likely to overglorify or expect more of the technology than they make
possible within their own pedagogies. In addition to asking the kinds of
questions that we raised earlier, these teachers are also likely to follow
Cynthia Selfe's advice about integrating technology into their own classes
in ways that reflect larger departmental and institutional goals. Selfe
explains that if computers are going to be an integral part of composition classrooms, they must be "influenced by an English program's philosophical values" (77).[5] If an English department's focus is collaborative
writing, then well-designed conferencing software can be useful in extending[6] existing classroom practices. For instance, a program modeled
after the University of Wisconsin's Studio Method, which is completely
collaborative (peer response), might well be strengthened using a text-
sharing program such as CommonSpace; however, a more teacher-cen-
tered classroom might not. Teachers using such technologies might also
assess whether students actually *do* become better thinkers, readers, and

writers as a result. We need more research in this area. These considerations are especially important for teachers using commercially developed software, because the pedagogy can seldom be imported with the
software. Thus, there may be heavy burdens on teachers, who must be
prepared to revise assignments, adjust pedagogies, give up previously
held assumptions, or even redesign an entire course. Critical inquiry, as
we define it, occurs on two levels, then: reconceiving the course and
reconceiving the *way* software engages students. The dialogic–critical
inquiry cycle is a dynamic process that will ultimately lead to stronger
pedagogies and stronger students.

It follows, then, that educators who are knowledgeable about the theories, research, and practices of their disciplines can best determine the
pedagogical and philosophical relevance of computer software and hardware. We have chosen contributors to this book (representing a range of
writing courses across several disciplines) who will discuss their theoretical positions and rationales for incorporating computer technology
into their coursework as a way to create better teachers and stronger
students.

By stronger students we mean those who engage in critical inquiry
and become inventive investigators who think insightfully, creatively,
analytically, and critically. Sometimes this process involves reading,
writing, thinking, and revising in various stages and over a period of
time. Other times it involves collecting data, examining emerging patterns, testing hypotheses, and developing methods of analysis. In still
other cases, it means knowing where and how to locate appropriate
materials and engaging in appropriate modes of discourse for specific
audiences.

The most effective computers and writing teachers use technology's
potential to strengthen students' interpretive, analytical, and problem-
solving skills. In some cases, computer-designed activities minimize or
eliminate problems previously unresolvable. In thinking about better
ways to teach the Borges short story "Pierre Menard, Author of *Don
Quixote*," Latchaw began to see connections between HyperCard's cross-
referencing capabilities, Borges's style, and reader interaction.
HyperCard's structure was powerful for Latchaw as a novice application designer because she could funnel students' attention toward a particular issue, facilitating recursive thinking while preventing cognitive
overload. Each issue can be built into its own "stack" with relative ease,
even for a novice. HyperCard's metaphor for design structure is a stack
of cards. At the most global level, a "stack" designates a group of "cards"
through which users can choose their own pathways. Each card represents a hypertextual "node," which is a screen full of information with

buttons, fields, and images for users to click on or read from as they move from node to node. Creating these stacks is relatively simple because the templates for all components (buttons, fields, etc.) already exist and because the scripting language that controls all of the program's functions is close to natural language and easy to learn. Latchaw was committed to developing the program because HyperCard's structure supported her pedagogy and even strengthened it.

A similar situation occurred with Grigar's Stein Project, a program designed to help students explore Gertrude Stein's *Tender Buttons* (see Chapter 2). Grigar's goal was to motivate and interest students in poetry that is commonly "ignored in most college curricula" because it is obscure, nonlinear, and confusing. The experimental nature of the poetry motivated Grigar to build an experimental program in Storyspace. Students could easily explore relationships between objects in poems and what critics said about those objects, and then add (input) their own ideas and reactions. Storyspace's metaphor is that of a web. Like HyperCard, Storyspace allows users to build multiple story spaces, or nodes, that are linked together into a hypertextual network of paths. Unlike HyperCard, however, Storyspace nodes are created with a single click of the mouse, and links are made dynamically with two clicks. Storyspace is more object oriented than HyperCard as HyperCard relies heavily on its scripting language. Because Grigar wanted to emphasize the objects in Stein's work, this program was the more appropriate choice. Storyspace also manipulates text much more easily than HyperCard (although HyperCard allows for more complicated structures). Grigar's web is so large that the ease of making links was a major decision factor. We particularly wanted to include Grigar's work because it is pedagogically sound, has been used successfully in the classroom, and is messy. The positive effect on students (becoming active readers, adding to their body of knowledge, forming collaborative groups, becoming devoted Stein followers) demonstrates that novice designers *can* use technology to improve learning even if design rules (see Chapter 6) are not strictly followed.

Although using computer technology as a mode of learning requires some investigation of software and design issues, it also means wrestling with hardware choices and availability. Will the system handle the program? Is the lab networked? Will there be sufficient technical support? These issues are explored in the chapters written by the teacher-designers. For instance, Latchaw and Galin had some difficulties in converting The Borges Quest from a PC to a networked system. Students were frustrated because they kept getting knocked off the network, some sections did not work, and network security features required Galin to restructure all writing components in the program. Latchaw and Galin were fortunate in that support staff was available for troubleshooting and problem solving. Eventually, these glitches were ironed out but not without a great deal of time and effort.

One way to encourage staff support is through a university or collegewide computer committee. A committee that is cross-disciplinary, representing both content areas and technological services, can support computers as a mode of learning when strong pedagogies are stressed and explored. At Shepherd College, such a committee will be basing future technology purchases on the soundness of the pedagogies. The committee is also exploring ways to encourage teachers to use computer technologies for their own projects. It is difficult to sell the idea to students when the teachers are not comfortable with and committed to experimenting with computer technologies. Another committee at Shepherd (the Pedagogy Committee) has awarded several grants that included hardware purchases: one to a biology professor for a cell biology class (the program shows the movement of chromosomes and other intercellular structures) and the other to a communications professor developing multimedia projects based on a phenomenological approach.

Other considerations involve time and space management. Will students have open labs and unlimited access to classroom labs, or will they have to share facilities with other classes? If the latter, the teacher may have to create a tightly structured schedule to accommodate everyone's needs. If remote communications are integrated into the course, will students have access to the accounts they need *when* they need it? Is the system too busy or overloaded? Do students have access from dorms or from home?

Another issue for instructors new to teaching with computers is whether to develop the program for their unique classroom contexts or for a commercial market. Most teachers will not be able to create publishable software. And even if they do, marketing should be a secondary concern. Deciding not to go commercial changes the nature of the work. For instance, in designing programs for the classroom, developers need not be overly concerned with polishing, obtaining copyright permissions, or reaching wider audiences. Furthermore, the teachers can focus on integrating the application into the work of the class. There may be secondary professional benefits. Some universities are beginning to count program development as scholarly work and/or service to the college.[7]

The biggest drawback to producing applications for the commercial market is that the kind of critical inquiry we advocate in this book is unlikely to occur. One only has to review commercial programs to test the validity of this statement. A large percentage of published software merely reproduces what already exists in print form: handbooks, text-

books, tutorials, and manuals. Sometimes such software is even counterproductive, as the Grammatik example demonstrated. These are the
kinds of programs that make Ted Nelson anxious about the glorification
of computer technology. Most of us, he says, lack a "deep understanding," one that will allow us to relate alternative structures, which Nelson
and other theorists see as necessary for learning (qtd. in Tuman 47).

One way of achieving that deep understanding is to explore the metaphors we use in imagining computers as a mode of learning. We have
been arguing that teachers need to examine their goals and purposes,
but we would add yet another reason: Conscious or not, the metaphors
we use determine the theoretical basis for our pedagogies and classroom practices. This is especially true when teachers consider bringing
computer technology into humanities classrooms, because the metaphors
of technology have been inherited from other disciplines. A case in point
is the tool metaphor, which has been inherited largely from computer
technology. Supporting this notion is the term *computer-assisted instruction* (CAI), which has dominated the area of educational computing and
implies that the computer is a teacher's helper, carrying out the related
roles and duties.

By nature, any metaphor is both enabling and limiting. It highlights
certain aspects of reality and conceals others. We do not mean to suggest that computers are not or cannot be tools. But this metaphor has
serious limitations. First, the term *tool* emphasizes the singularity of its
function. Some speak of computers as a writing tool, some as a tool for
thinking, some as a tool for transcribing, and some as a tool for revision.[8] Researchers and theorists usually employ only one of these metaphors. If, for instance, we say that computers are tools for revision, we
conceal their cognitive function.

Second, the importation of technology via the tool metaphor is likely
to mean the accompanying importation of a technique. And as many
researchers have pointed out (Nelson, Joyce, Kaplan, Sullivan, Hawisher,
Selfe), the techniques are commonly mechanical. "Traditionally, the view
of the computer as a tool, an implement as uncomplicated as a hammer,
has prevailed. The tool metaphor understands computers as simple and
predictable devices" (Hawisher and Eldred 110). Our favorite example
is an online grammar handbook, demonstrated at the 1991 Convention
of the Conference on College Composition and Communication, in which
glitzy images of broken cars represented fragmented sentences. Such
sensational graphics represent the image of the computer as "helpmate"
or "assistant" to teachers, thus concealing its function as an agent of
change (Sullivan 45).

As teachers, researchers, and programmers, we need to think critically about our metaphors. To return to Bakhtinian dialogics, each of
these roles and discourses must be considered in light of the others. How

do the metaphors that drive us as teachers relate to those that inform our research? And how can this interaction of meanings lead to a greater whole that enables us to become "agents of change"?

One answer to these questions is to imagine metaphors as ways to think. Creating strong metaphors, those that Max Black defines as interactive, fosters *new* ways of thinking. Black says the

> two subjects [terms of the metaphor] 'interact' in the following ways: (a) the presence of the primary subject incites the hearer to select some of the secondary subject's properties; (b) invites him to construct a parallel implication-complex that can fit the primary subject; and (c) reciprocally induces parallel changes in the secondary subject. (qtd. in Ortony 29)

Black then contends that "a metaphorical statement can sometimes generate new knowledge and insight by *changing* relationships between the things designated (the principal and subsidiary subjects)" (qtd. in Ortony 37). Ted Nelson spent years searching for the secondary subject he called *hypertext*; generating this term precipitated the development of a whole new field. The advent of hypertext has radically changed curricula, modes of learning, and teacher and student behaviors in many notable cases. Twenty years later, educators, inheriting the term from Nelson, are exploring its potential.

Only in the past few years have researchers begun stepping back to question the metaphor and examine its limitations. Michael Joyce, co-designer of Storyspace, has qualified the metaphor by defining *exploratory* and *constructive* hypertexts.[9] Joyce made this distinction in imagining the kind of work he wanted to do with his students. This is precisely what teachers need to do in bringing such forms of technology into the classroom. The point is, however, that one teacher's strong metaphor might be another teacher's weak one. For instance, we might want to question whether *exploration*, a common pedagogical term, is in fact a strong metaphor. What kinds of thinking has it enabled? Although it invokes the concepts of adventure, newness, depth, and alternative thinking, the *way* it is interpreted will determine whether real change in the classroom takes place. Metaphors are not *naturally* interactive; they become interactive only if we make them so. By the same token, we want to acknowledge that the tool metaphor can inspire generative ways of thinking, especially if applied dialogically. (See Grigar on Stein, Chapter 2.)

We have emphasized metaphorical, dialogical, and critical thinking to help teachers strengthen their pedagogies, research, and productivity by using computer technology. In asking contributors to discuss how integrating computers into their courses has strengthened teaching (*and* limited it), we hope to inspire and guide others into the world of technology. Because theory is not enough, however, we offer practical examples that have been used and tested. We hope that reading about other teachers' theories and practices will help our readers imagine how their own goals might be better served and how some pitfalls might be avoided.

Chapter Dialogics

In organizing this volume, we grouped the chapters based on technological similarities. Part II, "Teacher as Programmer: How, Why, So What?", highlights hypertext and hypermedia applications, while Part III, "Writing as a Social Act," emphasizes asynchronous communications and the role of collaborative learning. Although we have claimed a dialogic approach to technology, an interaction of multiple discourses and perspectives (including teaching, pedagogy, and research), we ask you, as readers, to draw your own conclusions based on the narratives, experiences, and projects under discussion—to speak back to the multiple voices, test them against each other, make connections to your own experience and ideologies. Explore for yourselves whether the chapters actually demonstrate a greater degree of dialogism, as we have defined it. Or is a new form of dialogism emerging?

We begin such an investigation by attempting to intervene in the master narrative or unifying impulse of the book's structure. We hope that the following analysis of trends, issues, gaps, and dissonances across chapters and sections will invite our readers to respond dialogically.

Integration

We have argued that computer applications should be integral to coursework and grounded in pedagogy. When new technological elements are introduced, the class structure changes, affecting the objectives and goals of the course itself. These changes may have a wider impact than on a single classroom, as teachers share their successes with colleagues, obtain grants for enhancing department or university facilities, and provide their students with computer-related experiences that are transferable to other learning contexts.

On examining our claims about integration across the chapters, we found that each teacher's rationale for incorporating technology had a clear pedagogical basis. Yet some projects were implemented more easily or more seamlessly than others. Grigar's Stein Project (Chapter 2) and Harrington and Condon's psychology stacks (Chapter 5) might best support the integration claim because, first of all, the applications directly responded to crucial problems, which were clearly defined. Grigar used the Stein Project to overcome a resistance to difficult course material, a major obstacle to learning. Harrington and Condon designed the psych stacks because psychology students were failing to complete their reports successfully. Second, the implementations were relatively efficient and effective because the designers understood course principles and had technological experience. We found that successful integration involved both technological and pedagogical expertise.

Latchaw and Galin's program, The Borges Quest (Chapter 3), was designed to help students read a difficult short story by Jorge Luis Borges. Having been developed by Latchaw and then implemented by Galin, integration was more difficult. At first Galin was unsure how the program would enhance the course. Furthermore, because it was a prototype when he started working with it and he had no prior experience using Macintosh machines, much less HyperCard, he found that adapting the program for the network and eliminating the bugs were unexpected problems that could not be resolved quickly. And because he used the program only to supplement the course, it had limited value for his students. As Galin modified the program, he made it more integral to the course, and, as a result, it began to serve the purpose Latchaw originally intended.

Doerfler and Davis's Confer Project (Chapter 9), a collaboration of teachers and students across five distant universities, began as a theoretically sound project but ended up being difficult to implement for a variety of reasons. Ultimately, logistical and technological problems changed the nature of the course in unexpected but positive ways. In this case, the technology transformed pedagogy, contradicting our premise that pedagogy should precede technology. Such contradictions often arise as print-based theories are superimposed on previously unimagined digital pedagogies. We encourage readers to reveal other gaps or inconsistencies they discover within these chapters or in dialogue with their own experiences.

Hypertext

Many designers, researchers, and theorists generally contend that constructive hypertexts provide more powerful learning environments than do exploratory hypertexts. In reviewing the chapters, we asked ourselves whether "good" hypertexts were always or should be recursive, user controlled, and open rather than more multilinear, guided, and closed. On what basis should we judge the success of a particular hypertext application? Harrington and Condon's psych stack is highly structured according to a series of linear strategies, which practitioners of psychology generally follow. Each section guides students through a strategy (Materials and Methods, Results, Analysis) corresponding to cognitive difficulty. The closed and guided nature of the hypertext, based on practitioner knowledge and pedagogy, increased student performance significantly precisely because of the linearity. The Stein Project, the most open hypertext discussed in the book, is partially exploratory and partially constructive. It was equally successful because students were given the freedom to make associative links, and they began to analyze and synthesize difficult literary material on their own. Many members of the class became lovers of Stein's work and good critical thinkers, which was Grigar's main goal in integrating the program. In this case, user control was an essential factor in student learning. However, the degree of openness had drawbacks; the hypertext was so collaborative that Grigar could not recover the original document. Furthermore, the potential for information overload was, at times, daunting and even risky.

The Borges Quest, though less open than the Stein Project, is guided at some points to avoid cognitive overload, to frame issues and problems, and to focus students' attention on reading strategies. The segments are not structured to teach a particular process, like the psych stack, but to help students investigate a difficult literary text. Like the Stein Project, The Borges Quest was intended to increase critical thinking skills and prepare students to write critical essays. However, it has been criticized because some segments are linear and program driven.

In some respects, the psych stacks (and to a lesser degree, The Borges Quest) might be considered a CAI application. Though we do not suggest that CAI applications should serve the computers and writing community at large, we argue that they can prove valuable in certain contexts. Harrington and Condon, trained in English departments, enlarged their spheres to include other disciplines, that value more traditional pedagogies than some included in this volume. Despite violating what is generally considered hypertext protocol for educational uses, the psychology students achieved remarkable success.

Trent Batson's graduate students, in "Rhetorical Paths and Cyber-Fields" (Chapter 10), theorize hypertextuality in its various forms and applications. They concur with our observations that linear and nonlinear hypertexts have different purposes that might be equally effective. They make interesting connections between hypertext and CMC, question the potential of hypertext communication, speculate on hypertext's effect on reading and writing, and envision new hypertext genres.

The explosive growth of the World Wide Web (WWW) within the past few years has supported such claims. Only a few years ago, hypertext theorists such as Michael Joyce, Jay David Bolter, and Stuart

Moulthrop claimed the superiority of constructive hypertexts based on authoring software such as HyperCard, Toolbook, Macromind Director, and Storyspace. The WWW has nearly replaced these aging technologies by virtue of its wide distribution, highly adaptable nature, information processing capabilities, and ability to provide a new and universal hypertext environment.

Bruce Dobler's journalism class (see Chapter 4) reflects the possibilities and limitations of this burgeoning domain. The hypertextual nature of the WWW is changing the way we interact, think, read, and write. As part of their curricula, students are being asked to design Web sites, engage in computer-mediated discussions, and share their essays, research, and ideas online. The very nature of academic discourse, genres, and conversation is being studied and re-envisioned.[10]

Collaboration

The computers and writing community generally privileges social construction of knowledge and, by extension, collaborative models of learning. Network and postmodern theory are commonly used to theorize these positions and practices. We have noticed that the essays in this volume generally support this common view of collaboration.

It is interesting to note that seven chapters were collaborative in the design, instruction, or implementation of the courses, and five chapters were co-authored. Most contributors incorporated technology to broaden students' experience (beyond the classroom), develop a sense of community, or enrich their knowledge. In the technical and nonfiction courses (Chapters 4, 8, and 11), students were either communicating with real experts in their fields, contributing documents for university publications, or simulating team projects in the workplace. The Internet, listservs, and e-mail transformed the nature of these classrooms. Michael Day's and Bruce Dobler and Harry Bloomberg's students have made contacts for jobs and research projects. For many students and teachers, collaborative learning erased boundaries: between school and the "real world," between students and teachers, between students and their peers, between experts and novices.

However, some of these gains resulted from confronting failures, renegotiating goals and expectations, and accepting unexpected outcomes. For instance, Tharon Howard insists that his chapter "is not intended to be a celebration of these four tools, nor are the projects . . . intended to serve as models of how to teach using these four tools." Instead, he emphasizes what did not work and highlights those issues central to collaborative projects in technical writing. By refusing to accept computer technology as an educational utopia, Howard analyzed weaknesses in technology and pedagogy; he used this information to create more effective learning environments for future collaborative projects.

For instance, he found that, while networked computer labs facilitate learning in some respects, ironically, they interfere with typical forms of social interaction. "[C]ontextual cues that students take for granted in traditional classrooms" are "strip[ped] away, . . .forcing students to state goals and assumptions that normally remain implicit" in those class-rooms. This weakness in the technology meant that "almost every aspect of [the] project's process had to be articulated and negotiated among students on each collaborative team. . . ." Students "learned more about . . . project management than [Howard] could ever have taught them in the traditional lecture/presentation classroom format" (212). Another incident proved equally instructive. When students used e-mail to share their résumés, they instantly lost boldface, italic, and font features. As a result, students became aware of the sound design principles Howard had been emphasizing. The limitations of e-mail foregrounded the form–content relationship that became visually apparent.

In addition to the three categories we have identified here, the chapters in this book might also be examined by considering how each use of technology can facilitate different kinds of practices. For example, Chapters 7 and 9 both assume that, as Kemp says, "Networked computer-based writing instruction is based on a rhetorical or social dynamic in writing." Yet Kemp's class emphasizes student writing and collaborative workshopping to the exclusion of outside texts, while Doerfler and Davis's interuniversity project worked hard to identify shared readings and projects to stimulate writing on the theme of liberal education. Noting how specific technologies and class experiments presuppose certain pedagogical practices can lead to revealing comparisons.

The dialogic nature of this text also offers interesting possibilities for analysis, unlike many books with Web sites currently available on the market. Our Web site (http://www.ncte.org/dialogic) features most of the supporting documents and related materials for the classes described in these chapters. The site includes syllabi, course descriptions, hand-outs, and software screen captures, as well as links to other online classes and resources. This breadth of materials provides the kind of rich context that books in print usually cannot afford to offer. Rather than using the WWW primarily to link related issues, our goal is to provide deep documentation and enable further research. We provide the raw data for each learning context discussed in addition to a range of related courses and resources already available online.

However, we use the research–database metaphor advisedly. In the spirit of a Bakhtinian dialogue, we invite readers to expand and enhance our Web site. Submitting additional links and materials via the interactive chapter forums and to authors' e-mail addresses will create additional voices, as multiple meanings and perspectives extend or resist the common view. We also hope to receive abstracts for work in other computer-facilitated classes to be considered for new chapters in a follow-up volume and expanded Web site.

We hope that this print–electronic publication will provide the kinds of interaction that forge "agents of change" as technology is incorporated into courses. If it encourages a dialogic of constant interaction among practitioners and the roles they play—pedagogue, researcher, programmer, end-user—then teachers will be more reflective and students will be better able to inquire critically, solve problems, and make decisions. If these interactions occur, then our primary goals will be achieved.

Notes

1. John Ciampa of the Rochester Institute of Technology developed this interactive videodisc program in collaboration with attorneys and Harvard Law School students. The program plots users' pathways as they solve their cases; it also allows users to follow an expert's pathway as a means of comparison. Initially, students could substitute Litigation for a class on the ethics and practice of law. Ciampa reported that students had to be pried from their chairs to give others a chance. The program was adopted by Duke University but has not been expanded because the platform used to design Litigation no longer exists.

2. There has been much controversy over this program. Some educators find it a useful tool and others an impediment.

3. Works such as Mina Shaughnessey's *Errors and Expectations*, David Bartholomae's "The Study of Error," and Barry M. Kroll and John C. Schafer's "Error Analysis and the Teaching of Composition" are seminal because they develop *philosophies* of error, not merely remedies by which mistakes can be classified and "fixed"; in fact, there can be many different causes for the same error. In many cases, only a tutor or teacher well trained in these causes (which can only be determined in face-to-face contact) can begin to diagnose what the problem is, why it occurs, and how to approach it. At this point in time, computers are not intelligent enough to make such assessments.

4. The controversy about grammar checkers has resurfaced in a recent e-mail exchange. Some teachers critiqued Grammatik for "rarely detecting comma splices," catching "so many nonerrors that students were confused," and "over-valuing the software's suggestions." The program rather than the student then becomes the decision maker, a pedagogically unsound practice. Some suggestions were to (1) include the teacher in the process in order to guide students toward decision making and to explain the origin of their errors and the limitations of the program, (2) use Grammatik as a supplement to handbooks and the

classroom, (3) use Grammatik as a proofreading tool for experienced writers only, and (4) consider adopting MLA's Editor, a software program geared to problems that college-level writers encounter. Editor tracks MLA style guidelines, common usage problems, gender-based terms, and clichés rather than performing syntactic analysis. It also has authoring capabilities, whereby the teacher can add documentation and advice.

5. Selfe advocates teacher-designed labs, even when teachers are technological neophytes. In *computer* labs, the computers come first; in *writing* labs, the writing comes first (8). Teachers should never lose sight of their primary goals and purposes. "Course content, including the purpose and structure of specific writing assignments, should shape the extent of computer support for any given writing-intensive task" (62). Sometimes teachers have to plan for unexpected changes, including radically revising assignments.

6. We caution developers about employing the "extension" metaphor, which too often results in the kinds of imitative programs we have demonstrated. However, Selfe's use of the term is more cognitively applied. In *Creating a Computer-Supported Writing Facility*, Selfe implies (though she does not directly state) that transformation may occur as a result of computer technology. We build on the idea of transformation in this volume.

7. At the 1993 Computers and Writing Conference (Ann Arbor, Michigan), this issue was discussed. Since that time, MLA has been working on a policy statement encouraging colleges and universities to acknowledge faculty involvement with technology for promotion and tenure purposes, and an NCTE committee has been formed to address these concerns.

8. Joan Latchaw conducted several interviews at Shepherd College on teachers' understanding and use of the tool metaphor. One respondent, a highly theoretical thinker, discussed Heidegger's hammer as a mental tool. It may be that more conceptual thinkers use the idea of "tools" to better advantage than do concrete thinkers. More research on this subject is indicated.

9. Drawing on the pioneering work of Vannevar Bush and Theodor Nelson and theories of cognition and artificial intelligence, writers such as Michael Joyce and Jay Bolter have identified two primary uses of hypertext: exploratory and constructive. Although Catherine Smith names them "passive" and "active" and Johndan Johnson-Eilola and Stuart Selber call them "contracting" and "expanding," each of these writers is referring basically to the same things. The first, and most common, Joyce defines as a "delivery or presentation technology . . . which encourages and enables an audience to control the transformation of a body of information to meet its needs and interests." He further explains that the transformation should include "a capability to create, change, and recover particular encounters with the body of knowledge, maintaining these encounters as versions of the material, i.e., trails, paths, webs, notebooks, etc." (*Sirens* 11). Netscape, the World Wide Web client software, functions as exploratory hypertext because it is designed precisely for exploring the Internet more efficiently. It works quite simply by offering a textual backbone with hot words and images.

Constructive hypertext, on the other hand, enables "scriptors" (a metaphor Joyce borrows from Jane Yellowlees Douglas) to develop a body of information that they map according to their needs, their interests, and the transformations they discover as they invent, gather, and act on that information. More so than with exploratory hypertexts, constructive hypertexts require a capability to act: to create, to change, and to recover particular encounters within the developing body of knowledge (11).

Rather than merely adding links to an already existing network of nodes, constructive hypertexts invite scriptors to design their own webs. Joyce explains further that "Constructive hypertexts, unlike exploratory ones, require visual representations of the knowledge they develop. They are, in Jay Bolter's phrase, topographic writing." See Chapter 2 for examples.

10.   Fred Kemp responded to a message on ACW-l sent by Linda Record, raising questions about the benefit of syllawebs. An excerpt from his response follows:

> Date: Fri, 12 Apr 1996 08:16:44-0500
>
> Actually, Linda, I see value in placing all aspects of a course on the web, including the syllabus, readings, student essays, grading criteria, grade distribution, and so forth. Check out http://english.ttu.edu/courses/1302/kemp/sp96/
>
> I haven't found the ready willingness to participate in the course because of the web that you describe (or, frankly, I expected), but that may be because I've tried something different, restricted much of the synchronous interactivity that I usually employ in favor of a sort of online task progression model in an attempt to make such a course as clear and as straightforward to those outside our knowledge community as possible. (The students are doing the work and increasing their facility with both words and the technology, but I don't think it's as much fun for them as it has been in the past.)
>
> We spend a lot of time improving our instruction (silly us) but not much time at all in translating what we are doing for those who don't have our backgrounds or expertise but who nevertheless have firm intuitive expectations about what we are supposed to be doing. Just as our students form for us a rhetorical constituency, so does the grim laity outside the door. Syllawebs and webbed course materials may serve both, but the juggling act gets profoundly more difficult.
>
> I always thought that classroom networks were going to lead to the salvation of writing pedagogy; now I feel that the Internet may lead to the salvation of the writing course itself, by publishing our efforts to the world. Society has not yet reached the critical mass of Internet users for such a dynamic to have much effect, and we still have too few courses online, but it's coming, for sure.
>
> Fred Kemp
> Texas Tech
> f.kemp@ttu.edu

Works Cited

Bakhtin, Mikhail. *The Dialogic Imagination: Four Essays by M. M. Bakhtin*. Trans. Caryl Emerson and Michael Holquist. Ed. Michael Holquist. Austin: University of Texas Press, 1981.

Bartholomae, David. "The Study of Error." *College Composition and Communication* 31 (1980): 253–69.

Ciampa, John. Personal Interview. 15 October 1994.

Hawisher, Gail, and Janet Carey Eldred. "Studies in Computer Mediated Communication and the Social Sciences: What Do They Offer Compositionists?" *Presentation Summaries from Ninth Conference on Computers and Writing*. Ed. Bill Condon et al. Ann Arbor: The English Composition Board, 1993. 109–13.

Hawisher, Gail E., and Cynthia L. Selfe, eds. *Evolving Perspectives on Computers and Composition Studies: Questions for the 1990s*. Urbana: National Council of Teachers of English, 1991.

Joyce, Michael. "Siren Shapes: Exploratory and Constructive Hypertexts." *Academic Computing* (November 1988): 10–14+.

Kaplan, Nancy. "Ideology, Technology, and the Future of Writing Instruction." Hawisher and Selfe, 11–42.

Kroll, Barry M., and John C. Schafer. "Error Analysis and the Teaching of Composition." *College Composition and Communication* 29 (1978): 243–48.

Ortony, Andrew, ed. *Metaphor and Thought*. Cambridge: Cambridge University Press, 1979.

Selfe, Cynthia L. *Creating a Computer-Supported Writing Facility: A Blueprint for Action*. Houghton, MI: Computers and Composition, 1989.

Shaughnessey, Mina P. *Errors and Expectations: A Guide for the Teachers of Basic Writing*. New York: Oxford University Press, 1977.

Sullivan, Patricia. "Taking Control of the Page: Electronic Writing and Word Publishing." Hawisher and Selfe, 43–64.

Tuman, Myron C., ed. *Literacy Online: The Problems (and Perils) of Reading and Writing with Computers*. Pittsburgh: University of Pittsburgh Press, 1992.

II Teacher as Programmer: How, Why, So What?

2 What Is Seen Depends on How Everybody Is Doing Everything: Using Hypertext to Teach Gertrude Stein's *Tender Buttons*

Dene Grigar
Texas Woman's University

Out of kindness comes redness and out of rudeness comes rapid same question, out of an eye comes research, out of selection comes painful cattle.

—Gertrude Stein, *Tender Buttons*

When I opened up class discussion about Gertrude Stein's *Tender Buttons*, my students responded with silence. On pressing them to talk about the assignment, many of the bolder students finally admitted that they had absolutely no idea how to read this poem. "What does it mean," one asked, "this 'painful cattle'?" These same students had very little difficulty discussing other modern poets found in their textbook. But this outside assignment, this slim volume of poems by a poet named Gertrude Stein who was not included in the required anthology, proved to be too obscure for their comprehension. "Oh, yes, I've heard of her. 'A rose is a rose is a rose,' right?" another brightly exclaimed. Who can blame these undergraduates for not understanding Stein when her work still remains an enigma to most scholars and critics?

For a literary figure who exerted so much influence on her contemporaries and followers, Stein is generally ignored in many college curricula. And probably for a good reason. Scholars such as Randa Dubnick point out that Stein's experimental approach to writing confounds the reader by its subversion of grammatical norms (Dubnick 28). Stein admits that her commitment to experimentation has as its underlying principle an "intellectual passion for exactitude in the description of inner and outer reality" (Stein, *Autobiography* 198). This process of description breaks from traditional conventions of writing and results in a somewhat cryptic writing style that is uniquely Stein's. So the question arises: How does a teacher of literature, a devotee of Stein's poetry, inspire students to read and love Stein's work? Determination to achieve this goal led me to teach Stein's *Tender Buttons* with hypertext, which resulted in my learning the value of hypertext as an instructional writing environment for the classroom.

During the previous semester, I had become fascinated with Stein's writing after reading a book of her selected writings. In particular I was drawn to *Tender Buttons*, a highly personal work in which Stein conveys her delight in sharing domestic life with Alice B. Toklas. *Tender Buttons* is divided into three distinct parts, each containing numerous poems. The first part, Objects, contains 108 poems, each describing various articles that Stein may have seen in and around her home. The next part, Food, consists of four sections. The first two poems, "Roastbeef" and "Mutton," serve as an overview of the entire first section. The second section of Food focuses on breakfast, the first meal of the day, and it contains eight poems. The third section of Food is called Lunch, which is the largest meal of the day for Europeans. The section contains twenty-seven poems, each describing a particular kind of food Stein may have eaten during that meal. Last, we find Dinner, which contains fourteen poems. The third part of *Tender Buttons* is called "Rooms," which is also a single poem that centers on rooms and those objects found in them.

At the time I was reading Stein's poem, I was in the midst of a hypertext project for translating parts of Homer's *Odyssey*. It occurred to me that the difficulty I was encountering in interpreting Stein's poetry is similar to the problems a translator faces when approaching a foreign text. Because hypertext provided an excellent environment for comparing and analyzing relationships between words in the *Odyssey*, I decided to design a hypertext program for *Tender Buttons* that would help me examine similar relationships among objects in Stein's poem.

Working with the hypertext software called Storyspace, I inputted parts of Stein's poem (specifically the first section, Objects), along with criticism surrounding the work, into spaces the software program makes available. I then linked passages within the poem that exhibited similar motifs or concepts and connected these passages to criticism that offered insight into the poetry. The result was a simple but thorough electronic document that was both intratextual and intertextual. The explorer of this Stein hypertext could navigate around the various spaces, reading her work, the comments made by scholars, and the multiple connections that I had made.

Working with Storyspace in this way expanded my understanding of Stein's poetry and engaged me in a way that was extremely compelling. For example, in order to visualize the ways in which Stein had structured *Tender Buttons*, I randomly chose four poems from Objects to link together with Storyspace's link tool. Positing that Stein structured the poem by building relationships among words or concepts she frequently repeated, I categorized these "relationships" by types, identified as specificity (colors, kind, pointing, description); spatiality (length, distance);

"visualness" related to seeing (clear, dim); negation (no, not, nothing); indeterminacy (if, order, cohesiveness); being/becoming (is, was, come, comes); orientation (out of, away); inclusivity (all, whole); and conjoining (and). Once I had done this, I looked for these relationships in the poems "A Blue Coat," "A Red Stamp," "A Carafe, That Is a Blind Glass," and "A Box." Then I made links among the poems with these words and concepts (see Figure 2.1).

After completing this task, I opened the box that contained "A Blue Coat," chose "color" from the text, and, using the navigate tool, shifted to the box containing "A Red Stamp," to which the color "red" had been linked. By clicking on any of the words describing "relationships," I could maneuver around the poems without stopping—in some cases, by following a circular path through all of the poems. I began to see that Stein's objects share specific qualities; however, on closer examination, I also became aware that these same objects never lose their individuality no matter how many qualities they have in common. For example, the poems "A Red Stamp" and "Red Roses" share a common color (red) and a description of cut flowers in need of being replaced. However, the white "lily" (with a woody stem to keep it upright in the container) leaves a

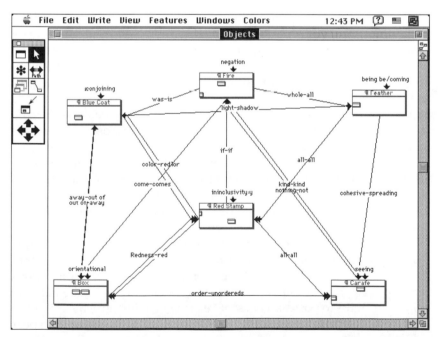

Figure 2.1. Links between Poems from Objects

dusty "red stamp," or red pollen, on the tabletop and its own white petals as it dies; this differs greatly from the "red rose" (with a less sturdy stem) that merely "collapse[s]." Thus, the ways in which these two flowers wither highlight both their similarities and their differences. Stein's observations concerning these two objects demonstrate her "passion for exactitude." Stein not only makes associations in order to be exact but also to determine differences. In "Composition as Explanation," a work in which Stein discusses her writing, she says, "and then everything being alike then everything very simply everything was naturally simply different and so I as a contemporary was creating everything being alike was creating everything naturally being naturally simply different, everything being alike" (520). Establishing links in the hypertext between Stein's words mirrors the associative quality of Stein's own ideas of meaning-making—that by looking at the common elements of objects, the unique qualities of each become apparent.

Because I had planned to teach my literature course in a networked Macintosh lab, I was looking for ways to incorporate available technology that would assist students in examining texts and ignite their interest in reading. Although I had already decided to include Stein's *Tender Buttons* among my required readings, it occurred to me that I could adopt my hypertext for the class. Being able to include hypertext in my curriculum provided an opportunity for me to investigate its use as an instructional tool. Because I fully expected my students to find Stein's work challenging—even impossible—I was interested in learning if Storyspace would make them more interested in Stein's writing and help them understand her work. Most important, like many teachers who are passionate about their subject matter, I wanted my students to feel the same enthusiasm for Stein that I felt. Allowing them to explore her writing in a hypertextual environment became my strategy for accomplishing these goals.

So that a clear picture of my pedagogy can emerge, it is important to discuss in some detail the electronic environment my literature students were working in. At that time, our lab, which was initially dedicated to writing classes, was comprised of twenty-one Macintosh II CIs networked with Novell Netware Version 3.11. We have been able to incorporate software programs such as Microsoft Word, WordPerfect, Apple File Exchange, HyperCard, and Timbuktoo into our classroom teaching. However, the system developed for establishing electronic folders has been particularly valuable for instructional purposes. The netware allows students to possess a personal electronic folder and be a member of a group folder, into which they can drop off or pick up work, do peer editing exercises, leave messages for classmates or for me, follow along with class discussions, and create or edit documents during class. During the previous fall semester, the department in which the freshman writing classes are housed had purchased copies of Storyspace for a graduate level course in rhetoric. Therefore, the computer technology available for instruction and the multiple copies of Storyspace made it possible to download my Stein hypertext into electronic folders for my students to read and work on individually and in groups. It also allowed me to check the progress of their work during class or later when I was in my office or at home.

To be honest, when planning my course I had been careful not to introduce Stein too early in the semester. Bringing her in midway through the course seemed wise because of the difficulty of her writing. Another advantage that became obvious later was that my students had mastered the computers in the classroom by that time. They were manipulating the Macs, word-processing programs, and electronic folders without much trouble. Consequently, introducing a hypertext document that I had already created did not cause much anxiety for students. In fact, it provided a way for me to teach my students how to maneuver in Storyspace without the intimidation of designing their own hypertext document, and it gave them a model for organizing their own material. However, I was careful to eliminate spaces of my document that contained or pointed to conclusions I had made, thereby allowing students to flesh out their own ideas when working on the project. What I retained of my work, for the most part, were some portions of Stein's poems, a few scholarly texts that discussed Stein's poetry, my bibliography, a glossary of terms, and many of the links I had made. Thus, getting them started on the project was not the major undertaking I feared it would be.

As mentioned earlier, when my students were first introduced to Stein, they floundered, unable to make sense of what they had read. When I realized that no class discussion was going to take place and that they all seemed to be waiting for me to tell them about the poem, I asked them to open the Stein hypertext from their electronic folders. From that point, I gave them basic instructions on how to work with the Stein hypertext and with Storyspace, and I told them they would develop their own hypertext in order to explore Stein. I also made it clear that students would be given ample time to conduct research on Stein and to explore her writing in their work groups, using the hypertext I had already developed to get them started. To assist with their exploration, I pointed them to the bibliography node in the Stein hypertext and to the annotated bibliography (in print form) produced by Stein scholar Maureen Liston. From there my students were instructed to identify parts of the poem and critical works they were most interested in investigating. We agreed on a deadline by which students would have their information inputted into spaces and material linked to their classmates' work. Because I had already organized my class into five groups comprised of three or four students who had been working together from the beginning of the semester on various smaller projects, there seemed to be less pressure on me to be present at every computer station answering technical questions and overseeing their contributions. My students were able to work through problems together and prompt each other to uphold their part of the project.

My plan was simple: Students would read the Stein hypertext and then add their own research and personal insights. Once again the only ground rules I established were that they had to find criticism that would assist their classmates in understanding Stein or *Tender Buttons* specifically, input the portions of the material relevant to the class project into Storyspace (documenting it as they would a printed text), and link their findings to those that other students were bringing in and to portions of the poem itself. I set no limits on the number of contributions they were required to make, nor was I adamant about them claiming authorship of the work they brought to the project. In fact, I thought that naming their work would detract from a smooth reading experience and undermine the collaborative process.

The final result of my class's work overwhelmed me by its scope and sophistication. To be honest, the most important outcomes of the Stein Project are not that my students mastered the technology of hypertext, focused on aesthetic principles when creating the document, and added a lot of information about Stein into electronic writing spaces, although they accomplished all of these things. Instead, they gained something much more valuable to the study of Stein in particular and of poetry in general. The process of linking Stein's own words and the words of various scholars within the hypertext document helped my students to see the larger picture—that is, the process that Stein went through to craft her work. Although they came to some of the same conclusions about the poem that I did, they found their own way. I had simply provided them a model and a space in which to create their ideas. They recognized that poetry, particularly Stein's poetry, was much more than an emotional response to some event; this was a revelation for many of my students who aspired to write poetry. They came to realize instead that poetry was the careful construction of words and ideas. Linking Stein's words to one another had led them to this discovery, and from this experience they could see the texture of her writing for themselves.

The work of one particular group stands out. Collaborating on the poem "A Fire" from Stein's Objects, one group member added the poem to the four other poems in the Objects box I had already created and linked it according to repetition of words and concepts, as I had done. What was interesting about this student's work was that I had not discussed with the class any of my insights on relationships, nor had I left any notation of this idea in my hypertext. However, this student noticed the way I had categorized certain words and linked them to words found in other poems. Comparing the words she selected in "A Fire" (shown here boldfaced) with my own from "A Red Stamp," we see that she understood the strategy I had followed in investigating *Tender Buttons*:

Me:
If lilies **are** lily white **if** they exhaust noise and distance and even dust, **if** they dusty will dirt a surface that has no extreme grace, **if** they do this and it is not necessary it is not at all necessary **if** they do this they need a catalogue.

Student:
What **was** the use of a whole time to send and not send **if** there **was** to be the kind of thing that made that come in. A letter was nicely sent.

Like me, she noticed that "A Fire" shared many of the same qualities the other poems possessed, and she was not afraid to take a risk with her ideas by linking her words to mine.

Another student in the group was bothered by the look of Stein's poetry and worked to structure the visual layout of "A Fire," presenting it in various ways (which she and others named A, B, and C). She created a box for each version and nested these boxes within the box entitled "A Fire," made by the student who had linked this poem with my own (see Figure 2.2). After examining version B, my student said that she noticed Stein had become increasingly more specific in the poem with "What was," "there was," and "A letter was." She believed that Stein moved from the general to the specific, and it was clear to her that specificity was Stein's aim. This insight, then, seemed to be derived from allowing students to play with the text both individually and within the group.

As my students came to understand from their research, Stein challenges us to participate in her subversion of language and to explore the many word relationships that she constructs. Scholar Jayne Walker points out that *Tender Buttons* is both a manifesto and a demonstration of the new mode of writing that it announces: "'Act so that there is no center' (*TB* 498)—this imperative produces a text that enacts the principles of fragmentation and difference and celebrates the freeplay of writing as a combinative game limited only by the systemic laws of language" (Walker xi). This kind of exploration invites active participation in the text and even intervention into its meaning—something that proponents

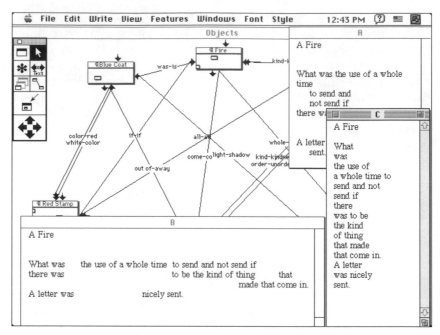

Figure 2.2. Student Restructuring of "A Fire" in Storyspace

of hypertext also maintain is true (Landow 71). And because scholars also claim that hypertext shows particular qualities of language, style, spatial relationships, and hierarchy in writing, hypertext provides an alternative method for analyzing Stein's experimental style, one that my students seemed to enjoy. For instance, a student from the group working on "A Fire" listed all of the nouns found in the poem and then commented that although Stein had used many, she did not use the noun representing the object described. It occurred to this student that Stein was pointing to the object by giving us clues, based on objects and descriptors commonly associated with that object. For him, *Tender Buttons* was a series of conundrums that we were invited to solve—something he seemed to enjoy doing. Although the Stein Project (as it came to be known) produced some minor problems, my students said they enjoyed *Tender Buttons* because they had found exploring the poem with Storyspace to be fun. Success with the project can also be attributed to the informal tone I had set. Using Storyspace seemed to establish an atmosphere of playfulness, which is evident from the way the group exploring "A Fire" collaborated freely with one another without being too concerned about changing Stein's text or linking their work with mine.

It is important to note that my students came to understand that Stein relied heavily on the sense of sight when discussing the various objects, food, and rooms mentioned in *Tender Buttons*. Ulla Dydo tells us that "what she describes is what she sees, which always includes the process of seeing. And the process of seeing is inseparable from the process of saying" (Dydo 44–45). For Stein the empiricist, seeing is knowing. Understanding that Stein's scientific training influences the way she strives to explain phenomena made all of us aware of why her work is not widely understood and has not achieved the prominence it deserves. This kind of seeing is closely connected to the process of doing, something Stein knew innately while writing these works. And this discovery could only have been made if someone painstakingly linked word to word and phrase to phrase, a task undergraduates seldom undertake. My students were able to participate in this activity specifically because Storyspace offers a system that makes large portions of text easier to read, retrieve, and link *and* provides a fluid environment in which users can maneuver comfortably. I am not saying that analyzing Stein cannot be done without Storyspace; however, I do not believe that an enterprise such as linking text within *Tender Buttons* and outside of it to its critical works could be accomplished with the same economy of space and time that hypertext offers. In fact, some of my students mentioned that they had always felt overwhelmed by research, not so much because of the work it entails but because of the problems that arise in organizing material derived from multiple texts. The amount of space (and paper) it would have taken to chart the many associations my students and I discovered in Stein's text would have been too laborious a task to complete in one term without Storyspace.

Although the sense of sight plays a significant role in Stein's approach to poetry, my students also came to realize that as a poet she is concerned with building relationships between words through the use of sound. One particular group studied the restructuring of the poem "A Box" that I had left in one of the spaces, and they commented on some of the internal rhyme:

Out of	kindness	comes	redness and
Out of	rudeness	comes	rapid same question,
Out of	an eye	comes	research,
Out of	selection	comes	painful cattle.

Analyzing alliteration, consonance, and assonance prompted one of the students to remark that the rhyme united the work. Some students noticed that the alliterative repetition of the letter R found in lines 1–3 ("redness," "rudeness," "rapid," and "research") links together these three lines. The last line containing the words "selection" and "painful cattle" seemed odd to them at first when viewed this way, but when my students found the consonance connecting "selection" to "kindness," "redness," "rudeness," "same question," and "research," they suggested that Stein may have connected all of these words in order to emphasize "painful cattle" (which did not seem connected to anything in the poem, further convincing them that this phrase held some magical significance that would unlock the meaning of the entire poem). However, after identifying the assonance that connects "painful cattle" to "rapid same" (which one of my students astutely commented was a reversal of the two A sounds of "painful cattle"), they became more attuned to the poet's careful crafting of words and relationships (see Figure 2.3).

The process of designing a hypertext document seemed to invite my students into the playful spirit of Stein's writing, and they came to love her work because of it. No longer were they daunted by the meaning of "painful cattle" (which they finally decided meant "tanned leather"); instead, they focused on the process she undertook to create poetry like

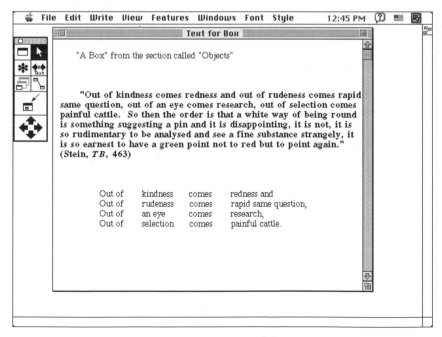

Figure 2.3. Student Restructuring of "A Box"

Tender Buttons. They also became familiar with Stein's relationship with Alice B. Toklas, their vacation together in Spain that inspired this particular work, Stein's training in science, and the philosophies that grounded her experimentation with words—facts and concepts that enriched their understanding of her work. In one particular case, a student who had just finished reading another student's box containing Stein's biography commented that Stein had retained her interest in biology. It seemed to this student that Stein liked to dissect what we see, leaving everything but the object of her attention in place. The student quipped, "Like taking out a heart, but leaving the body." Insights like this made me aware that Storyspace had indeed assisted my students in learning.

At the same time, however, several problems arose while working with hypertext in this way. The most obvious disadvantage is the unwieldiness of the document. Because I did not direct the way in which my students inputted or linked their work, the Stein Project is visually demanding. With its 101 spaces and 345 links, the Stein Project takes up a lot of space on the computer screen and, therefore, must be reduced to fit. This results in very small print that is difficult to read. Furthermore, my students developed so many links that it is impossible to see all of them easily (see Figure 2.4). Because of the way one can choose to follow links, the size of the document would not ordinarily be a problem—but my students were not very careful about naming links. In some cases, the names are so similar that it is impossible to differentiate among them. For example, many students were interested in Stein's use of repetition. Consequently, they created a "Repetition" box and connected this word to multiple locations on the document. They then named each path "Repetition," making it impossible to identify which example of repetition the path leads to (see Figure 2.5).

Managing the various versions of the Stein Project that were being passed around the class forced me to spend a great deal of time sifting through them all in order to guarantee that we had at least one version of the hypertext that represented everyone's contributions; however, there were potentially forty-three versions of the Stein Project available. Despite my attempts to avoid confusion by limiting the number of copies we were working with, multiple versions of the Stein Project still exist and are not immediately recognizable even to me. One of the many claims about hypertext is its open-endedness. Having access to forty-three different texts seems to corroborate this claim. Because I have used the Stein Project in subsequent literature and composition classes, allowing students to add, subtract, link, and unlink text, the document continues to take on new shapes, increasing and diminishing in scope and size.

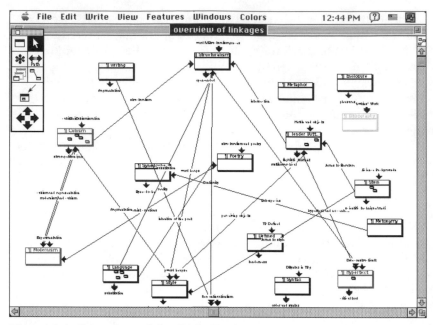

Figure 2.4. Overview of the Stein Project

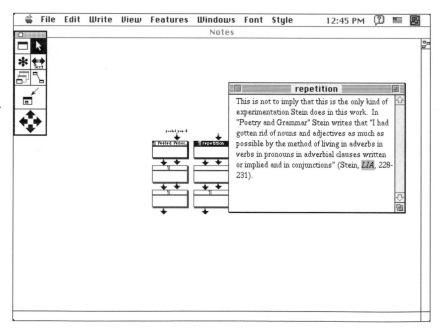

Figure 2.5. Repetition Box Created by Students

Scholars have also posited that hypertext is multihierarchical and therefore decenters the text (Landow 66–70). Being unable to locate my own work or voice among the many student versions of the project convinced me that hypertext does indeed have the capability to democratize a classroom. The one drawback to this feature of hypertext and to the way I set up the classroom assignment is the impossibility of grading in a traditional manner. Because I could not determine the individual authorship of the various spaces and links—an important consideration when attaching grades to papers—I was forced instead to evaluate the groups, based on collaborative presentations that focused on the insights they gained from their experience in researching Stein and in the development of the hypertext. In fact, I did not announce the presentations in advance, which encouraged a spontaneous discussion. Some of my students compared my surprise to a "pop test," but when the groups presented their findings and discussed their work, they demonstrated a sophisticated level of understanding of Stein's poetry.

Because this was the first time I had used hypertext in the classroom, other instructional problems emerged that I had not anticipated. Initially, I had set aside two class periods for a discussion of Stein, but as the project got underway, it became obvious that I had to rearrange my course to find more time for it. The general rule I follow is that I can eliminate work from a syllabus, but I should not add to it. Therefore, I had to make it clear to my students that I was trading work on the Stein Project for comparable work scheduled later in the course. At first many students were dubious about this proposal, but after they had become involved in the project, they did not seem to worry about this change in the workload. They actually produced more work when they created the hypertext than they would have if we had followed the original syllabus. The time it took to research Stein, read the books and articles, input the material, link their work, and meet in groups was much more extensive than the time needed for the third essay I had planned. With class time set aside for working in groups and visiting the library, the Stein Project took over four weeks to produce. Students spent approximately 340 hours on this project, a significant amount of time for a summer course.

I should also add that some of my students had access only to IBM computers at home or at their offices, and the version of Storyspace that we were using requires Macintoshes. Even those students with Macs could not work at home because none of them owned copies of Storyspace. This forced my students to complete most of their work on campus, which they had been loathe to do prior to this project. Although a few grumbled about the inconvenience, the complaining died down when they realized I intended to give them class time to work.

One last comment concerns my approach to teaching Storyspace by allowing my students to model my own work as they designed their portions of the project. Because many of my students had never touched a computer keyboard—much less heard of Storyspace— before arriving in my class, I was careful not to overwhelm them with hypertext theory or technology. By eliminating philosophical discussions concerning the claims made about hypertext, I demystified it. Just as I did not spend long hours discussing the theoretical notions underlying word processing software such as Microsoft Word, I avoided talking about linearity, open-endedness, and hierarchies—concepts associated with hypertext— figuring that these terms should emerge naturally as students worked with the tool. Therefore, instead of introducing hypertext as a theory, I showed students a version of my own Storyspace document. Furthermore, by providing students with my hypertext as a starting point to expand on, I gave them an idea how to organize their text and set up links. Doing this also removed any anxiety they may have felt if they had been forced to design their own hypertext from scratch. Although much debate surrounds the use of modeling as an educational strategy, my goal was to give my students an opportunity to investigate and expand on ideas about Stein by using my hypertext document as a point of departure for their own work. I had also emphasized at the beginning of the project that they were not limited by formal constraints. As a result, my students' insights took many different shapes, including the formal essay, poetry, journal-style entries, and dialogues with each other, Stein, and me. Lastly, I should mention that one of my students whose poetry I had been reading throughout the semester became much more particular about her art after working with the Stein Project. She remarked to me later that she had no idea that poets crafted their work in the way Stein obviously did. After we completed the Stein Project, I saw far less of her poetry because she claimed to be taking more time to write. For her and other students, then, hypertext provided an environment that helped them improve their own writing. Most important, they enjoyed their work.

One last example from my students' work may highlight the excitement that this project sparked. A group had been working on Stein's interest in modern art; one student in the group came up with the idea of locating examples of art that Stein had collected or art by artists she admired. With a little sleuthing based on the bibliography I had provided, the student found scholars who discussed Stein's connection to Picasso's Cubism. This investigation also led her to Matisse, another artist whose work Stein collected. My student then decided that she would show the relationship between Stein's use of color in the Objects poems and Matisse's bright reds, blues, and greens. This exploration took her to the poems "A Red Stamp," "A Red Hat," "A Blue Coat," and "Red Roses." She photocopied pictures from an art book and labeled various parts of the paintings with text from Stein's poems. Thus, this student physically linked text to pictures in much the same way that Stein connects words to images.

Although hypertext is increasingly being used in the classroom to teach everything from languages to mythology, it is still a new technology—one that has become popular among academicians only since the mid-1980s. Perhaps as we get closer to understanding and accepting alternative writing systems like hypertext, we will get closer to understanding and explaining experimental poets like Stein who test the boundaries of language. Hypertext can help us explore those boundaries. As Stein herself reminds us in "Composition as Explanation," "The only thing that is different from one time to another is what is seen and what is seen depends upon how everybody is doing everything. . . . Nothing changes from generation to generation except the thing seen and that makes a composition" (516). By using hypertext in my classroom, my students recognized that the process of "doing" the Stein Project helped them to see a little more clearly the "thing" called *Tender Buttons*. It helped them to see how Stein played with language and ideas, and it offered them a space in which to join the scholarly voices discussing Stein and *Tender Buttons*. What they had viewed originally as "meaningless nonsense" (as one student initially called Stein's poems) was instead revealed to them as an ingenious game in which they were invited to participate. In the end, making meaning from Gertrude Stein's poetry was reward for their effort; the zeal they displayed and the discoveries they made were mine.

Works Cited

Dubnick, Randa. *The Structure of Obscurity: Gertrude Stein, Language, and Cubism.* Urbana: University of Illinois Press, 1984.

Dydo, Ulla. "Gertrude Stein: Composition as Meditation." *Gertrude Stein and the Making of Literature.* Ed. Shirley Neuman and Ira Nadel. Boston: Northeastern University Press, 1988.

Landow, George. *Hypertext: The Convergence of Contemporary Critical Theory and Technology.* Baltimore: Johns Hopkins, 1992.

Liston, Maureen. *Gertrude Stein: An Annotated Critical Bibliography.* Ohio: Kent State University Press, 1979.

Stein, Gertrude. *The Autobiography of Alice B. Toklas.* 1933. *The Selected Writings of Gertrude Stein.* Ed. Carl Van Vechten. New York: Vintage Books, 1990.

————. "Composition as Explanation." 1926. *The Selected Writings of Gertrude Stein*. Ed. Carl Van Vechten. New York: Vintage Books, 1990.

————. *Tender Buttons*. 1914. *The Selected Writings of Gertrude Stein*. Ed. Carl Van Vechten. New York: Vintage Books, 1990.

Walker, Jayne. "Introduction." *The Making of a Modernist: Gertrude Stein from* Three Lives *to* Tender Buttons. Amherst: University of Massachusetts Press, 1984.

3 Voices That Let Us Hear: The Tale of The Borges Quest

Jeffrey R. Galin and Joan Latchaw

Composition teachers bringing technology into the classroom have tales to share. Like many others in this book, our story resonates with the inevitable complexities, excitement, and frustrations inherent in computerized instruction. Only by confronting these difficulties will computer technologies serve as agents of change. The tale of The Borges Quest reveals the transformation that can occur when the voices of researchers, teachers, students, theorists, and technologists interact.

We use the metaphors of Bakhtin's dialogism (specifically, the notion of multivocality) and Donahue and Quandahl's interactivity to argue that integrating computer technology into the classroom can be transformative. However, dialogism is not a transparent concept. It is easy to claim that we hear different voices in computer-facilitated learning; all students *seem* able to participate equally. Yet, just like traditional class discussions, synchronous communications (such as chats or MOOs) privilege certain voices over others. For example, students with attention deficit disorders cannot follow the rapidity of the dialogue, and poor typists do not get heard in cyberspace. When we get caught up in the liberatory rhetoric of empowerment and decentering, we can lose critical perspective of our own practices. If technology is, in fact, going to cause transformations, we need to look for disruptive moments (and voices) that unmask our belief systems. The disruptive nature of dialogics often opens up the possibility of examining our practices.

Interactivity is another metaphor that enables critical inquiry, sometimes dialogically. In *Reclaiming Pedagogy: The Rhetoric of the Classroom*, Donahue and Quandahl make a distinction between affiliation and interactivity. Affiliation maintains the status quo: Composition teachers use critical theory to support what they are already doing, thus jumping on the theory bandwagon. Likewise, when composition teachers use technology in their classrooms to support what they are already doing or merely to demonstrate cutting-edge practices, they are often jumping on a bandwagon—the technowagon. Experimenting with theory and technology may hold potential value; so may exploring new ways of reaching, engaging, or challenging students. However, to do either just because it is possible, without much forethought or preparation, is not likely to improve pedagogies or serve students. On the other hand, an interactive approach—in which theory or use of technology grows out of and engages pedagogy—"offers us a voice that lets us hear ourselves: a way to interpret our own practices" (Donahue and Quandahl 6). We have been able to revise as well as interpret our teaching practices through the dialogic interaction among students, teachers, scholars, and technologists (with their multiplicities and stratification of language).

The resulting tale of The Borges Quest (a HyperCard application) illustrates this interactive process—how the introduction of computer technology into teaching can alter classroom practice. The multifaceted nature of this project (from its subject, to its design, to its classroom use) grows out of the countless interactions between students and teachers, designers and composition theorists, teachers and technologies, designers and technologists. The interaction of these Bakhtinian "voices," all with differing ideologies, languages, politics, and practices, represents the intersection of critical theory, hypertext theory, cognitive theory, and pedagogy. Latchaw initially designed the HyperCard program to help students in her Basic Writing course think, read, and write about Jorge Luis Borges's short story, "Pierre Menard, Author of *Don Quixote*," a story that is itself dialogical in its parodic stylization[1] and structure. Like the story, the program is interactive in Donahue and Quandahl's sense of the term because it represents a way to resee and revise habitual practices. Students find that the program provides ways to revise how they understand reading and writing practices as they build interpretations of the text. Galin found that using the program served the same purpose for revising his teaching practices that the story served for pushing his students to revise their ways of reading and thinking.

This chapter is a dialogic narrative that weaves the program's design with its development and subsequent implementation. The first part of the narration focuses primarily on the interactions of teachers, cognitive theorists, composition theorists, and computer programmers that led to the creation of The Borges Quest. The second part explores the interactions among teacher-designers who adopt software and the students who use it. Interwoven throughout are the twenty rules of thumb (in bold type), important pedagogical and technological principles. The interaction of the two narratives, while not heteroglossic in the true sense of a comedic novel, still provides a multivocal story for teachers who hope to integrate computer technology into their teaching.

Cognitive Framework

Under the best circumstances, teachers should make their underlying goals and assumptions explicit; doing so informs their choices for bringing technology into courses and enables them to make necessary revisions along the way. Whether or not these assumptions are clarified, they are always present, embedded within departmental practices or prior experiences. Therefore, **pedagogy should precede technology**. Latchaw clarified her assumptions when constructing a Basic Writing course sequence. The tale begins with the creation of a course sequence called "The 3 Bs: Berger, Borges, and Buber"—long before her interest in computers. The sequence was grounded in four key principles of composition theory: that reading and writing are interdependent; that writing is critical thinking; that one assignment builds on another sequentially; and that basic writers are capable of engaging in intellectually rigorous, term-long projects. Latchaw chose Jorge Luis Borges's "Pierre Menard" as a critical text because it challenged students' assumptions about reading and writing, just as Martin Buber's *I and Thou* and John Berger's *Ways of Seeing* challenged assumptions about art and visual perception. While higher order cognitive processes—skeptical inquiry and alternative interpretations—are essential for critical thinking, they are extremely difficult for less experienced readers and writers. Traditionally, good students have been taught to paraphrase, summarize, find the *real* meaning, outline, freewrite and express feelings, and structure their points logically and clearly. Rarely have they been encouraged to think while they read, to talk back to the text. For teachers, as well as students, that is a risky and unfamiliar business. Latchaw's course sequence was designed to push students to do both the traditional and more critical work. Thus, the sequence grew from an interactive relationship between cognitive theory and composition theory.

The success of the sequence was marked by the five teachers who chose to teach it and the resulting work that students produced. Three of the five teachers chose to meet weekly to discuss assignments, students' papers, and methods of presentation. This collaborative effort produced multiple revisions of assignments, significant discussions on theory and pedagogy, and a lasting professional relationship between Galin and Latchaw that would greatly affect the development of The Borges Quest two years later. Furthermore, three Basic Writing course students from two different classes won awards in university-wide writing contests for essays written in response to this sequence during the two years it was used. Thus, collaboration dialogically interacted with revised pedagogy, student writing, and the professional lives of teachers.

Despite these successes, students were frustrated reading "Pierre Menard" and, at times, resisted engaging with this difficult text. "Pierre Menard" is a ten-page short story from Borges's collection called *Ficciones*. The first part is a brief enumeration of Menard's *visible* life works, including a two-page bibliography. For example, item (e) of the bibliography is "a technical article on the possibility of enriching the game of chess by means of eliminating one of the rook's pawns. Menard proposes, recommends, disputes, and ends by rejecting this innovation" (46). The second part is an exposition on the significance of his *invisible,* subterranean literary feat. The narrator carefully teases out how Menard, a French Impressionist writer, took on the task of rewriting Cervantes's novel *Don Quixote.* He first tried to become Cervantes but found that too easy; after destroying numerous drafts, Menard settled for a rereading of *Don Quixote,* a linguistic duplication yet not a translation. Skilled readers or literary critics might describe the story as a parody of scholarly pretensions, or as a theory of reading. They have seen the genres before. However, students have to develop different strategies of reading because they have not seen the genres and because no literary or scholarly agendas are likely to leap out at them.

At this point, the tale intersects Latchaw's work as a Ph.D. student, adding yet another dialogic strand (teacher-student). It occurred to her that writing a computer program for "Pierre Menard" would help her by fulfilling a graduate language requirement and by offering her students strategies for reading. This convergence of interests provided Latchaw with the *hook* she needed to begin investing the time and energy it takes to explore possible uses of technology for teaching. This hook, which differs from one teacher to another, greatly influences the philosophical and practical approaches that teachers take as they begin to integrate computer technology into teaching.

For Latchaw, if composition theory provided the philosophy undergirding her pedagogical principles, then cognitive theory and hypertext theory would provide the methodology to implement those principles. Thus, it made sense for her to spend time building a HyperCard application for her students: first, as she would be gaining professional credit for her work, and second, as no other hypertextual authoring applications were readily available at the time (1989).

Latchaw's foray into cognitive theory research sheds light on how her students became more proficient readers and writers. Recent theory shows that both background knowledge (local knowledge) and higher-order strategies such as reasoning and inquiring—(global knowledge) are essential in acquiring more sophisticated cognitive styles of learning

(Smith and Lansman 21). Cognitive theorists recognize that novices in a domain lack a sufficient knowledge base, which is critical for pluralistic thinking (relating various concepts, considering alternative meanings). A weak vocabulary slows down reading, decreasing comprehension and, by extension, critical thinking. One student said prior to the development of The Borges Quest, "The main problem, what confused and even angered me because I got frustrated, was large words like 'fallacious' and 'monograph.' It takes too much [time] to look it up and when you do it gives you a paragraph. . . ." While some definitions are straightforward, others require some speculation about the use of language and even authorial intention. So in addition to presenting the Borges story "Pierre Menard," which can be read within The Borges Quest, Latchaw built a dictionary of terms, names, and foreign words the students might not understand. Picking up on Borges's playfulness with the reader (and he had us sleuthing interminably in libraries), Latchaw entered "Madame Henri Bachelier" into the dictionary: "At this time, no information has been discovered about the mysterious Madame Bachelier. Something may turn up at any scholarly moment. Or it may not." Students learn that even reading a dictionary might be an interpretive act.

Such interpretive reading demonstrates a cognitive style of learning, which promotes integrative thinking, whereby students are encouraged to look for relationships among things in a relativistic world rather than perceive their surroundings in isolated bits of information. They are also expected—in our courses—to become inventive writers, which requires thinking insightfully, analytically, and critically. Galin states boldly in his course description that "Thinking is a requisite of this course." He would destroy the myth that Basic Writing is a skills course, and he invites students to "question habitual ways of thinking, to move beyond obvious responses, and to develop [their] own strategies for posing questions about the reading, writing, and thinking they do."

Theoretically, The Borges Quest fits this model of inquiry nicely. First, the title of the story itself elicits doubt because Cervantes, not Pierre Menard, wrote *Don Quixote*. And within the story, the characters continually wonder and inquire. Menard, the subject of Borges's short story, questions the literary canon—the glorification of Cervantes's classic text. His supposed technical article on the possibility of enriching the game of chess by removing one of the rook's pawns (which he eventually rejects) subtly ridicules academic scholarship (46). Through parodic techniques, the narrator himself questions what it means to *see*, gain knowledge, and interpret. Menard calls for a new way of reading, urging us to "run through the *Odyssey* as if it were written after the *Aeneid*" (54).

Second, the Quest poses problems, contradictions, and ambiguities. For example, in the Quest section called Authorship, students find the following message:

> Dear Investigator,
> It seems that many of our readers assume that
> the narrator and the author, Borges, are one and
> the same. We have reason to suspect a problem
> of dual identity, which has recently come to our
> attention. However, some of our other investigators
> have disputed this claim. Your job for today is to
> test this assumption and write a report of your
> findings to your supervisor.

In using the computer program, students embark on a literary investigation. They become sleuths, picking up on clues, tracking them down, and then writing reports to their supervisors. Sleuthing, a playful process, comes to mean close reading: searching out linguistic distinctions and rhetorical tropes, making inferences, and drawing conclusions. The opening screen poses the challenge they have before them, a focus that is maintained through the rest of the program (see Figure 3.1). The quest metaphor, by emphasizing a process of reading (through questioning and testing claims), opens the text rather than restricting it to a particu-

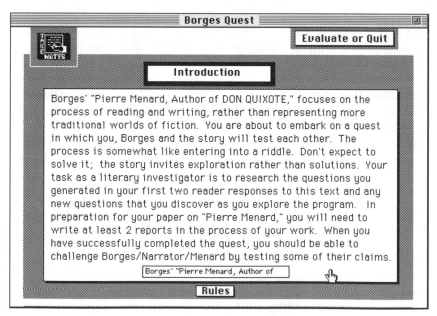

Figure 3.1. Introductory Screen for The Borges Quest

lar meaning. Playing the role of investigator, students are asked to "embark on a quest in which [they], Borges, and the story will test each other." The process of reading (and writing about reading) is thus conceived as an active challenge, whereby neither the text, author, narrator, nor reader has ultimate authority. The quest might lead in any number of directions: opening another path (area of investigation), putting up a roadblock (finding flaws or contradictions in the narrator's account), or reinforcing the surface (textual interpretation).

As students move through chosen paths of exploration, they may take notes at any time, but they will eventually find themselves (like any agent) accountable in writing. After completing an investigation, questers are asked to report on their discoveries. The instructions for one such report state, "As the senior sleuth on this case, your help is needed in investigating the identity of Pierre Menard." The clues are historical, biographical, and fictional material that the students must sift through to arrive at a hypothesis. Students learn associational thinking by linking information across segments (spaces) and by evaluating its validity. They learn that even historical facts are subject to inquiry. (Did Borges invent, interpret, or discover Menard and Madame Bachelier?) The associational thinking that hypertext supports enables students to construct theories about the story and processes of reading. Thus critical thinking strategies are embedded in the design. Yet strong pedagogy cannot exist in a vacuum. In this case, it was supported by an interaction between cognitive theory and critical thinking. With its multiple cross-links and references, hypertext is an ideal environment for preventing cognitive overload, supporting student-centered learning, and encouraging associative thinking. Hypertext can be imagined as a database that lets users connect screens of information through associative links, or as a computer-based medium for thinking and communicating. Jeff Conklin defines thinking as the developing and rejecting of ideas at different levels and points, each idea depending on and contributing to others (32). It is a serial, nonlinear process. Because it can link nodes of thought, references, annotations, and visual aids, hypertext can help the user "build a flexible network to model his problem or solution" (Conklin 33). It cuts across traditional boundaries, merging, for instance, the library, classroom, and movie theater by providing an ideal environment for associating disparate bits of information, a skill that often eludes students.

Latchaw initially designed a guided, exploratory hypertext to minimize student frustration, which was her original incentive for developing the program. (We acknowledge the criticism that such guided applications violate the openness of hypertext protocol; certain pathways in the program are linear and "force" interactions at certain points. In a few cases, the program suggests a particular order of investigation to provide interpretive and analytical strategies. On the other hand, hypertext is often criticized because users get lost, confused, and overwhelmed by unlimited pathways, sometimes forgetting their initial purpose or thought process. For these reasons, Latchaw imposed some limitations, valuing the pedagogy appropriate to her course over general theories of hypertext.) Thus, the hypertext technology grew out of pedagogy and by the same token, engaged pedagogy in unexpected ways when Galin adopted The Borges Quest.

Because the structure of The Borges Quest focuses on certain issues and techniques in the story, it funnels the user's attention toward one particular facet at a time, thus preventing cognitive overload. Students can explore issues of authority, humor, or genre without being overwhelmed because their attention is directed. The program's segments (the story, a bibliography of Borges's works, a dictionary of unfamiliar terms, humor, authorship) are structured to engage students in specific critical thinking, reading, and writing activities (see Figure 3.2). These activities were designed to help students focus on the issues and themes of the Basic Writing assignments and course. Thus, the program was initially integrated into the *objectives* for the course rather than existing as an isolated, supplemental application. However, it had not yet been integrated into an actual course, an important distinction addressed in the second part of our narrative.

In using the computer program, students embark on a literary investigation. And like sleuths, they only solve one case at a time, unless they themselves decide that a side investigation is necessary. Ideally, a hypertext application allows users to take control of their learning processes by linking diverse screens of information or queries, following a line of thought, doubling back, or checking out a reference.

Hypertext is consistent with current theories of reading and writing because it is interactive, recursive, and user controlled. In posing problems, contradictions, and ambiguities, The Borges Quest guides learners to interact with their own thoughts, the programmer's queries, and other texts and resources. It helps users learn *how* to argue and "read against" (Bartholomae and Petrosky 11).

Many teachers reading the description of The Borges Quest and the Basic Writing course in which it was used may counter, "We could never do that kind of thing in Basic Writing here." At the University of Pittsburgh, such teaching sequences are common. Though no one else in our department was working with similar technologies at the time, Basic Writing sequences in the department commonly ask students to ques-

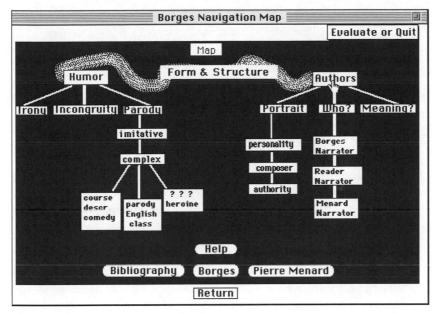

Figure 3.2. Map of The Borges Quest

tion assumptions in these ways. One faculty member, observing Galin's class and reviewing a teaching sequence he developed that included the Borges text, wrote, "He [Galin] has composed an ambitious sequence of assignments on the issues of authorship and authority, and the papers I've seen from this section suggest that his sequence has prompted his students to do some powerful thinking and writing" (Teaching Evaluation, Fall 1990). We all know, however, that pedagogical assumptions differ from institution to institution. What is valued at Pitt may be taboo at other institutions and vice versa. The point here is that pedagogical assumptions made in one academic context are not necessarily transferable to other, even similar contexts; thus, **technologies are not necessarily transferable from one institution to another**, and, whether or not underlying pedagogical assumptions are made explicit in a piece of software, **all computer applications are built around such assumptions**.

We would not expect teachers at other universities to be able to use The Borges Quest in their classes without at least holding similar pedagogical goals and without the kind of tacit support that we received at Pitt for doing this work. Likewise, though individual teachers might be able to use such a program in their own classes, **one measure of its success in that new context will depend on the degree to which it corre-**

sponds with the teacher's and the department's teaching practices. Although there are certainly exceptions to this rule, most teachers starting out with technology (particularly experienced teachers experimenting on their own) can expect to do so within the constraints of their current teaching practices.

Galin had sound pedagogical reasons for using The Borges Quest, many of which reflected departmental values. He did not want a program that, like many tutorials, would be used to find *the* meaning of the story. Rather, he wanted one that would help students discover new ways of reading. "Pierre Menard, Author of *Don Quixote*" challenges students' assumptions about form, structure, authorship, narrator, and voice, demanding that they rethink these relationships. Furthermore, because of its difficult vocabulary and numerous allusions, students must negotiate meaning in context and build their papers on carefully chosen evidence from the text. Not only was Borges's story a pivotal text for Galin's "What Is an Author?" teaching sequence, but the HyperCard application also lent itself nicely to developing the kinds of critical strategies, such as question posing, that he was already asking his students to implement. In his course description, he asks students to become "active" readers of texts by "looking for questions" as they read, "rather than looking only for answers." He explains further that "Doing this kind of active reading opens places in a text for further exploration, as we make room for our own thinking and ideas." Because The Borges Quest was set up as a literary investigation, like a riddle that is not meant to be solved but rather "explored," students are pushed to develop strategies of reading and composing that may not be apparent to them when they are at home reading by themselves. Also, the response-type "Reports" scattered throughout the application looked as if they would be useful preparation for upcoming journal and paper assignments on "Pierre Menard." The interaction of reading theory, student-driven learning, hypertext, and critical thinking made The Borges Quest an appropriate choice for Galin's class.

However, no teacher is going to undertake the kind of work Latchaw and Galin did to develop an application for a specific classroom context unless **institutional supports and incentives are in place to reward the amount of time and energy it takes to develop such software**. Teachers who have tried to integrate technology into their classes to serve more than just a supplemental function know this to be true. The work that Latchaw and Galin undertook to build The Borges Quest represents the extreme case. Latchaw invested several hundred hours one summer to develop the design and build a beta version of the program. Galin spent another eight hundred or so hours honing, redesigning, adding to, and scripting the stacks over a period of about five years. Although the program now serves its purpose well, it still needs a great deal more work. Inconsistencies in design and bugs in scripts remain. Furthermore, parts of the program were designed but never built. Both Latchaw and Galin were able to negotiate partial fulfillment of graduate language requirements for their programming work. This reward provided enough incentive for them, as graduate students, to invest their time. Gaining professional credit for such development is an entirely different problem that will not be addressed here.

Clearly most teachers are not going to undertake the kind of development required of The Borges Quest, no matter how great the rewards. Most will choose from a wide assortment of Internet-based and local-area network-based software, primarily whatever is supported on their campus. But even these kinds of applications demand unexpected amounts of time to integrate effectively into a course. Teachers must still choose appropriate applications and learn how to use them before they ask their students to do so in order to anticipate problems, avert mistakes (whenever possible), identify technical support personnel, and effectively integrate the technology into their course. In other words, **teachers need to be aware of the availability of and access to hardware, software, or wetware (technical and pedagogical support) before assigning work to students**. Students need reassurance that someone will be responsible for helping them upload a homework assignment, if necessary. Sure, we teach our students these techniques, but often they forget, leave the training materials at home, or fail to check the files posted on a Web server. And faculty need to know to whom they can turn when they have a question or a problem or need technical support for their classes. The importance of developing good ties with campuswide technical staff cannot be overemphasized.

Even when the application is pedagogically sound, the technical support sufficient, and the departmental goals congruent, teachers must expect to make adjustments. **If teachers expect technology to transform the work of their classes, they are more likely to rethink their teaching practices.** "Expect" is the key word in this statement. Often what we see or discover is affected by what we expect to find or to happen. For example, if teachers expect to substitute previously valued activities (using word processors, turning in assignments, sharing student texts, or supplementing a course reading) with corresponding electronic forms, then the technology has little chance of causing them to reflect critically on their pedagogy or course structure.

For instance, if we use e-mail simply as a new context for assigning and collecting work, then it is likely to have little impact on the way the class is run; in fact, Galin found that some students refuse to do the work. Why use e-mail when more traditional methods are easier or more expedient? If, on the other hand, we expect e-mail to modify our practices, we might ask ourselves why students are not participating in online discussions or submitting work electronically rather than express anger when students do not comply. We may find that students do not know how to use e-mail effectively because they were trained by someone unconnected with the course. Typically, computer information services personnel lack pedagogical and/or disciplinary expertise. For this reason, we argue: **If the technology is important enough for use in the course, then it is important enough for use in class.** Some teachers argue that training can be conducted outside of class, and to some degree this is true. But, as we all know, all learning and working environments are unique. For instance, if students need to know how to transfer a file to their accounts, rather than simply learning the Macintosh program Fetch, they are often taught all there is to know about FTP (file transfer protocol). When more information than necessary is provided, students often face cognitive overload and fail to learn even the simplest tasks.

Furthermore, when we prepare our students technologically and witness their difficulties, we can isolate the problems and determine realistic expectations for using various forms of technology. Most important, by taking time to integrate this training into the work of the course, we are forced to weigh the costs and benefits of using the technologies. Thus, we find ourselves reconceptualizing the very kinds of work that students are to turn in. We could begin commenting electronically on papers, extending class discussions, and encouraging small group work among students outside of the classroom. We might require electronic submissions so that everyone could revise the same text simultaneously to demonstrate multiple perspectives. The following activities, which are becoming essential to any basic writing course, often demand different technologies: e-mail, synchronous chat, and World Wide Web. **Because no one application will ever be sufficient, a suite of technologies is ideal.** Through a process of trial and error, teachers can find the set of technologies that help them best serve their students and their own pedagogical aims. In determining what training is necessary and why we have taken time to provide it, we can reflect critically on the ways technology, as an agent of change, helps us reexamine our work.

Asking the following questions activates that reexamination, a dialogical process in which goals, purposes, and expectations can undergo radical or more moderate shifts.

What is the nature of the course?

Why is the technology being introduced?

What can the computer do that cannot be done better in other ways?

What implications, consequences, and results might be expected in the computer-facilitated course?

Classroom Trials

Over the course of five class trials and reflecting on the failures and successes, Galin came to understand that The Quest offered a way to "interpret [his] own practice[s]" (Donahue and Quandahl 6). It eventually became an agent of change in his classroom. The technical and pedagogical problems Galin and his students initially encountered in using The Borges Quest led students to help him rewrite all five assignments on the Borges story and change class pedagogy from individual wrestling to collaborative exploration. He would revise every button, field, card, and stack of the program as well as develop additional components.

In response to questionnaires from the first two classroom trials, most of the assignments were revised. Galin clarified goals, made connections between them more explicit, and framed the class work more as exploratory investigations than as individual products to be turned in. The most dramatic changes in course pedagogy and developments in The Quest itself, however, are best demonstrated through his work with one student.

Before working with Ron, Galin had had little investment in The Borges Quest other than as a supplemental tool for his students and a favor to Latchaw; therefore, he had little incentive to "re-envision" the application. That first term, only two students out of eighteen chose to use the program as a supplement to their class work. The second time around, Galin decided to eliminate an assignment and require all students to write two of the embedded reports within The Borges Quest as part of their work with "Pierre Menard, Author of *Don Quixote*." Standing in the computer lab with his students, Galin realized that there were so many bugs in the software that students could not use the program effectively. Thus, in preparation for the third class trial, he did finally spend time learning how HyperCard functions by working about sixty hours to resolve system problems, edit out bugs, and add superficial visual effects to make the application more user-friendly for students. In learning about HyperCard, he became interested in making structural changes to the program. One of his most difficult students, a prison guard coming back to school, provided him with that opportunity.

After the last class of the semester, Ron sat down with Galin to point out a place in the program that had made possible an important breakthrough in his writing—realizing the importance of supporting claims for his audience. The fact that Ron sat with Galin at all is worth noting. He was a difficult student who was vocal and dominated class discussions and, when frustrated, would shut down his own thinking processes. (He would tell himself he just could not do the work, which would send him into a tailspin.) In the process, he also often shut down class discussion by asserting his position, not listening to others, or making snide comments.

Talking with Ron about his work after class that day, Galin mentioned significant changes in Ron's writing that had occurred a few weeks earlier and coincided with using The Borges Quest. Galin wondered what had made these changes possible. Before the change, Ron tended to defer to authorities or rely on clichés rather than perform the kind of close textual analysis that the assignment required. He had written in a previous paper:

> Donald F. Bouchard gave an explanation of what he understood an author to be and a reason for his feelings. He wrote: "To learn, for example, that Pierre Dupont does not have blue eyes, does not live in Paris, and is not a doctor does not invalidate the fact that the name, Pierre Dupont, continues to refer to the same person: there has been no modification of the designation that links the name to the person." What this means to me is that a name does not make a person an author, only the works that are attached to the name. 'A rose by any other name would smell as sweet.' This old cliché sums up the thought that he was trying to make the reader understand in my opinion.

Ron's first move to explain the quote is an appeal to authority. He is quoting from two pages of a Foucault essay that was handed out as optional reading for students who wanted a source for statements that Galin made in the course description about Foucault's theory of authorship. Notice Ron's gesture to explain the quote: "What this means to me . . ." and "in my opinion." In a characteristic Basic Writing move, the real work of making connections has been done off the page. Only the final result of a complex train of thought is apparent, and the primary justification for it is Ron's own opinion. For further authority, Ron turns to an "old cliché," which again is a substitute for his much more interesting, but absent, thinking processes. Galin's comments in the margins of Ron's paper point to this discrepancy. He wrote, "As I read this quote (a really interesting one at that) I see him saying that no matter what an author's background or personality, the relationship between the *name* and the person remains the same. I just don't see what in this quote gets you to 'works that are attached to the name.' How did you make this step to 'works?'"

In the following passage, Ron works a bit more closely with the text in one of his reports from The Borges Quest on the role of author as narrator in "Pierre Menard, Author of *Don Quixote*." Notice the ways he is struggling with quotes and how he is trying to make sense of them. To explain his claims that "the narrator seems to have made up most of the information in this story" and that he has a "vivid imagination," Ron attempts an analysis of the narrator's use of pronouns about a third of the way down his page:

> He is trying desperately to pull us along into his mystical webb of intrigue. As we read further in the story he states, "For evoking [plebeian delight] in anachronism, or (what is worse) charming us with the primary idea that all epochs are the same, or that they are different." In this pasage he is now referring to himself and other writers of noted works. He could mean the reader, but his primary concern in this excerpt is with the professionally involved person (of the literary field).

Though Ron has not quite worked out his argument here, for a journal response he has worked hard. Notice that Ron does not appeal to authority outside of the text. Instead, he tries to piece together a reading by tracing the web of pronouns that Borges uses to toy with his readers. Ron implies this playful relationship when he suggests that the narrator is pulling "us along into his mystical webb of intrigue." The quote Ron uses from the text is jarring. It starts in the middle of a line and actually leaves out a couple of words, the two marked with brackets. But the move Ron makes with the quote is the kind of move Galin wanted to see him make. Ron's gloss of this sentence focuses on the pronoun "us," as he argues that the speaker is "referring to himself and other writers of noted works." The "us" he defines here is a special kind of reader, "the professionally involved person (of the literary field)." Ron stops short of demonstrating how he makes this association, though words such as "anachronism" and the idea of "charming us" with a paradoxical method of reading were likely part of his thinking. Even though he has not offered his full thinking processes here, he has at least identified specific words in the quote from which to build his *own* analysis. This is a first for Ron. In commenting on this journal entry, Galin tells Ron that he has begun to do the kind of analysis required in the course: "Slow, careful analysis and attention to the text are the kind of work you'll be expected to do in most classes you take."

No matter how dialogical we aspire to make our classes, we are nonetheless trapped within institutional expectations that frame our courses, particularly those of a basic writing class in a university setting. The story we offer here about Ron's success can be read as a resistant student submitting to disciplinary expectations. The student becomes the antagonist (to be trained), while the teacher and his hegemonic academic discourse serve as the protagonist (the educating force). If the story ended here—the student as good learner—the technology would serve only as a foil for the teacher to better achieve his aims.

In this case, however, a crucial dialogue between Ron and Galin ensued about Ron's success that would push Galin to rethink his teaching and use of technology in the classroom. In effect, this conversation reversed the teacher–student relationship, even if only temporarily, when Ron began to make suggestions about ways to improve The Borges Quest and student work with the program. Ron, the struggling student, became the protagonist, and the teacher, with his hegemonic academic discourse, became the antagonist. Although Ron's success is small—he neither completely overthrows the strategic relations of power that define his marginal position nor affects course changes for the current semester—he does push Galin to reexamine practices for future courses and leads his teacher to realize that **dialogics in the computer-facilitated classroom are not always revolutionary, but they can be transformative**.

The full story of this conversation is worth retelling because of the ways it demonstrates the dialogical potential of bringing technology into the classroom. For numerous reasons, Galin did not have a chance to discuss this journal response with Ron until the course was over. On that last day, standing outside the classroom, he mentioned how impressed he had been by the shift in Ron's writing. Ron picked up on the comment immediately and offered to demonstrate what in The Borges Quest had triggered the changes.

It is worth noting here that the reason Ron sat down to work with his teacher was to develop his own writing, not to discuss programming issues. Furthermore, it was Galin's role as a teacher that enabled their conversation, not his role as a programmer; however, Galin's recent investment in The Borges Quest as a programmer compelled him to take up Ron's offer. (The dialogic interweaving of these roles made the conversation possible.) The meeting was significant because Galin had made at least three prior classwide appeals for students to meet with him and identify problems in the program. No one had volunteered. Thus, only the interplay between the roles of teacher and programmer gave Galin both the access to Ron's way of thinking and the impetus to pursue them.

Ron's way of thinking was challenged by a W. C. Fields joke in The Quest. In a section called "Incongruity," a joke by W. C. Fields made it possible for him to understand that saying, "In my opinion . . .," was not enough to justify a reading of a text. After an explanation of *incon-*

gruity as a "conflict between what you expect and what actually happens," the joke is offered: "Someone asked the famous comedian, W. C. Fields, 'Mr. Fields, do you believe in clubs for young people?' He replied, 'Only when kindness fails.'" This concrete demonstration offered Ron an example of how different meanings can affect the reading of a particular text, suggesting that meaning is seldom self-evident and often needs explanation.

When Galin asked Ron how he had made this connection to his own writing, Ron told a story of frustration and struggle. Explaining his frustration at trying to read "Pierre Menard, Author of *Don Quixote*," Ron said that The Borges Quest had only made things worse. He could not figure out why he was being asked to use it or what he was supposed to do with it. And, like his other outbursts in class, his frustration shut down his thinking processes. Then, one day over spring break when he was in the computer lab doing other work, he decided to sit down and look at the program once more, this time without the pressure of fulfilling an assignment. As he wandered through the application, his anger absent, he discovered the section on incongruity. Something clicked.

Ron wanted to help future students avoid the frustration with the story and the program that he had faced. He suggested that students work in groups of three for the initial demonstration session, adding that these groups should be out-of-class study groups, assigned by the teacher so students would "stay on task." Furthermore, he recommended that each of the three students choose a section of the program to explore, while the others offer input. Taking turns in this way, three sections would get preliminary examinations during the introductory session. In addition, this arrangement would enable peers to help each other adjust to the application, solve any problems, choose issues to explore, share ideas, discuss the story itself, and work collaboratively on writing their papers. Ron helped Galin realize that **students, too, can be seen as colleagues for support and collaboration**.

In addition to helping Galin revise class assignments and pedagogy, Ron also helped him to conceive two new HyperCard stacks that have greatly enhanced The Borges Quest and its future role in the Basic Writing course. Galin spent about a year developing these stacks, revising them during each use in his classes. The first is an online questionnaire, an evaluation of the program that can be accessed from every screen and that allows students to review their own comments from previous sessions. Galin cannot be in the lab to get feedback from every student, and Ron helped him realize that an online questionnaire would serve a similar function. Besides, it makes more sense to jot down thoughts as they arise than to try to remember them later (see Figure 3.3).

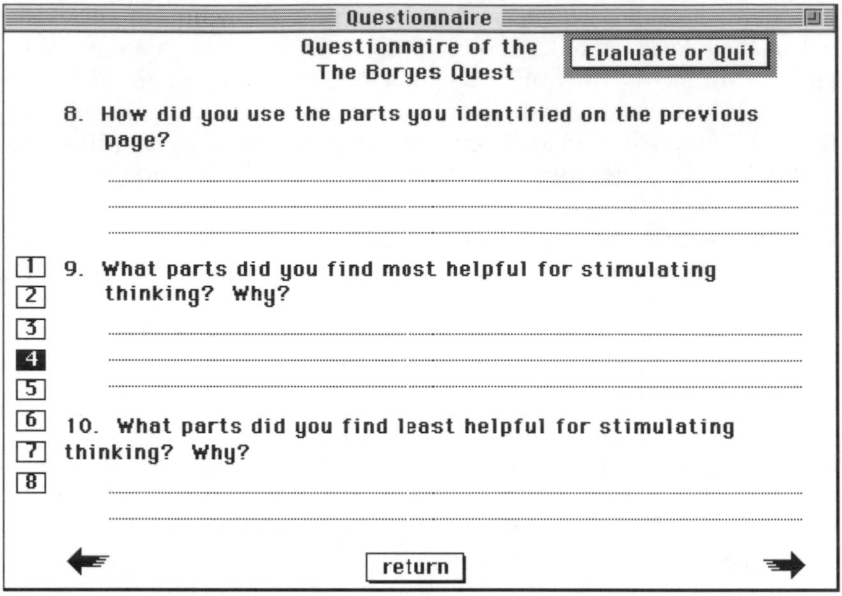

```
┌─────────────────────────────────────────────────────────────────┐
│ ▓▓▓▓▓▓▓▓▓▓▓▓▓▓▓ Questionnaire ▓▓▓▓▓▓▓▓▓▓▓▓▓▓▓               ▣  │
│              Questionnaire of the    ┌─────────────────┐          │
│              The Borges Quest        │ Evaluate or Quit │          │
│                                      └─────────────────┘          │
│     8. How did you use the parts you identified on the previous   │
│        page?                                                      │
│        ..........................................................  │
│        ..........................................................  │
│        ..........................................................  │
│                                                                   │
│  ┌1┐  9. What parts did you find most helpful for stimulating     │
│  ┌2┐     thinking?  Why?                                          │
│  ┌3┐     ........................................................  │
│  ■4■     ........................................................  │
│  ┌5┐                                                              │
│  ┌6┐  10. What parts did you find least helpful for stimulating   │
│  ┌7┐  thinking?  Why?                                             │
│  ┌8┐     ........................................................  │
│          ........................................................  │
│                                                                   │
│   ◀━━            ┌──────────┐                              ━━▶    │
│                  │  return  │                                     │
│                  └──────────┘                                     │
└─────────────────────────────────────────────────────────────────┘
```

Figure 3.3. Sample Questionnaire Screen

The second stack Ron helped Galin conceive is more complex. Called "Notepad Space," it has functions similar to those in the hypertext program Storyspace. With no prompting from Galin, Ron said that he would prefer taking notes in an online notebook because, once all of the notes were entered and each student had spent additional time developing these notes and adding others, papers for the next assignment would almost be written. "It would be," he said "just a matter of rearranging sentences and paragraphs, developing gaps, and Voila! a paper." Notepad Space does all Ron asked for and more: It enables students to sort through all of the notes and reports they have written throughout the program, make selections, throw them into workspaces, and edit them further (see Figure 3.4). Also, students have the capability to organize these notes graphically by building a network of linked fields and writing their papers with the aid of pull-down menus (see Figure 3.5).

Latchaw and Galin had talked previously about developing a "Notebook" that would be accessible from various locations in the program. Galin, however, had never envisioned a notebook space in which students, in addition to taking notes, could sort, develop, and structure them into a paper while remaining within the program. Furthermore, Galin had not designed a collaborative assignment within the course sequence prior to Ron's suggestions.

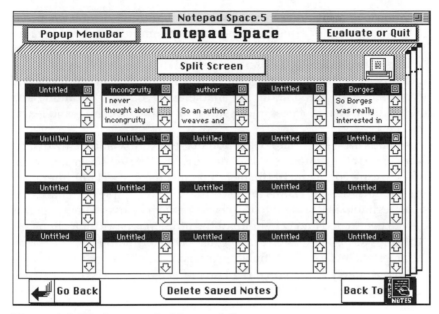

Figure 3.4. Workspaces in Notepad Space

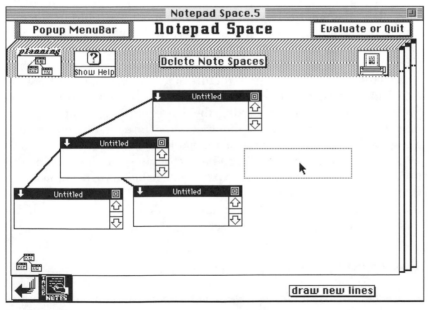

Figure 3.5. Notepad Space Organizational Page

Thus, Ron helped Galin **understand that restructuring class pedagogy is essential for effective integration of computer technology into teaching.** Galin redesigned his assignments and reconceptualized his courses. Also, Ron helped Galin understand that collaboration in a classroom using technology necessitates dialogue between students and teachers. Such collaboration can enable all involved to examine and modify their own practices and assumptions about teaching and learning.

Perhaps most important of all, Ron made clear to Galin that **we must work to hear the dialogics of the computer-facilitated classroom, even while we are cognizant of the fact that most teaching is not liberatory for students (despite claims to the contrary).** The complexities that computer technologies bring into the classroom can be overwhelming. It is easy to get excited and caught up in the utopian rhetoric of technology. Although terms such as *decentering, democratizing,* and *empowering* can be important metaphors, stimulating teachers to rethink pedagogies, they are just as likely to reinforce the fears of skeptics who consider such terms excuses or rationales for faculty to play with technology in their courses. And classroom experimentation may indeed have marginal value. **Teachers must explore the metaphors they use in understanding computers to facilitate learning.** For instance, if we expect students to use word processors for writing essays, we are imagining "the word processor" as a tool, a service to the course. We do not question assumptions about the way we teach. Thus, it is unlikely that word processing will have much impact on the way we teach. However, if we imagine word processing as an agent of change for writing, we can begin to explore how it might re-envision the composing process (i.e., how immediate access affects our claims, structure of ideas, even the questions we ask). Failing to ask such questions often leads to adopting utopian metaphors, which tend to propogandize the (false) glories of computer technologies. We do not advocate one metaphor for everyone but instead argue for understanding how our metaphors determine the ways in which we act and think. Finding a balance among the rhetoric, institutional practices, and our drive to experiment enables us to hear the voices that simultaneously reflect authorial intentions and unmask and destroy these same belief systems. We cannot leave this work to chance. It demands our attention from the outset.

Taking Stock

As teachers of Basic Writing, we never know what is finally going to reach a given student. When we are willing to interact with students like Ron, exciting transformations can occur. Nor do we know which new teaching practices will result in significant reevaluations of our teaching practices. In this tale of The Borges Quest, we have tried to demonstrate what can happen when teachers are willing to take risks such as introducing new technologies into our classrooms and collaborating with students. No other student, in seven years of teaching, has helped Galin gain as much access to his own assumptions about teaching as Ron has.

Finally, Ron made Galin realize that **for on-going professional development, inspiration, and publication, forming networks of support locally and nationally is essential.** When Galin first undertook the revision of The Borges Quest, he could not have accomplished what he did without the help of someone in the library at Pitt who was also working on HyperCard projects.

Equally as important, without forums either for presenting his work, such as at conferences, or for discussing his frustrations with others in the field, Galin might have given up using the program altogether after that first term. **Sharing discoveries, failures, and insights with others is essential.** Galin joined the listserv, Megabyte University (MBU), at about the time that he piloted The Borges Quest in his class. He asked others what they did to solve certain classroom and technological problems and engaged in long discussions on issues he had considered a great deal but had never expressed in a public forum. After two years of active participation, he developed friends within the field with whom he could collaborate on projects.

Developing a critical mass of supportive colleagues within the department and campus is essential. Anyone who has written a grant for a computer classroom can testify that department and program chairs and deans need to be persuaded that a lab serves important goals. Skeptics abound. The more colleagues who can be convinced to explore technologies in productive ways, the easier it will be to encourage others to test the waters, hold the skeptics at bay, and get deserved recognition toward advancement and tenure. As professionals using technologies for teaching, we need local support for our work to be valued, and we owe it to ourselves to become part of the larger communities of support.

Given this support, some teachers might argue for jumping on the technowagon, expecting a smooth transition into technology without much pedagogical reflection. Although this strategy may work in some cases, the possibility that technology will drive pedagogy is too risky. That technology should engage pedagogy is clearly illustrated in the tale of The Borges Quest. The interplay among researcher, programmer, student, and teacher demonstrates why it takes several semesters to integrate any technology effectively into a given class. It follows that **technical innovation is a gradual process within learning environments.** Any given innovation that a teacher brings into the classroom is unlikely to work as planned the first time despite proper preparation. Not many of us want to admit this, especially teachers who have spent hundreds of hours developing software for their specific classroom contexts. Generally, no matter how prepared a teacher is, a minimum of two semesters is needed to integrate a given technology effectively into a course. As we state in Chapter 1, the dialogical give and take of teachers as pedagogues, researchers, and programmers is essential to integrating technologies into the classroom. Even the simple task of introducing e-mail into a course requires trial and error: Today the server is down; tomorrow updated software will be installed; next Tuesday five machines in class will have disabled operating systems. Even when all the hardware and software are working properly, the teacher might simply forget to include the space and period after a copy command in UNIX, preventing students from performing the most rudimentary function— transferring a single file. A small mistake like this can ruin an entire class plan.

It follows, then, that **effective teaching with computer technology is a great deal of work.** There is no reason to reproduce efforts accomplished more efficiently through other means. If the technology is well justified, **teachers should plan to spend a minimum of forty preparatory hours familiarizing themselves with any applications that students will be expected to use.**

A few years ago, Louie Crew, associate professor of the Academic Foundations Department at Rutgers University, wrote in an e-mail exchange, "I would like to see a law that condemns every person who buys [we add 'or designs'] software for someone else to have to use that software herself for at least 40 hours" (1992). He was speaking of style checkers when he made this comment; however, his point applies to any computer-aided instruction (CAI) application. He explains further:

> Remember the story about the drunk walking around a street lamp looking for his keys. An officer approaches and offers to help. After about ten minutes, the officer says, "Are you sure this is where you lost them?" "No," the drunk replies, "I lost them over there, but the light is better here."

"Too many CAI tasks," Crew explains, "are blocks away from the keys." Adapting software to your own institutional context takes a great deal of careful consideration and often departmental and university negotiations. And the software can be adapted successfully only when the teacher knows what it can do. As a way to justify designing a computer program, Latchaw's dissertation advisor asked, "What can computers do that other methods can't?" This question has informed every computer project that both she and Galin have undertaken or will undertake in the future.

This sort of inquiry is necessary, given how fast technology changes these days. We also know how quickly theories of discourse, representation, and textual practices shift. Staying ahead of the technology curve is seldom possible, but exploring and questioning our own assumptions on a continual basis reduce the likelihood of falling into stagnant practices that once served political or cultural contexts. Most teachers tend to teach the same ways that they were taught. **Good teachers know that when they have settled into a system, it is time to look for new challenges**. But we have to listen hard and interactively to hear other voices "that let us hear ourselves." Only then will we discover and recover pedagogy.

Note

1. In "Discourse in the Novel," Bakhtin writes that the incorporation of heteroglossia and its stylistic use in the comic novel are represented by two features: (1) The "multiplicity of 'language,'" (311) voices from all walks of life, and (2) the incorporation of these languages and their concomitant socioideological belief systems that simultaneously serve both to reflect authorial intentions and to unmask and destroy these same belief systems. Bakhtin explains further that "In most cases these languages . . . that are authoritative and reactionary—are (in real life) doomed to death and displacement" (312). Various forms of parodic stylization of incorporated languages are the results of these displacements. "Pierre Menard, Author of *Don Quixote*," a parody of the seminal heteroglossic novel, *Don Quixote*, dissembles all notions of textual ownership. Authorial intention becomes voice. And the authoritative languages of news media, academic writing, serious literature, personal discourse, and so forth, are all dismantled and displaced.

Works Cited

Bakhtin, Mikhail. "Discourse in the Novel." *The Dialogic Imagination: Four Essays by M.M. Bakhtin*. Ed. Michael Holquist. Trans. Caryl Emerson and Michael Holquist. Austin: University of Texas Press, 1981. 259–422.

Bartholomae, David, and Anthony Petrosky. Introduction. *Ways of Reading: An Anthology for Writers*. David Bartholomae and Anthony Petrosky. 4th ed. Boston: Bedford/St. Martin's, 1996.

Borges, Jorge Luis. "Pierre Menard, Author of *Don Quixote*." *Ficciones*. Ed. Anthony Kerrigan. New York: Grove Press, 1962. 45–55.

Conklin, Jeff. "Hypertext: An Introduction and Survey." *Institute of Electrical and Electronics Engineers* September 1987: 17–41.

Crew, Louis. E-mail. 30 May 1992, 12:23. Edutel.

Donahue, Patricia, and Ellen Quandahl. "Reading the Classroom." *Reclaiming Pedagogy: The Rhetoric of the Classroom.* Ed. Patricia Donahue and Ellen Quandahl. Carbondale: Southern Illinois University Press, 1989. 1–16.

Smith, John B., and Marcy Lansman. "A Cognitive Basis for a Computer Writing Environment." *Computer Writing Environments: Theory, Research, and Design.* Ed. Bruce K. Britton and Shawn M. Glynn. Hillsdale, NJ: Erlbaum, 1989.

4 How Much Web Would a Web Course Weave if a Web Course Would Weave Webs?

Bruce Dobler
University of Pittsburgh

Harry Bloomberg
University of Pittsburgh

The last presentation of this year's Founder's Day symposium was by Bruce Dobler, a published author and associate professor of English who became one of the first instructors on campus to make work on the Internet part of a formal credited class. Last year, Dobler and Harry Bloomberg, a CIS systems analyst, collaborated on a new course that is unlike anything that the English Department has ever offered. Indeed, there is not another course available at the University that could even come close. The course, titled "Topics in Electronic Media," offers a mixture of computing, publication design and writing instruction that never would have been envisioned in the days prior to the Internet.

—Tim Fitzgerald, *Connections!*

The World Wide Web is essentially a gigantic engine for publishing—with global distribution. As a writer, Dobler finds this a compelling and irresistibly charming notion. He wanted to get his hands on such an engine and learn how to make it run. As a teacher of writers, particularly young professionals who hope to go on to become magazine writers; editors; journalists; technical, corporate, public relations, or advertising writers, if not writing teachers themselves, Dobler felt that a course in the theory, practice, and implications of creating content on the World Wide Web was simply a practical and responsible offering for a university nonfiction writing program.

On the practical side, we find ourselves in the midst of a revolution in providing and receiving information, ranging from scholarly resources to the latest news, from raw data to poetry—a revolution in how we will train, teach, learn, communicate, do research, and publish. We will see changes in the way we shop, and in how we are entertained and a dramatic transformation in how we will interact with each other and even with our government. The great need, the hot prospect, the new job opportunity of our time, especially for those in communications and writing, will be providing content for the World Wide Web.

This revolution in providing content touches writers ranging from the nuts-and-bolts journalist to the most esoteric scholar. We are making our journalism students aware of a shift from the standard "who-what-when-where-why" pattern to a new form that involves creating stories with hyperlinks to other text, to images, to sounds, and to video clips. The whole notion of a news story is being rethought and reinvented. Already, the eight major newspaper chains have joined in a single enterprise that, by the time you read this, will bring some 180 newspapers online, providing local, targeted editions for the metro areas they will serve, along with discussion groups and up-to-the-minute news, a combination of your local paper and something perhaps resembling CNN and talk radio. Magazines such as *Discovery Channel On-line* are changing the way feature stories are conceived and presented. Even for those who do not think, or need to think, about restructuring information for a hypermedia–multimedia environment (and I am thinking here of scholars and academic writers), the World Wide Web is opening up new venues. Scholarly, professional, corporate, and popular journals, along with new electronic journals that exist only in cyberspace, are moving to the Web partly because the cost of hard-copy printing and distribution makes Internet publication economical, and partly because the Web allows broader distribution and easy updates. On the Internet, a journal can be a living and growing document, with threads of discussion added to it day after day, or responses and alterations made at a moment's notice.

For researchers in all areas, the range of the Web and the Internet's other resources, such as gopher sites, Usenet, and Listserv discussion groups, as well as active online discussion in MOOs and various real-time chat rooms, create an interactive research space. Documents that would have remained unpublished or published to limited audiences are finding their way into worldwide distribution because the Web makes that possible. Web browsers (the software that allows you to "see" Web pages) can also find gopher sites and the vast, archived resources contained in the ten million gopher files spread around the world on over five thousand host computers. Join a Usenet or Listserv discussion group and you can not only read discussion threads, but you can also pose questions to a worldwide audience and get answers—a research tool that scholars, journalists, students, hobbyists, parents, teachers (the list could go on and on), and anyone needing a specific piece of information could not have dreamed of two decades ago. And Web browsers such as Netscape, the favorite tool of some 70–80 percent of Web users, have built-in Usenet access.

Supposedly, we are no more than six degrees of separation from any person or piece of information we need. The Internet, with all its communication and information tools—e-mail, electronic discussion groups, gopher, Internet Relay Chat, and the World Wide Web—puts those six degrees of separation into overdrive for us as teachers and researchers. To cite one example of how this power to conduct interactive research has transformed the way people find or disseminate information, we would suggest the example we see repeated more and more often: Someone makes a desperate appeal for help on a medical situation and gets responses from electronic discussion groups, as well as information from Web and gopher servers, that otherwise might well have remained inaccessible. Quite literally, some people are doing research—or supplying information to seekers—that has saved lives. In less dramatic situations, the Internet and the Web are providing new sources of research materials, whether in the form of online expertise or online documents. It is not a matter anymore of using computer searches to locate existing documents buried in some far-off library or archive. The Web is providing documents and resources that simply *do not exist in any other form*, resources that would be too expensive to publish on paper or CD-ROM. Right now—and not in some distant future—doing research without looking for resources on the Internet is, in most cases, not really looking hard enough. Despite the seeming anarchy of the Web—its transitory nature, its built-in information overload and search tools that cannot, as of yet, provide absolutely reliable and exhaustive results—we will find more and more useful materials moving into this ever expanding cyberspace.

Although it may seem merely fashionable or faddish to call anything that looks sufficiently new or different "a revolution," the World Wide Web, even in its infancy, is truly something new under the sun. We have not seen anything since the invention of printing, the harnessing of electricity, and the ubiquitous sprawl of television to rival the impact of the Web, and the Web itself is already undergoing a revolution that will transform the way many, or most of us, use computers and software.

The transformation of the Web, and Web browsers, began in late 1995 and took hold before the end of 1996. Here is what was happening:

- APIs (Application Program Interfaces), such as Adobe Acrobat and Macromind Director, were built (or "plugged") into browsers, such as Netscape, allowing you to run and display multimedia applications as though your computer had a preloaded CD-ROM.
- Java, software "applets" that download automatically, began to perform various functions such as interactive spreadsheets, word

processing, and database searches. The applets resided on the Web server but were able to run on most browsers on any platform, just as though you were connected to a powerful inhouse server loaded with hundreds of software programs.

- Scripting language allowed nonprogrammers to create simpler versions of Java applets as a normal part of writing HTML, turning even low-tech Internet users into software designers and authors.

All of this represents a profound paradigm shift from regarding the Internet/Web as a mechanism for electronic publishing to redefining the Internet/Web as a *platform* (just as, say, Sun workstation, Macintosh, or PC computers are platforms) and considering the various browsers, such as Netscape, to be the *operating system* (such as UNIX, Mac OS, or Windows).

This shift from publishing to a combined platform and operating system not only broadens the usefulness of the Internet and Web browsers, but it may also even lead to $500 PCs that do not need much in the way of storage or an operating system or software, PCs that operate as terminals connected to a worldwide network full of software, highly specialized applications, multimedia files—and an even richer variety of electronic publications than we have today.

Because Web applications are already essentially platform independent—running nearly as well under Windows and under the Macintosh operating system as on powerful UNIX machines—resources created at one location can be accessed across the campus or across the globe. Therefore, courseware or publications created on one site are not limited by specialized software or hardware. This easy, almost effortless exchange, this built-in ubiquity, is essential even to the current information revolution. If it plays on your system, it will play in Peoria.

Topics in Electronic Media

We have already moved into an environment in which ideas, images, sounds, video and animation clips, and hyperlinked documents have become increasingly commonplace. Beyond the practical implications of these changes upon changes, it seemed a matter of simple responsibility to give our professional writing students a way not only to decipher this audiovisual environment but also to manipulate it, control it, and become proficient in navigating through it. The course we have been teaching helps students understand how to gather information, how to design and shape that information usefully, and how to create content that is effective and, we hope, elegant, useful, and powerful.

As you might well imagine, setting up such a course takes not only some delicate navigating through the academic environment, with forays across disciplines and administrative levels, but it also demands hard work and commitment from the faculty member involved. Getting yourself up to speed is a job in itself; you will have to master the basic technical issues just to get a sense of what you might expect from the course and the students. To actually teach the course, you will have to gain some proficiency with both hardware and software.

That done, you can begin to pull in support, both administrative and technical, as well as to consider the hardware and software you will need and the classroom space you will require for such a course to prosper. Speaking bluntly, for most of us in the liberal arts, a hypermedia production course will require some months of preparation. You have to decide for yourself if offering such a course is worth the time and energy.

Although we did not know it when we first began, the minimum requirements for the course probably break down into the following elements:

- E-mail and UNIX accounts for *everyone* in the class
- A computer classroom, with Internet access, available for *every* class meeting
- Public computer labs, with Internet access, *readily* available on campus
- At least one flatbed color scanner with Adobe Photoshop or the equivalent
- Some kind of support person(s) to answer technical questions about UNIX and CGI scripts
- An *already-established* Web server on the university's file-sharing system

In addition, you will find it desirable to have access to:

- A slide scanner
- A small-to-moderate budget line to cover the cost of Kodak PhotoCDs (100 slides for about $100)
- Computers with Adobe Photoshop or equivalent *and* with CD-ROM drives
- Sound and video equipment to convert audio to *au* and/or *wav* files and video to *mpeg*, *mov* and/or *avi* files

If you do not have the minimum requirements, the course probably is not feasible. Without the slide scanner or the budget for some PhotoCDs,

you will be limited to handling prints for your images. Without the sound
and video equipment, you will obviously have to forego audio and video
clips on your Web pages. On the other hand, students can at least download such clips from other sites and use them in their pages for demonstration purposes.

We had most of the above on hand before we began, and we quickly
gathered up the rest (the slide scanner and a moderate budget) as we
put the course together. Here are the steps we took, from initial concept
to the first day of class:

1. In January, Bruce Dobler asked Harry Bloomberg if Bloomberg
   could get him a copy of Mosaic so that he could see the World
   Wide Web. Bloomberg did, and he showed Dobler several interesting sites during the month.

2. In February, Bloomberg suggested we might offer a one- or two-
   hour Web seminar as part of the university's Quick Start program.
   At this point, a nonfiction topics course for fall had failed, and
   Dobler needed to provide a new topic or course. Dobler told
   Bloomberg that if Bloomberg could in any way assist, Dobler would
   like to do a whole semester on Web publishing. Dobler went to the
   department chair and the Writing Program head and got the okay.
   Our department advisor suggested that students be allowed to
   claim the course as either a topics or internship requirement.

3. Bloomberg got permission from CIS (Computing and Information
   Services) to co-teach and otherwise support the course. We scheduled the new offering in our journalism lab, which has twenty-
   three networked Macs, and began talking about goals. We would
   teach students the basics of HTML and send them out as interns to
   put on Pitt's World Wide Web server various academic units, such
   as Sports Information, Semester at Sea, Alumni Affairs, Pitt Magazine, The Pitt News, and a campus tour.

4. During March and April, we gave Web demos to these various
   units so that they would take on the student interns. We also discussed, at length, the problems in dealing with already published
   material, in terms of permissions for photos and copy and the difficulties of dealing with files in various formats—and the question
   of getting the finished product. In each area, someone would accept the responsibility of having the final say before any Web site
   could be published.

5. Working with Bloomberg, Dobler spent May through August learning how to scan images on both a flatbed and a slide scanner. At
   this time, no one seemed to be certain at what resolution the initial
   scans should be made, or if 72 dpi (dots per inch) was indeed suf-

ficient for final scans (it was). It was clear that we could not have twenty-two students discovering how to scan on a trial-and-error basis; we would have to settle on a step-by-step routine that would produce adequate results. In addition, we tried various Web editing programs, and Dobler learned basic UNIX commands as well as file management and editing. By the end of summer we had scaled back our estimation of what the students might accomplish. We originally had thought we would put three Pitt publications online, but it became obvious we had to choose one and make sure it worked.

6. During the summer, we also made sure that Mosaic would work in our classroom and got it installed in the public labs, and both of us tried working with HTML editor programs that might be made available to students. We settled on Hotmetal for the X-Windows/ UNIX environment and on BBEdit Lite with HTML extensions for the Mac.

7. Just before classes began, we put the syllabus online as a Web document, with links to various useful sites, including several guides to writing HTML. We arranged for some class sessions to be held in the UNIX lab, so that the students could make use of Sun workstations, and some to be held in our TEC (Technology Evaluation Center) Lab, where students would find scanners and a support staff.

For most of you reading this now, the Web is not so mysterious and some of these steps can be eliminated. What cannot be eliminated is the necessity for the faculty member to feel generally comfortable in a technical environment—and for the technical support person to stretch in the other direction, to provide nontechnical explanations, simple metaphors, and lots of patience. Some liberal arts majors want to know, for example, why you would spend a lot of time talking about "eunuchs" as an operating system.

Our course announcements had to reflect the liberal arts background of our students and the advisors, as well as of other colleagues. Just to make sure we would make the enrollment, considering that this was a new course offered at the last minute (in academic time), we ran an ad in the school paper. Figure 4.1 depicts how we described our hypermedia class.

As it turned out, though, not all students felt that e-mail used alone was "just fine." Evan, the one graduate student in the course, found that

> too many people . . . are quite simply not proficient enough in computer [terminology] to be included in this new technology. Indeed, that is what I found difficult about the course. I am not computer

> NEW Magazine/News Internship Course: Electronic Publishing on the Internet!
>
> ENGWRT 1403/8403 Topics in Nonfiction: Electronic Media
> 3 credits— M/W 4-5:15 PM— CL G-26— Instructor: Prof. Bruce Dobler—
> Technical Support: Harry Bloomberg, CIS.
>
> Pitt Magazine, The Pitt News, Sports and Information Publications, programs such as Semester at Sea, and various Southwestern Pennsylvania Travel and Information Bureaus, will be publishing on-line electronic versions of newspapers, magazines and brochures over the World Wide Web. Students in this internship will learn how to research, design and publish such hypermedia documents using text, images, video/movie clips and sound bites. Course provides technical support—so if you can use e-mail and a word processor (or are willing to learn), you'll do just fine.
>
> Requirements: Magazine 1 or News 1—or the equivalent—or permission of the instructor.

Figure 4.1. Course Catalog Description

> literate. I use E-mail and because of my writing, I can't do without a computer for publishing, etc., but the hypermedia class really was loaded with new terms and technologies which can only be compared to a foreign language.

This problem could be remedied, according to another student, Jennifer, by reminding the computer support person that this is, after all, an English class. "Don't get more technical than necessary. Explain the technicalities students needed to know but not those that they don't. If you find yourself saying 'you don't really need to know this but . . . , ' then don't say it." Jennifer makes this point for a good reason. "The technology was cool. It really wasn't hard, but we were given so much unnecessary technical information that we often got bored and quit paying attention to information that would have been really valuable."

For other students, the technical difficulties had more to do with priorities—too much to learn and do in a single semester. Sara, a graduating senior who is now publishing an online magazine with classmate Patricia, wished the course had been offered over two semesters.

> There are things that take more finesse to do, such as image-maps, mail-to forms, etc., that just can't be covered in one semester. I'll explain: what needed to be taught were the basics. This was done, in a fine way. Once everybody learned the basics, they needed time to experiment with this new knowledge. I know that [Bruce] and Harry took a session to try to teach us how to do image-maps, but at

that point in the semester, most of us were past the point of caring to learn new things—we were too busy getting our projects finished, etc. I now regret that I didn't pay more attention to what Harry was telling us, although I really do believe he was being too technical at that point. Anyway, things like that take more time, so I think a two-semester hypermedia course would alleviate this situation. The first semester, teach the basics (because most people don't know UNIX or how to use their e-mail). Once these are learned, let the students experiment. In the second semester, move on to more complicated things (like adding sound and video; those sessions meant nothing to me).

Sara was an outstanding student in the first year of this course, and we asked her if getting on top of the technology had been a struggle for her given that she had no computer background beyond e-mail. She said:

At first, I was going to answer "no," it came easily to me, but the more I thought about it, the more I realized that wasn't true. It WAS difficult, and a struggle. The reason I did well is because I spent so much time experimenting. My page did not look right the first few times I did it. The thing about me is, I won't stop until something is exactly the way I want it to be (a virtue or a fault, depending on your viewpoint). I sat in that computer lab in between classes, after classes, before classes, until I learned everything I needed to know. To be honest sometimes I skipped classes because I didn't want to leave in the middle of a project. I spent more time on this course than any other I took at Pitt. Part of it, I suppose, is the excitement of learning something completely new. Also, the fact that your work can be seen across the world probably had something to do with it. You ought to warn your future classes that they won't succeed if they're not going to put a lot of time into this.

The UNIX commands and the HTML tags were relatively easy to learn. What was much, much harder was dealing with technical equipment. The scanner was tremendously hard to learn how to use, as was Photoshop. Transferring files was another pain in the butt. Part of what makes it hard is that it's something so new; the people who know how to use it (computer consultants at the TEC lab, etc.) were kind of frightening because there's this notion that 'normal' students hold of computer science majors. That they're geniuses and we'll never be able to understand them. That said, the people in the TEC lab were extremely helpful, once I got past that initial fear of talking to them.

Beyond dealing with varieties of technophobia and the inevitable problem of introducing a new technology to the classroom—technology getting in the way of teaching—we also relearned an old lesson about learning and motivation. People generally want to learn the things they feel they really need—not the things they may, theoretically or really, need, but the things they truly *feel* they need. That first semester, we

probably spent too much time insisting on teaching technology before
the students really had a solid sense of why they would need it. The
second semester, Bloomberg took the lead, speaking in a language the
English majors could understand.

> We're going to learn some technology in here. We're going to learn
> to write HTML so we can design web pages and publish them. But
> first we are going to *look* at some websites out there on the Net and
> see what's good and bad and exciting and useful. We're going to
> consider what you can do on the Web and why you'd want to do it.
> And then, when you've got a feel for the Web, we're going to spend
> some time learning *how* to create Web documents. After all, you
> wouldn't want to go out and write a bunch of poems until you had
> read—and thought about—some poetry.

In the student evaluations of that first semester, many students mentioned that they wished they had gotten started on their internships
sooner. The second time we taught the course we moved up the timetable, and that seemed to work better. Even in a course in which technology comprises much of the content and ways of working, teachers
must be alert to the risk of technology taking over or acting like some
noisome interloper that stands between you, your students, and the real
work. As long as you are aware of the problem and can adjust, experience will gradually show you ways to maintain balance. Sometimes this
may mean abandoning some aspect of the course or courseware you
thought essential. We used an HTML editor that we thought deserved
the two class sessions it took students to learn it. The editor seemed
powerful, offering preview features that allowed students to see on screen
what they were designing and that featured a built-in HTML syntax or
grammar correction, which precluded writing faulty HTML. But, like
some incredibly pedantic grammarian, our editor also precluded writing some "normal" HTML that it had not really considered before, refusing to save or write files it didn't approve of. Worse, it sometimes
persuaded itself of errors that neither Dobler nor Bloomberg, nor an
online HTML checker, could discover. Despite the time we put in, we
finally had to admit to the class that this editor was not such a great
idea; the second semester we didn't even mention the offending editor.

At times like this, when technology breaks down, emphasize the pioneering instinct, the exploration, the new frontier—and not the fact that
for the moment, we are all hopelessly lost!

In both semesters, it took about a month for students really to grasp
the basics of HTML, Web design and a handful of necessary UNIX commands to make the technology and course content come together. For
the third semester, at the request of perhaps a third of the students and

despite the wealth of up-to-date online resources available, we assigned a textbook for the course. The title is indicative of the growing impatience all of us had with getting everyone up to speed: *Teach Yourself Web Publishing with HTML in a Week,* by Laura Lemay.

On that first day of class, as in every course you teach, you need to let students know what you are going to expect by the end of term, how much work the course requires, what sort of work, the level of participation, ways in which learning will be demonstrated, what is due at the end, and how different elements will be graded. With any new course, anticipating all of this can be tricky. Add a new and evolving technology, and your job gets trickier still. The first semester we were able to teach our students just about *all* of the existing HTML tags in use. During the second semester, beginning in January 1995, we found that the number of HTML formatting tags, or extensions, had at least doubled. By the start of the fourth semester, in January 1996, the best we could hope for was to teach the basics and at least expose students to the more advanced HTML extensions and their implications in Web design. Nonetheless, we would be testing our students on what remain the essentials: HTML basic tags, headers, lists, anchors, and inline images. Of all these, the theory and practice of creating *anchors*—links from text or an image in one document to files or to other documents—lies at the heart of hypertext; and we must be absolutely sure that our students understand how to create and manipulate those links.

It seems apparent to us that with technology, testing truly teaches. The students need tests, early and often, as a diagnostic. And, for the first time in some twenty years of teaching, Dobler felt that he had the tools to give a test in which students were learning as they sweated through the exam. The test created a situation in which students suddenly had—and felt—a genuine need to use all of their skills early in the semester. We did not test enough the first time around, and we ended up with some students who, at the end of term, still could not reliably create a hyperlink to another document or put an inline GIF image on the page with a link to a larger JPEG image. In essence, they managed to muddle through by asking others, including lab technicians, to help, without actually learning the basics of creating a Web document. This did not happen the second semester.

To illustrate the nature of these tests, see Figures 4.2, 4.3, and 4.4. We handed out a sheet of plain text, no bold, no italics, no large type, no photos, no bulleted or numbered lists—just text. Along with the text, we handed out a finished Web page, using the same text but with all the formatting done, including pictures. We also gave them a list of UNIX filenames where they could get pictures and Web site addresses to which

---

Here is my HTML test

Section One: The Basics

I have worked hard learning how to do HTML and I am making bold strides forward! Among the things I am learning to do, is to create a bulleted list, and to include links on this list. Here is an example:

A bulleted list.

  Link to my home page
  Link to Pitt's main page
  Link to the syllabus

Numbered list: Three useful websites

  ABC News online
  New York Times online
  Yahoo Home Page

Section Two: Intermediate

Again, we have done all of this in class.

There are ways to adjust font size to make text larger or smaller.

                Send me email: yourname+@pitt.edu

                    Last revised: 5/20/98

Below...a horizontal rule...can you make one like it?

Section Three: Advanced

POEM
from the depth
of the dreamy
decline
of the DAWN....

Figure 4.2. Plain Text

they could create links. Then, on the lab server, we showed them where they could retrieve the plain text file and gave them some choices:

1. Move the text into your UNIX account and mark it up using the Pico editor.

2. Retrieve the text using the BBEdit Lite HTML editor and then either copy and paste into UNIX or use Fetch to move the file directly.

3. Use the Netscape browser to look at your file as you work to see if the formatting is doing what you want.

Figure 4.3. Finished Page

Figure 4.4. Notes for URLS, etc.

To hand in the assignment, all students had to do was bring the finished file up on Netscape, go into View Source to display the HTML, and print out the result on the lab computer (making sure their name was added to the top of the text file).

One student finished, with no errors, in twenty minutes. Most got about forty to sixty percent done within the hour. A few became hopelessly lost but came to see us in the office to go over every line of their test. By the end of the term, almost everyone in the class could create a solid, working Web page with the essential markup tags in the right places. If you are clear on what exactly students need to know, and if you can find a way to communicate it, test it, and reexplain it, your students will be less anxious and you will keep the technology where it belongs—as a tool, not an obstacle.

Along with working on technical skills, however, you must work closely to see that students are creating a design that will make sense. Bloomberg's long experience in the software industry served us well in this course. Sometimes academics forget that writers occasionally produce a job that has to satisfy a real-world customer—and meet deadlines. This practical course put that dynamic to a final test for all of us.

"What I found over the years," Bloomberg tells the students, "is that the earlier in a project that you make a mistake, the more it costs to correct later on." The solution? "What we need to do in a course like this is to storyboard the design first, to see where the links go, to see how the site is connected, to get a sense of whether the information structure is going to make sense. And then we have to build what's called a rapid prototype."

A rapid prototype is essentially a skeleton with some skin on it and a few working organs. It looks like the real thing, but only some of the parts work. You might create a homepage with all the links apparently in place, but, if you click, only a few of them actually work. But those working links will take you to another page with perhaps another dozen or so links, again only a few of which work. Show this to a class, a teacher, a customer, and you can, by clicking on the few active links, easily demonstrate how the site will look and work. It is much easier and, in business, cheaper to make changes when you work with this rapid prototype. Some Web designers also speak of this as "proof of concept."

Having made a few simpleminded errors early on *and* replicated them a few hundred times in the course of a year as he created the English Department Web site at Pitt, Dobler reflected on Bloomberg's wisdom for hours, going through perhaps four hundred files and making tiny changes, the same tiny changes, one . . . at . . . a . . . time.

It is precisely because of Bloomberg's rule (the earlier the mistake, the more costly the fix) that you, as teacher, must act as team leader and project coordinator for your students, whether they work alone or in small groups. And to act in this way, to be a useful presence in storyboarding and demonstrating the rapid prototypes, you must be on top of the material and the technology. You have to put in the time up front or *everyone* will pay for the early mistakes.

Another mistake that we made in the first semester had nothing to do with technology or design. We erred, grievously in a few cases, by assuming that we could simply set up the students in teams, let them pick a leader or work in whatever cooperative way they chose, and send them on their way. As many of our students find out when they begin their professional careers, however, teamwork plays a much more significant role in the working world than it does in the academy. Schools typically put great importance on what an individual working alone achieves, but we find when we begin teaching or writing for a corporation, or doing much of the world's work, that the ability and agility of cooperative, constructive interaction—in short *teamwork*—carry the day. The lesson we learned was so simple that we do not know how we forgot it: Teams need leaders. A team without a leader, with no clear lines of authority or, minimally, no model for action, quickly turns into a mob or a melee. After a semester of alibis, finger-pointing, complaints, and uncertainty, Dobler, as faculty member, had to put the blame on himself. Along with HTML and Web design, we needed to teach teamwork, and we began the second semester by offering our own examples from jobs we had done and the kinds of jobs the students would do. Dobler and Bloomberg split the projects, acting as team leader-coordinator for the teams under them.

Most of the teams quickly found someone who was willing to lead in a particular area, settled on how the work would be divided and who would do what, and arranged for meetings at fairly regular intervals to keep the project moving. Teams reported to Bloomberg and Dobler, and the entire class was asked, team by team (along with some individuals who had one-person projects), to demonstrate the rapid prototypes shortly after midterm.

This time we had fewer problems, but Sara's first-semester experience, working on a Web site for Pitt's Nationality Rooms, revealed some remaining weakness in our plan.

> Working in teams was frustrating. It was probably a good idea, considering the work load, but a lot of times I felt like I was making an extra effort and the others weren't. I also felt that they weren't sticking to the layout. I didn't want to be the "boss," but I ended up feeling that way and I think some of the others resented that fact. But we should have all stuck to the plan we conceived of our first meeting, and two of us did, while two of us didn't. Another thing is, I think you should make it mandatory that we meet once a week. I really think that's important. The groups should have to sit down together and discuss what's going on. That makes it possible to head off problems.

We will follow Sara's advice next time around by discussing our expectations for the semester: what we consider HTML/UNIX basic competency and how we will measure the quantity and quality of individual work—and how we will expect individual students to function when working as part of a team.

For our course in publishing on the Web, our goals are that students create by end of term two projects that are in fairly good working order.

The first project, one that begins the first class session, is to create a personal homepage that demonstrates at least the following:

- several hyperlinks, both to other pages on the student's own site and to homepages outside of Pitt
- a personal picture (to show that the student can scan an image and save to proper format)
- an inline, GIF image with link to a larger JPEG image of same
- link to either audio or video clip
- basic HTML text formatting, including:

  -headers

  -bold and italic text

  -bulleted and/or numbered list

  -preformatted text

  -hard rules

  -paragraph and line breaks

  -centered text
- some advanced HTML extensions such as:

  -backgrounds

  -text in color

  -tables

  -font size
- error-free HTML

The final project does not have to be complete but should function well enough to demonstrate the site or act as "proof of concept." Because of the fluid, open-ended quality of designing Web sites (nothing ever seems finished!), it is important, not only to be clear about expectations but also to stay in close contact with every student and every project throughout the semester and to be responsive and flexible as unforeseen problems suddenly arise.

Another set of expectations (and occasional surprises) will also affect this class: What will the liberal arts instructor expect of the computer support person (whether full- or part-time), and what might someone with a technical and even nonteaching background expect of the instructor and students? The first question suggests its own answer. The liberal arts instructor, most likely the sole official instructor for the course, bears ultimate responsibility for syllabus, students, and grading. And that liberal arts teacher will likely lean heavily on the computer expert for technical support throughout the term. But both need to hear the other. As this course started, Dobler and Bloomberg sat down well ahead of time, talked out the goals, and worked on the syllabus. Both agreed that the computer expert would probably handle most of the classroom presentation and discussion in the first few weeks, and experience proved this true. But what did this all look like from Bloomberg's perspective, before, during, and after that first semester? And how does he see the interaction now? "If I had to write a headline about myself," Bloomberg says, "It would go something like this: **Unexpected Peace Dividend: A Former Defense Engineer Becomes an English Instructor.**"

From the Collaborator's Perspective

When Bloomberg decided to leave the defense industry to join the staff of Computing and Information Services at the University of Pittsburgh, he never dreamed that he would end up as a member of Pitt's English Department. After all, engineers stereotypically enter the profession because they relate better to hardware and mathematics than to human emotion and expression. Engineering students take liberal arts courses only when forced to by degree requirements, and then with great disdain. Some of the worst writing Bloomberg has been forced to read has been written by engineers. One particularly memorable engineering paper he read while working on a guided-bomb project described damage caused by a smart bomb as "target signature modification."

According to Bloomberg, however, current technology does not permit successful contributors to be pigeonholed into a particular discipline. For example, a brilliant engineer might design a WWW page that works perfectly in terms of transferring data efficiently to the Internet and meets every requirement of HTML, but it might do a poor job of communicating a message to a reader. Likewise, the English writing major knows all about communicating a message to people but doesn't know how to unravel the mechanics of the problem. To use a non-Internet example, an engineer could design a billboard that would glow brightly and survive hurricane winds but communicate nothing. The English major would know what to put on the billboard but wouldn't know how to plug in the lights so that others could read it.

The most important words in developing a successful Web page are *collaboration* and *multidisciplinary*. The engineer and English major both need each other to succeed. But they speak different languages and view

problems from different perspectives. Bloomberg's job was to try to overcome this gap and to allow Dobler's students to use the necessary tools
to create a Web page.

Unfortunately, these tools were developed with engineers in mind,
not liberal arts majors. This proved to be the biggest stumbling block in
the entire course. The students grasped the basics of HTML easily
enough, but they found the mechanics of development troublesome.
Among the problem areas were UNIX, distributed computing, and
HTML developmental tools.

UNIX

Bloomberg likes to think of UNIX as an operating system that was developed by hackers for other hackers. The UNIX user interface was designed with this community in mind, not the community of English
majors who grew up using a Mac or Windows GUI. Depending on one's
point of view, UNIX commands are either terse or cryptic. Our class
found commands such as *ls*, *cd*, *mv*, and *rm* most confusing. The case
sensitivity of commands does not help either. Bloomberg suspects that
for many of our students, this was their first exposure to a command-
line computer interface. He had grown up with these kinds of systems,
and it was difficult for him to understand what it was like *not* to grow
up staring at a C:> prompt.

Another UNIX concept confusing to English majors is directories. Pitt's
Web server requires that all Web pages *must* be in a user's public/HTML
directory. To an engineer, this is a trivial requirement to meet. However,
this was a great source of confusion for our students, particularly early
in the semester. Many students would write a perfect piece of HTML,
only to have a Web browser be unable to read it because it was in the
wrong directory.

Directories are also confusing in collaborative efforts. Pitt uses a form
of file-sharing on its UNIX systems called Andrew File System (AFS)
that makes it easy for students to work in a common directory. However, moving files from student accounts into developmental directories was not easy. The UNIX commands to copy files from a student
directory into a common directory are something like the following:

    cd ~bdobler/public/html/sas

    cp ~wlsst13/public/html/.html*

Such commands were beyond the grasp of most of the class and usually
required some assistance from Bloomberg.

Distributed Computing

All of the scanning tools and the best HTML development tools are hosted on Macs or PCs. But all files and images eventually must be moved to the UNIX system. Some students never understood why this was necessary, and the mechanics of file transfers were a source of great trouble. Ultimately, we spent a lot of class time just covering how to transfer images to UNIX. Still, one student spent hours scanning six images, only to botch the file transfer from the scanning station to UNIX (we suspect that he transferred the files as MacBinary rather than Raw Data). Despite a great deal of effort, we were not able to recover the corrupted images, and, by the time the problem was noted, the images had been purged from the scanning station's temporary disk area.

HTML Development Tools

To avoid the problems of file transfers, we initially teach our students how to write HTML in UNIX with a text editor named Pico. Pico is already familiar to many of our students because it is the same text editor used by the Pine e-mail program, the most popular mail program at Pitt. Pico is easy to learn and was not a major source of trouble for students. However, it requires them to enter every single character of every HTML tag. Although this is acceptable for small Web pages, a power tool to reduce the drudgery of generating tags seemed like a good idea.

We have used two HTML tools. The first one, BBEdit Lite is Mac based. The mechanics of using BBEdit on the English Department lab machines were confusing, however, and although the tool could generate HTML, it would not check HTML syntax. A student could use BBEdit Lite to write incorrect HTML. The other tool we tried was a UNIX workstation-based package called Hotmetal. In theory, Hotmetal should have provided many advantages over PC-based tools. It read and wrote files directly to the student's public/HTML directory, so the problem of file transfer was completely eliminated. Hotmetal also enforced very rigorous HTML syntax. With Hotmetal, it is impossible to write syntactically incorrect HTML.

At the time, Hotmetal was Bloomberg's favorite HTML development tool, and he thought it would be of use to the class. So we arranged to use a UNIX workstation lab, and Bloomberg attempted to teach our class how to use Hotmetal. The first problem is that Pitt's UNIX workstations (various flavors of Sun SPARCs) run a GUI called X-Windows. X-Windows was developed at MIT with the hard-core UNIX community in mind and is completely different from GUIs on Pitt's Macs and DOS machines. For example, to open a UNIX session, the student must either type "xterm -ls" from inside a terminal window that already exists, or move the mouse to an area of the display that is not already covered by a window, hold down the middle mouse button and then scroll down a menu until "xterm -ls" is found. Bloomberg has a SPARC on his desk; it is the machine he uses for his daily work. He uses X-Windows so much that he forgets how difficult it can be to learn.

The next problem was that because Hotmetal was not an officially supported software package at Pitt, we needed to instruct the students in its use by copying a short UNIX script into the directory that contains their programs. Finally, Hotmetal proved to be too exacting to be useful. The slightest error in HTML would result in a cryptic error message that was not of much use in identifying the problem. Also, Hotmetal's interface proved to be difficult to learn. So, at least for our class, Hotmetal turned out to be a failed experiment.

We now teach BBEdit Lite and Pico, and we are evaluating a promising new tool called HotDog. Even if we should find the perfect HTML development tool, we would still teach Pico because we think it is important that students understand what functions the tools perform before they start to use one. It is also easier to make a small change to a Web page with Pico than to transfer the file to a PC, invoke a tool, make the change, and transfer the file back.

In addition to problems with development tools, another difficulty needed to be overcome—culture. Bloomberg had been computing so long and dealt on the job with so many computer-literate individuals that he tended to forget that not everybody has an intuitive grasp of computing and computers. For our class, he needed to teach computing more slowly and to relate computer technology in terms that English majors can understand. He also needed to eliminate anything that was not absolutely necessary for students to meet the minimal requirements of putting a page up on the Web. This meant no neat but tricky shortcuts, a minimum of explanation about why something worked, and a lot of repetition. In other words, he needed to view the computer as a tool to an end and not an end in itself.

So, were we successful? Every student (except for one with a medical problem) was ultimately able to place a page on the Web. However, we learned that students fell into three categories:

- Those who quickly grasped computing concepts and seemed to possess an intuitive feel for computers;
- Those who could master the necessary UNIX and HTML tool incantations by rote and get the job done;

- Hopeless cases who, no matter how hard they tried, just did not have it in them to understand computing (these students needed help from their classmates to get any sort of Web page up).

Although the title of the class scared off most members of the third group before they even registered, a few of them still enrolled. That first semester we had difficulty identifying these people because they were usually afraid to admit they were in over their heads. They would sit in the back of the class and nod their approval at whatever computer jargon was thrown in their direction. The next semester, however, we learned that an easy exam on UNIX and HTML fundamentals within the first few weeks helped us identify these people; we could then keep a close eye on them and offer assistance.

Ultimately, we found that it is indeed possible to teach English majors how to develop Web pages but we also learned that we had to be prepared to spend a significant amount of time and effort dealing with computer-related issues. Dobler says that he really needs a full-time computer person to co-teach the class and Bloomberg agrees. Bloomberg can quickly resolve computer problems that would take Dobler a bit longer to solve.

Student Reaction to Collaboration

"Our class," Bloomberg concludes, "is a prime example of the benefits of the collaboration between technical and liberal arts people." In student feedback on our interaction during the semester, a few students mentioned that they found one part of the dynamic between Bloomberg and Dobler very confusing. Sometimes Dobler would begin to explain, step by step, how to do something, and then Bloomberg would interject, "There's actually another way to do that," and then begin to explain. Or Bloomberg would begin to explain something and Dobler, feeling that Bloomberg was being too technical, would interrupt and either suggest a simpler way to do things or give a simpler explanation (the "liberal arts version"). Such cross-talk is confusing and makes note-taking impossible. We had to learn to let the other teacher talk and then see if anyone had further questions. If you teach technology to students who do not have a technology background, be aware that many of them, even the most eager, are under genuine stress. This is particularly true when students deal with software and hardware that simply will not function if so much as a single character or operation is missing or in the wrong order. Generally, in a writing class, we make room for a variety of approaches, readings, responses, arguments, and even, to borrow a computer term, a certain amount of fuzzy logic. Computers are not so forgiving.

One student, Paul, who found a full-time job writing HTML for a Web design and presence company, offers advice to students who want to succeed in a course in which technology is part of the content and not just a tool.

> Students have to practice. At home, in the campus labs, at the TEC center—they just have to practice scanning, loading images, working with HTML and UNIX, moving files around, experimenting and generally seeing what happens. I had a big interest in computers before I took the course. Even so, I spent a lot of time outside the class just practicing. It might help if the instructors assigned more homework—and checked on it. Maybe a textbook would help. But the students really need to get involved if they want to get on top of this material. I learned how to do this and it got me a job—doing what I like to do.

The payoff for the hard work—the real delight both of teaching and taking this course—occurs about two-thirds of the way through the semester, as the projects begin to take shape and the students see that they are actually publishing, that this engine called the World Wide Web is displaying their work over a global distribution network, and that their friends at Pitt, and around the world, can actually see what they have created.

It is clear that this course is preparing many of our students for the new ways in which information will be presented. Students looking for positions as technical writers tell us that half or more of the listings they see ask for familiarity with HTML and the Web. Paul found his job immediately, and two other students, Sara and Patricia began publishing their magazine, *Marbles*, with the hope that it would lead to work.

As magazines and newspapers go online, new writing and editorial strategies will also emerge. The Discovery Channel's online magazine (*Discovery Channel On-line*) bills itself as offering "Originally Produced Interactive Stories with Film, Music, Photography and Illustration." Talk with the editors of this magazine and you will discover that they are engaged in creating a new structure for feature writing, one in which the main body of a story, which they call the spine, might be eight hundred words long, with several hyperlinks to information pages (called jumps) totaling another eight hundred to twelve hundred words. In the first half-year of this magazine, readers and editors and writers are educating each other, issue by issue, in what would make useful links, what belongs in the spine, what belongs in the jumps, what constitutes useful continuity and coherence. When the 180 or more major U.S. newspapers go online, the old five-W lead will still work, but the rest of the story may look very different and may also include sound and audio clips as well as pictures.

In the early days of film, directors made movies of plays, with the camera fixed and at a distance. The so-called "grammar of cinematography" developed in fits and starts, with arguments over whether audiences would understand close-up shots and cutaways to action going on at the same time. Audiences must learn, too. The shower scene in *Psycho,* which bewildered many moviegoers who saw it back in 1960, plays easily to viewers today. Likewise, when television first went national, most news shows were simply radio with a television camera pointing at the anchorperson while he or she read story after story. Today we are in the process of reinventing magazines and newspapers and books, along with advertising, information texts, and reference works—in short, we are finding the structures and audiovisual syntax that allow us to communicate effectively in a multimedia world. When you teach a course in which students write, design, and shape material for the World Wide Web, you will come to understand this quest, this challenge, this excitement, in a direct and practical way. And so will your students.

For Bloomberg, who has worked in a variety of software engineering situations, rapid change and constant upgrades are the norm. Obsolescence in the academy comes more slowly, though even that process seems to have speeded up, with one theoretical revolution coming so quickly on the heels of another that words such as *new* and *neo* and *contemporary* lose their luster in a hurry.

Dobler, in his many years of university study and then teaching, of working as a public relations writer and as a freelancer, and of writing novels, nonfiction, poetry and news stories, has had to learn one structural system after another. The adjustments began with the General Writing course in the late '50s, getting oriented to style guides for term papers and theses, then moving through the structure of short stories and novels, writing press releases and news stories, writing features (and various kinds of features tend to fall into certain patterns), creating grant applications, and probably dozens of other jobs that asked for a different structure, a different emphasis, a different style.

Writing in this new hypermedia–multimedia world seems to call for teamwork—not working alone in a cubicle, but rather working in a dialogic, connected environment. And such work certainly calls for some basic skills in design and image manipulation. Ideally, multimedia students should be offered cross-disciplinary courses in which writers, communications majors, graphic artists, library and information science spe-

cialists, students in education, and computer science majors work together in small teams, just as they would in an electronic publishing
agency or project team. Isolated work does not really fit this new paradigm. Dialogue, collaboration, communication, cross-disciplinary exchanges—these are probably going to become more and more necessary. In the new media, whether on the Web, on CD-ROM, or in some
software or network application, talent, energy, ideas, and technology
must converge. We must learn to be both specialists and generalists.

As magazines, newspapers, radio and television stations, along with
advertisers and public relations marketing efforts and online journals
from arts, sciences, technology, medicine, and every conceivable direction, meet somewhere in cyberspace, it becomes clear that *your* multimedia is going to look, sound, feel, and behave a lot like *my* multimedia.
CBS and *Time* and *The San Francisco Examiner* and Pitt's English Department and Sara and Patricia's online magazine share, and are published
in, the same space with the same tools at the same time to the same
general audience.

What this commonality of multimedia expression will mean for the
future is anybody's guess, but in the next decade, the explosion of ubiquitous hypermedia publication will surely be the stuff of papers, disser-
tations, conferences, articles, books, and online explorations. Nobody
has ever seen anything quite like this before. "Freedom of the Press,"
according to Joseph Liebling, "is guaranteed only to those who own
one." For the first time in history, that guarantee, robbed of its irony,
applies to just about everyone reading these words. We are in the middle
of a transforming event, as powerful as the invention of movable type,
electricity, radio, and television—and the engine that will drive this revolution can (and possibly should) be a part of your classroom or at least
your curriculum.

Today at Pitt, we are discovering, right along with our students, learning from them as they learn from us—and from thousands of other pub-
lishers big and small—how to move and think and operate in this multimedia publishing system. We are inventing ways of creating, managing, understanding, and presenting content for worldwide distribution.
And when, as happens in a world of transformation, we cannot immediately figure things out, we are learning to live with and to love our
confusion. A little patience goes well with technology.

Work Cited

Lemay, Laura. *Teach Yourself Web Publishing with HTML in a Week.* Indianapolis:
    Sams, 1995.

5 Don't Lower the River, Raise the Bridge: Preserving Standards by Improving Students' Performances

Susanmarie Harrington
Indiana University–Purdue University at Indianapolis

William Condon
University of Michigan

The project we describe here produced a series of four HyperCard stacks used by students in Psychology as a Natural Science, an introductory psychology course at the University of Michigan taken, for the most part, by nonmajors seeking to fulfill general education requirements. At the University of Michigan, English Composition Board (ECB) faculty fulfill part of their teaching assignment in the Writing Workshop, a service which offers writers half-hour conferences to discuss any writing project. Our first contact with these psychology students occurred when they began flooding the Writing Workshop, where they had been required by their teaching assistants to come after having failed, many of them miserably, on their first writing assignment (a formal research report). Our writing faculty noticed that not only had these students handed in poor work, but they also had little, if any, understanding of the assignment, and most were demoralized by the harsh comments their TAs had written on their reports. The faculty helped individual students as best they could, and as the numbers of psychology students coming for appointments remained high for several weeks, our conversations in the faculty lounge soon focused on the problems we saw, the solutions we attempted, and our growing sense that the psychology TAs were not well equipped to handle the writing problems their students faced. Bill Condon, at the time Associate Director for Instruction, contacted the psychology professor to learn more about the nature of the problem and to offer our assistance in preventing similar predicaments in subsequent semesters. Although the Writing Workshop's primary mission is to provide help for students, when extensive writing problems seem connected with one course, the ECB does offer to assist faculty. Since our dean was encouraging contact across departments and programs and had a special interest in developing instructional technology, we proposed using our expertise in conferencing with students and developing HyperCard stacks for writing assignments to assist the psychology professor in looking at the problems her students faced. She accepted our offer, and the collaboration began.

As we talked with Theresa Lee, the psychology professor, we discovered that she had included writing assignments in this large lecture course to give beginning students the chance to use writing as a way to learn how psychologists think; we also found that while she had attended the ECB's annual seminar for faculty teaching advanced writing-intensive courses, her TAs had no instruction in the teaching of writing and found their students' writing problems simply inscrutable. The writing assignments the professor valued became a huge burden for the dedicated, yet inexperienced, TAs. Lee asked us to devise a way to support writing in the curriculum without creating added instructional burdens for the psychology TAs; thus, we opted to create HyperCard stacks for the students to use as they completed the assignments. We called in a software designer (Matthew Barritt) from the university's Office of Instructional Technology and an ECB colleague with experience in psychology (Helen Isaacson) to help us achieve this aim. The software would provide flexible instruction for students and enable them, we hoped, to produce written reports more closely matching their teachers' expectations; when students could accomplish this goal, their TAs could concentrate on clarifying assignment requirements. Our purpose here is not so much to describe the particular software we created but to outline the main concerns other teachers should consider in assembling interdisciplinary teams to support writing in the disciplines. We begin with a brief description of our own work before moving quickly into a consideration of guidelines for development teams.

The Project

Designing software to support writing in courses across the disciplines requires more than the drill-and-practice structure that is so depressingly common in much content-area software. In addition, attention must be paid to discipline-specific and course-specific writing assignments. Such software has to move beyond what Brazilian educator Paulo Freire has called the "banking" model of education, in which teachers present content to students, who will passively listen and learn (*Pedagogy of the Oppressed*). The resources we have designed involve students as practitioners in a field of study and encourage them to attend to psychology's processes as well as its products. We worked to develop software that would help "[s]tudents learn what it is that scholars do: How historians, mathematicians, and authors write, think, and solve problems . . . how to use tools that facilitate the process of scholarly work" (Kozma and Johnston 14). Early studies dealing with the effects of computers on students' writing stress that computer-assisted instruction should focus on the "planning activities a writer uses" (Barker 114). This model fit nicely with our belief that students might benefit most by mimicking professionals' composing processes. Thus, the HyperCard stacks we created provide a bridge that allows students, who often write as "outsiders," to learn how "insiders" think and write.

Our first step involved developing "a detailed description of the processes the student needs to acquire" (Larkin and Chabay 160) by talking with the psychology professor, Theresa Lee, and her teaching assistants, examining published models they suggested, and comparing samples of successful student responses with unsuccessful ones. We soon learned that students who were successful quickly grasped factors that differentiated writing in the social sciences from writing in the humanities; this was evident even in the titles that students chose for their work. One failing report was titled "A Taste of the Day," in contrast with a successful report titled "A Comparative Study of the Preferences of Students among Different Colas." Although perhaps awkwardly worded, the second title nevertheless acknowledges the scientific convention that titles should summarize the research problem, using appropriate key words. This and other scientific conventions had been ignored, or not sufficiently internalized, by students whose reports failed. These unsuccessful reports, however, addressed what the students, thinking like laypersons rather than psychologists, took to be important issues. Several students' research reports, for instance, questioned what they viewed as ethical problems in a double-blind experiment in which the participants were led to believe they were doing one thing, while the researchers were interested in another. But this type of questioning had no place in the assignment, and these introductory students needed extra help determining which kinds of questions were appropriate for the formal report and which were better raised in their discussion sections. Because the students' failures on their research reports acted as the catalyst for this project, we will draw most of our discussion from this assignment, although we would note in passing that students had similar difficulties with the other class assignments, which required them to analyze readings as well as perform experimental research. The four stacks we ultimately developed address these issues for each assignment.

Overall, the problems with the research reports were twofold: (1) The sections of the report were not well differentiated, if at all, and (2) the

prose was obscure and rambling. Most students, working from the out-
line in their coursepacks, did at least use all of the required subheadings
(Abstract, Introduction, Methods and Materials, Results, Discussion,
Conclusion), even if they did not use them accurately or appropriately.
Material that belonged in Results, for example, often could be found in
Discussion; Abstracts did not contain enough information; and Introductions contained the analysis of Results rather than a rationale for the
experiment. Some students omitted sections altogether or omitted some
sections but retained others. Many students felt that the sections of the
research report only required organization of material, and we joined
them in this perception at the beginning of the project. Yet as Faigley
and Hansen note:

> Learning to write a report of a psychological experiment [is] not
> simply a matter of mastering a four-part organization and the ap-
> propriate jargon and style; students also [have] to learn how to for-
> mulate hypotheses, to design ways to verify or reject hypotheses,
> and to choose and interpret the results of statistical tests. (142)

Students had to learn new ways of mastering material, which included
a different approach to writing tasks. And the outlines provided in the
coursepack stressed only the organization of a research report, not the
process it represents. The coursepack provided a brief definition of each
part of a research report; for example, "Abstract: summarizes in less
than 100 words the research report." These definitions, which at first
seemed adequate to represent the nature of the written product, failed
to provide students with the direction they needed to actually write the
reports. Anne Herrington's work on assignments argues that teachers
need to help students find "a guiding question or problem to solve, to
avoid the problem of student work that report[s] rather than analyz[es]
. . . information" (248). Likewise, assignments must help students see
how to form the questions that define the contents of each section of a
formal report, if that is the genre required in class. As we worked with
students, we came to realize that they needed help with the complex
thinking that underlies the formal structure of a report—a conclusion
that will surprise no one familiar with research in writing across the
curriculum.

The Software

Herrington's work led us to consider the ways in which we could help
the psychology instructors sequence the writing tasks while actively
involving students in the sequence. Heeding Larkin and Chabay's in-

junction to "Let most instruction occur through active work on tasks" (161), we wanted, most of all, to produce software that would do more than *tell* students how to fulfill their assignments; we wanted an application that would give them support as they actually worked to fulfill their assignments. Our writing teachers' instincts told us that learning to think and write as practitioners was a deceptively complex undertaking. We would have to separate this complicated process into a sequence of manageable tasks, following Larkin and Chabay's advice to "limit demands on students' attention" (163). Then students would be able to combine the smaller chunks into a complex but organized whole. This process led us to the notion of cognitive chunking—breaking down a complex assignment into small units so that students could concentrate on one at a time. Once the chunks were drafted, students could manipulate them, thus learning that the order in which writers need to write is not always the same as the order in which readers need to read. In a sense, we drew from both a cognitive approach to writing, which stresses the intellectual tasks involved in writing, and a social constructionist approach to writing, which stresses the ways in which dialogue and collaboration produce knowledge. Drawing on the work of Oakeshott, Vygotsky, and Bruffee (summarized in Bruffee), we sought to involve the students in a kind of dialogue that would help them see the ways in which normal discourse in psychology functions; we attempted to structure the dialogue "indirectly by the task or problem" that the professional psychologists had defined (Bruffee 644).

Thus, each card of the HyperCard stack contains two main features: the top half of the screen provides information about one part of the assignment (students can click on boldfaced words to see definitions of key terms), and the bottom half of the screen provides a writing space or work area, where students can make notes that can later be saved in a word processing document. Furthermore, students can click on different buttons to see an example of a research report, and they can move forward or backward as needed (see Figure 5.1). The information at the top half of each screen, or card, helps students write and ask questions as professional psychologists. Each card mimics the kinds of questions that the professor or TA would ask were each student to come in for a conference. By engaging in this "dialogue," the students compose and write—create knowledge, in fact—the way professionals in the field of psychology do. Questions lead them through a consideration of their experimental data and toward a preliminary conclusion. But students begin the Research Report stack by considering the Materials and Methods section first; this is the easiest section to understand and to write, and our collaborators in the field told us that is where most practition-

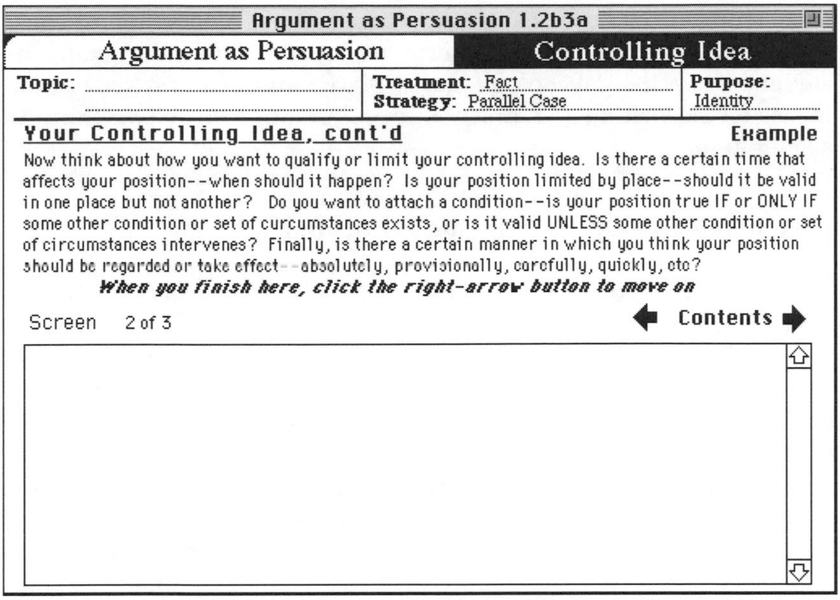

```
╔══════════════════ Argument as Persuasion 1.2b3a ══════════════╗
║        Argument as Persuasion        │      Controlling Idea     ║
╠══════════════════════════════════════╪═══════════════════════════╣
║ Topic: _____│ Treatment: Fact    Purpose: ║
║ _____│ Strategy: Parallel Case   Identity ║
```

Your Controlling Idea, cont'd   **Example**

Now think about how you want to qualify or limit your controlling idea. Is there a certain time that affects your position--when should it happen? Is your position limited by place--should it be valid in one place but not another? Do you want to attach a condition--is your position true IF or ONLY IF some other condition or set of curcumstances exists, or is it valid UNLESS some other condition or set of circumstances intervenes? Finally, is there a certain manner in which you think your position should be regarded or take effect--absolutely, provisionally, carefully, quickly, etc?

When you finish here, click the right-arrow button to move on

Screen   2 of 3   ← Contents →

Figure 5.1. Argument as Persuasion

ers begin. Students then work through cards that prompt them to make notes toward their Results, Analysis, and Discussion sections; each section of the report has several cards demonstrating the kinds of thinking necessary to create (the form and content of) the final report. Students follow a similar series of questions for note–taking before writing their Introductions. Finally, they write their Titles, Abstracts, and Bibliographies. This process mirrors the order professionals use and leads students to write the more easily understood portions first.

As students used the software, their performances improved significantly. Before we introduced the stacks into the class, one-fifth of the students failed their research report assignment, and fully one-third of this class of 250 students were required to revise because their performances were so weak. The median grade on that assignment was 5 on a scale of 10, or approximately a C. In the first term that stacks were introduced, grades rose markedly. The median grade rose to 4.3 on a scale of 5—a B+. (Note: Professor Lee changed the grading scale from a 10-point to a 5-point scale for reasons that are not relevant to this discussion.) In addition, only 2 of 250 students were required to revise their reports, and no student was required to come to the Writing Workshop for assistance. (On an ancillary note, this fact meant that the stacks helped us make more efficient use of Workshop time because other students could now take advantage of the appointment slots previously dominated by students from the psychology class.) As a result of improved performance on the writing assignments, course grades rose by two-thirds of a letter grade.

Designing Software, *R*edesigning Curriculum

To claim that the software we developed was the sole cause for this improvement would oversimplify the intellectual work demanded of the psychology students. Although the HyperCard stacks are the most visible product of this collaboration, the curriculum development that grew out of this project is as significant a product as the software. The time we spent in conversation with the psychology professor and TAs and the technical support staff enriched the course curriculum in crucial ways. For one, our attention to the cognitive chunks in each assignment helped the professor and TAs clarify what they wanted to teach. More important, our attention to the demands of each writing assignment led Professor Lee to reorder the assignments, thus providing the sequencing that Herrington argues is so important for student success. A series of four meetings at the beginning of the software design process was devoted almost entirely to the discussion of curriculum and assignments, and the exchange of expertise—our knowledge of Herrington's work, for instance, and the psychologists' knowledge of their discipline's concepts—enabled us to redesign the course together. The tight fit between curriculum, classroom instruction, and software development raised the students' performance levels. The revised course provided HyperCard stacks for students to use outside of class if they chose and sequenced assignments that built on students' strengths.

Before we began the software development project, the course included four writing assignments. The first, which had proved so difficult for the class, required students to conduct cola taste tests in discussion sections and then to write a formal report that examined the relationship between variables such as age and gender on cola preferences. Next, students wrote a critical analysis of an essay by Stephen Jay Gould criticizing creationism. This critical analysis was much more like the assignments students had grown accustomed to in high school and in other college classes; this genre may not vary much from discipline to discipline, especially in introductory courses. But Gould's critique of evolutionism and creationism provoked emotional responses or raised religious issues for some writers, and those stresses—from addressing a topic irrelevant to the course's mission—often resulted in poorly written essays. The third assignment returned to experimental issues and required students to conduct a naturalistic observation, and the fourth assignment was another critical analysis of a film and reading.

Just as the software required students to change the order in which they wrote their research reports (beginning with the Methods section rather than the Introduction), our collaborative meetings prompted the professor to change the order of her assignments. She now asks students to write a critical analysis first because they already possess most of the skills they need for this assignment. Furthermore, she asks them to analyze a flawed and problematic research report rather than an essay on a controversial subject. This revised assignment builds on students' familiarity with the task while introducing them to the new genre of the research report. In the second assignment, students use this newly acquired knowledge to carry out and report on the cola taste-test challenge. In the third and final assignment, students work together to design observations that they carry out and write up separately. With our support, the psychology curriculum retained its emphasis on writing, but did so in a way that encourages a greater degree of student success.

The consulting process, then, not only helped improve one course, it also helped the ECB carry out its mission of promoting more effective writing instruction across the curriculum and of encouraging faculty to incorporate more writing into all courses, not merely those designed to meet our college's upper-level writing requirement. Both parties benefited. Psychology as a Natural Science is now a better, more popular course and one that is more pleasant to teach; both students and teachers appreciate a class in which students, on the whole, can learn from their assignments rather than be frustrated by them. The ECB acquired a great deal of knowledge about writing in the field of psychology, knowledge that helps our Workshop faculty respond more effectively as students bring assignments to us for assistance. We also learned more about what faculty in the disciplines—even those who, like this psychology professor, had taught upper-division writing-intensive courses—know about using writing as part of their course curricula. This information helps us design better faculty and TA workshops to help instructors develop more effective courses that fulfill our upper-level writing requirement.

The principal benefit, however, is that we discovered a way to raise the level of students' performances to meet their teachers' high standards. The resources we developed make more information available to students about the content of the assignments, but more important, they offer more information about the patterns of thinking that guide those assignments (see Figure 5. 2). Even before the introduction of our stacks,

⌐   **Psy 170:   The Research Report**

The Methods Section: Procedures   **Example**

Explain exactly how the experiment was conducted at each stage, including the instructions given to
the participants. If an experiment used **experimental and control groups**, for example, this
section would explain how the subjects were divided between groups; for a **double-blind study**,
this section explains exactly how the study was set up and conducted. You should provide enough
detail in this section of your report so that someone else could duplicate your work. Draft a
description in the space below.

Screen   3 of 19   ← Map

One group of students administered the taste test to the remaining students in the class. Neither
group knows which soda is which. They are labeled with colored dots and the order of tasting is
randomized. Subjects are asked to taste each soda and rank them by preference. They are also
asked to try and identify the sodas by name.

Figure 5.2. Example of How Stacks Define Assumptions Underlying Tasks

some students were performing at a high level. Some caught on to the
new genres, the new set of requirements, the new criteria by which their
writing would be evaluated. But most did not. Many students in the
class failed at the guessing game long before they failed their assignments. They had little experience writing in a specific discipline, and so
they simply did not see that the assignments were asking for a new (to
them, at least) genre of writing. Thus, they wrote in their usual manner—meaning they wrote an essay similar to the ones they had written
for English classes—and they failed. They did not produce writing that
met their teachers' expectations. As it turned out, they were capable of
addressing those expectations if someone made those expectations
clearer. The stacks gave all students equal access to the assumptions
underlying the tasks, assumptions that define how psychologists think
and write. Given that access, the students performed well. More of them
learned what their teachers wanted them to learn, and more of them
performed at a high level.

   In the end, then, our story is really about access of several kinds. The
heart of such a project lies in giving more students the ability to succeed, to learn, to perform at the level their teachers expect and demand.
The process of redesigning the course's curriculum to make the learn-

ing path more accommodating and designing learning aids (the HyperCard stacks) created the kind of access to knowledge that a good course should provide. In a different sense, we also expanded the access that professors in other disciplines have to expertise in writing instruction, as well as the access that ECB faculty have to knowledge about writing in the disciplines. If two experts are better than one, then involving professors from different disciplines is also better than limiting input to only one discipline. We learn from and benefit each other, directly and indirectly. These benefits generate more writing in more courses, and they create a context within which we can assure that good practice is built into individual courses and into our writing program as a whole. In addition, such projects open our program's access to resources by generating a higher institutionwide stake in our success. When efforts benefit a single course or a single department, they naturally attract less interest than efforts that benefit the institution more broadly. By involving faculty and staff from different departments, we ensure that more people know about the initiative and that the successes are more visible. Thus, they create more opportunities, and they raise the stature of the collaborating units. Of course, the opposite is true as well: failures, if they occur, are also more visible, and they can be equally detrimental. Our project was made possible because our dean was committed to helping create connections across departments and programs and because she was committed to funding those efforts.

Conclusions

So what can people embarking on similar projects do to help ensure success? What information is needed? Our experience leads us to identify several factors in a successful development project:

1. Institutional support is crucial

Perhaps the first and most basic concern for faculty getting involved in designing software for their own or others' use is the need for institutional support. This support begins with time, of course—time to conceive of, design, and carry out the project—and that means funding released time or, as in our case, summer appointments. In addition, the institution must be ready to include the products of these efforts in evaluating faculty for retention, merit raises, and promotion and tenure decisions. It is crucial that software development be viewed as a form of curriculum development and design, valued by the institution in the same ways that more traditional forms of curriculum development are.

2. Technical expertise should be readily available

Perhaps more crucial to the success of such a project is support in designing the project and technical support in bringing it to fruition. In our case, though we had some experience designing software and a fairly advanced—for humanities faculty—acquaintance with HyperTalk scripting, our project would not have been possible without the assistance of Matthew Barritt, an instructional design expert and HyperCard wizard who was made available to us by a cooperative arrangement between the College of Literature, Science, and the Arts and the university's Office of Instructional Technology. He contributed expertise in instructional design that complemented our expertise in designing writing assignments and the psychology professor's disciplinary expertise. Barritt worked with us as we designed the software and when we reached the end of our scripting ability, he stepped in to implement our designs. Thus, our collaboration had a third partner, and his involvement was crucial, enabling us to carry out the project without becoming sophisticated programmers. It is important that faculty be able to use their expertise in software development, whether that expertise be technical or disciplinary; our institutions must help us make connections with people whose knowledge complements our own.

3. Students need to be able to use the software

Although this may appear to be stating the obvious, it is important to remember that technical support involves infrastructure. Software is useless if students cannot run it or if the institution has not ensured that students have easy access to computers and other computer-related resources. For instance, students must receive sufficient training and support as they are working with the software. When software is designed to be used outside of class, it must be easy to use, even for a novice. Weakness in any of these areas—funding, design and technical assistance, or infrastructure—will weaken the project, making faculty less likely to embark on it and lowering the likelihood that even a successful product would benefit the students.

We are all too familiar with the problems that lack of infrastructure can cause. The first semester we distributed these HyperCard stacks on the campus network the university, without warning, changed the way software was made available on the network. Approximately 250 psychology students visited public labs during the weekend, only to find that the detailed directions they had for using the stacks did not work— and that the computing center's staff knew nothing of the project. We now distribute the stacks on disks (sold with the students' coursepacks) and educate lab staff.

4. Listen well and ask good questions

Collaborating with a faculty member outside one's discipline raises special challenges, especially in terms of a project like this. Developers are likely to begin projects for their own classes with enthusiasm and specific expectations for the writing tasks. When developing software for another teacher's class, however, one must be willing to listen and learn about that discipline—something that is no surprise to anyone who has worked in any successful writing-across-the-curriculum program for any length of time. We examined the psychology assignments in terms of the course and the discipline, and that meant looking at ways other people think and write. Our first impulse was to use the HyperCard stacks to get students thinking about the conceptual issues underlying the assignments: We jumped to the Analysis section of the research report and the critical sections of the critical analysis assignments, for instance. But our work with Professor Lee led us to set the expectations aside and to structure the stack the way *she* saw her course and discipline functioning. These periods of listening and observing can be profitable but frustrating. In an initial meeting, we felt that Professor Lee and teaching assistants laid too much blame for the students' failure on the students; they probably thought we were far too interested in the nature and order of the writing assignments. We were fortunate, however, in that we had enough rapport with Professor Lee and the TAs to influence course design in major ways; once the professor committed to redesigning the curriculum—something she had not planned to do when she agreed to help with the software development—the frustration abated. Ultimately, exchanges such as these are one of the most rewarding aspects of such a venture, because all parties to the collaboration learn about other disciplines.

5. Be willing to talk

Any collaborative effort means paying attention to team building. Without involvement from everyone associated with the final product—designers, developers, and end users—from the very beginning of the initiative, problems are sure to arise. Initial decisions about what is possible, for example, limit the outcomes, even if an early attempt is discarded in favor of a later idea. And moving from one concept to another can only create confusion and delay. Without early investment, collaborators will never feel as if they are equal stakeholders in the outcome. Assembling a team from the earliest possible stages of development helps ensure a smoother, more productive development process and one that is infinitely more pleasant and amenable. Our collaboration was uneven in that Professor Lee was involved in the stack construction only at the early and late stages; a stronger model—one that institutional constraints did not permit—would have all members of the team equally involved throughout. In our particular case, the work of development fell much more heavily on the writing faculty and instructional design specialist than on Professor Lee; ideally, a more effective collaboration would spread the burden more equitably and allow the exchange of ideas to flow both ways. Because we invested more time in the project, we came away with a greater knowledge of psychology than the psychology professor and TAs did of our discipline.

6. When you think the software is finished, test it—and test it and test it and test it again

The final concern in projects like ours, in which the developers are *not* the primary teachers, is that the users of course software (teachers and students) will not be completely familiar or comfortable with the application. All developers want students to use the applications with ease, but a teacher-developer is often in a better position to help students with problems that may arise than we were. When software developers assist other faculty, the software must work flawlessly; initial problems with implementation could cause students or faculty to reject a promising application. This fact makes the effort more closely resemble commercial software development because, once the product is finished, it passes out of the developers' control. Thus, the early versions (beta versions) need to be field tested. When the beta version is ready to use, selected students are chosen to try the software to see where they experience difficulties. The development team should monitor that initial use to discover where access problems occur and subsequent problems that emerge when the software is handed over to 250 students who know little or nothing about the authoring system or interface they are using. After this more robust test, the problems have to be corrected, and the software has to be reworked carefully and completely in order to ensure that its use will be as transparent and problem-free as possible. Finally, the team has to develop enough documentation to allow students to use the software with ease. Once all these conditions are met, the software is ready to fly the nest.

Works Cited

Barker, Thomas T. "Studies in Word Processing and Writing." *Computers in the Schools* 4 (Spring 1987): 109–21.

Bruffee, Kenneth. "Collaborative Learning and the 'Conversation of Mankind.'" *College English* 46 (1984): 635–52.

Faigley, Lester, and Kristine Hansen. "Learning to Write in the Social Sciences." *College Composition and Communication* 36 (1985): 140–49.

Freire, Paulo. *Pedagogy of the Oppressed.* Trans. Myra Bergman Ramos. New York: Continuum, 1970.

Herrington, Anne J. "Assignment and Response: Teaching with Writing Across the Disciplines." *A Rhetoric of Doing*. Ed. Roger Cherry, Neil Nakadate, and Stephen Witte. Carbondale, IL: Southern Illinois University Press, 1992. 244–59.

Kozma, Robert, and Jerome Johnston. "Toward a Technological Revolution in the Classroom." University of Michigan: National Center for Research to Improve Postsecondary Teaching and Learning (NCRIPTAL), 1990.

Larkin, Jill H., and Ruth W. Chabay. "Research on Teaching Scientific Thinking: Implications for Computer-Based Instruction." *Toward the Thinking Curriculum*. Ed. L. B. Resnick and L. E. Klopfer. Washington, DC: Association for Supervision and Curriculum Development, 1989. 150–72.

6 The Seven Cs of Interactive Design

Joan Huntley
University of Iowa

Joan Latchaw
University of Nebraska at Omaha

Our view of education as critical thinking involves considerable mental exertion, by which the learner questions, challenges, speculates, and theorizes. To exploit such critical thinking, designers, users, and teachers must collaborate. When the teacher *is* the designer, he or she will be better able to determine how technology can enhance active learning, that is, help students to perform a function, respond to directives or challenges, draw conclusions, or solve problems—all elements of critical thinking. Educational computer programs should engage as many human qualities as possible (intellect, emotion, cognition, perception) to promote the kind of learning advocated in this book. Therefore, design principles that exploit such human potential are likely to produce more effective and successful computer programs. Because this book is directed toward teacher-developers, our chapter focuses on creating instructional applications for specific classroom purposes; however, we include the possibility of designing educational software for commercial markets. This chapter will discuss applications and Web pages developed for a variety of audiences, beginning with the smaller audiences of classrooms and courses and moving toward more general audiences on Web sites.

Representing twenty years of design experience, the seven Cs we offer as guidelines are correctness, creativity, consistency, clarity, consideration, coherence, and curiosity. In general, if you follow these guidelines, you will not be flooded with an overwhelming number of concerns and details; however, as designers you will have to consider how they interact and sometimes weigh one principle with another. Some of the categories may overlap; for instance, a cognitive issue (under clarity) may apply to a perceptual issue (under consistency). The important point is to consider the consequences of the choices you make. The interactivity of the principles and the consequences of design choices will be discussed using graphics from The Borges Quest, the Stein Project, the psychology stacks (for Psych 170), and the journalism Web site (for the Topics in Nonfiction course). Our critique is not meant either to glorify or condemn any particular software package but to demonstrate how design enhances (or could better enhance) the projects under discussion. It is helpful both to consider the pedagogical goals of teachers and to imagine naive users embarking on new experiences with little expertise.

The degree to which designers seek perfection will depend on the market targeted, the purpose of the program, time constraints, and collaborative opportunities such as creating design teams. Marketability of published software depends on sound design principles, which can be perfected through design teams, sufficient funding (for support and equipment), and beta testing. Adequate resources are necessary to ensure success: Unless users rely on software support, they are generally on their own. Therefore, the programs must be user-friendly, intuitive, and self-explanatory. They must also be enticing and interesting. However, trying to smooth out every design issue may drive even an experienced designer to distraction. In fact, it may be impossible for designers to consider every principle outlined here in developing one application. For instance, more menus (greater navigational depth)—though undesirable—may have to compensate for spatial limitations on the screen. Or regional/local considerations (defining the knowledge of a particular group, a convention of "correctness") may have to be ignored in appealing to a general audience. But, in general, commercial designers must achieve a high degree of accuracy, if not perfection.

Educators, on the other hand, rarely have the luxury of time or adequate resources to develop a polished product for their classrooms. The good news is that perfection is not usually possible, essential, or even desirable in some cases. (Following the rules is not always advisable; sometimes charting your own course produces a better designed document, as some examples here will illustrate.) Teachers are generally available for dialogue or questions of navigation, clarity, and consistency—in person or by phone or e-mail. And constructive hypertexts, in which students add to the existing material, will necessarily be messy. Messiness is a pedagogical imperative, as the Stein Project demonstrates.

Therefore, the purposes of computer applications must be weighed against the design principles. Applications can be targeted for very different audiences, each with a different need. Those needs can be determined by analyzing the program's purpose, its targeted audience (including publishability), and its emphasis on process or product. If the application is developed for commercial markets (a more general audience), then product perfectability is fundamental. Most of the seven design principles should be considered. For instance, a more general audience targeted for a Web site will demand creativity and curiosity in the graphical interface. The "genre" that is developing on homepages must capture a user's attention even to be noticed. If, on the other hand, the application is developed primarily for the classroom (a narrow audience), some design principles will be more important than others. For instance, Susanmarie Harrington and William Condon's psychology stacks are used by a number of teachers in the psychology department. Although the developers were under time constraints, certain principles were primary, considering the number of teachers and students using the application. In this particular environment, consistency, coherence, clarity, and consideration were adhered to rigorously. Creativity and curiosity are largely absent, but in this case they may be relatively unimportant. An instructional focus might even emphasize process over product. In fact, the Stein Project is not really a "product" in the usual sense of the word because it changes from one term to another as students modify, even restructure, the Storyspace web. In this case, curiosity with consideration (collegial respect) takes precedence as students become co-authors; consistency, clarity, and coherence are largely ignored.

Creativity, Curiosity, Consideration, Consistency (in Single Classroom Applications)

If we want to engage our students as colleagues, guiding them into our disciplines and engaging them in research projects, then the computer programs we use, or adopt, and the applications we design for classes should highlight the principles of creativity, consideration, and curiosity. Applications can inspire students to become our co-investigators in literature and composition courses. The designers of The Borges Quest and the Stein Project wanted to make challenging and frustrating texts more accessible to students through the creative playfulness of the software. Therefore, curiosity and creativity (highly valued by professionals) were primary principles. Consideration offers students the respect too often reserved for faculty.

As both The Borges Quest and Tharon Howard's fantasy quest illustrate, creativity, which can enhance meaning, usefulness, and interest, is often aligned to or inseparable from curiosity. Perhaps the two most important issues to consider in developing students' sense of themselves as learners are their decision-making abilities and their skepticism about blindly accepting privileged views. These two important aspects of critical thinking can be exploited through curiosity. The design can signal to students that what they do really makes a difference. In The Borges Quest (Figure 6.1), choosing the character traits for Pierre Menard will determine the profile that students construct. The resulting character sketch will help them make critical distinctions between author, narrator, and character.

By posing questions to spark curiosity, the program provides a challenge that requires students to use what they have learned, as The Borges Quest demonstrates in Figure 6.2. Notice that the screen is filled with questions and question marks. The teacher-designers wanted students to question long-held assumptions about authors and to become co-investigators by puzzling over the apparent contradictions presented within the program. By clicking on the three different buttons to the right of the screen, students find contradictory historical explanations of Pierre Menard, which pushes them to reexamine their expectations.

Curiosity can be piqued by providing little structure, few guidelines, and no direct challenges. (Breaking the rules of consistency and clarity is purposeful here.) The Stein Project, because it was designed as a re-

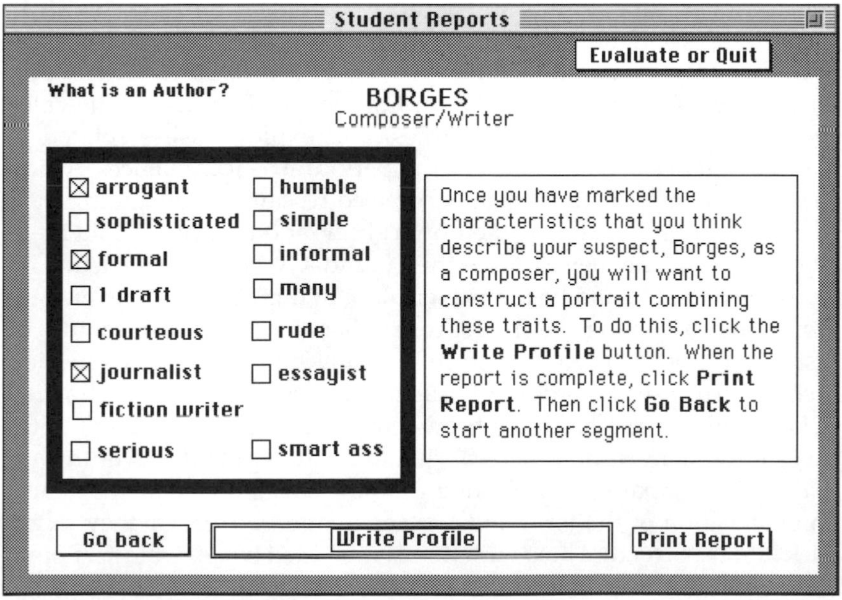

Figure 6.1. The Borges Quest—Student Reports

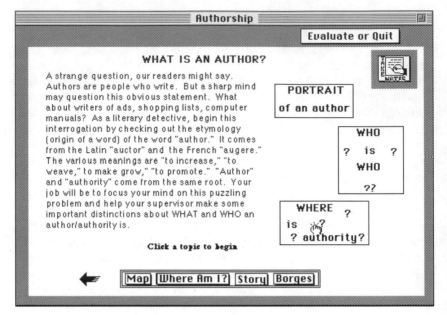

Figure 6.2. The Borges Quest—What Is an Author?

source and exploratory tool and because students add to and modify it, is constantly changing. Creativity, though it would enhance the application, was largely ignored—perhaps because the project was so labor intensive. Dene Grigar designed the application initially as a space in which to conduct research, gather sources, and explore issues related to Gertrude Stein's poetry (i.e., historical period, artistic influences, critical theory). She invited students to become co-researchers by adding their own connections (via links), their own observations, insights, and interpretations, and any new sources they found. Overlaying a structure on the information would be too prescriptive in this case and prevent students from becoming the model researchers Grigar had in mind. For instance, the box labeled "Structure" explains that "There is no one hierarchical structure of words or of usage. Because of the use of abstraction in her writing, Stein has often been compared to Cubist painters." Students have many options here. They might attempt to discover the *reason* for the comparison by clicking on the Cubism box, which contains an explanation of the term and four embedded boxes. Or they might click into the Structure box, with three embedded boxes: Objects, Room, and Food. Objects is divided into sections, such as "serving items for the table," including the object and a corresponding line or phrase of poetry.

1. a carafe: "A Carafe, That Is a Blind Glass"
2. a container: "Glazed Glitter"
3. a coffee pot: "A Piece of Coffee"

If students have looked externally at Cubism and internally at pieces of the poem, they might discover something interesting about Stein's method.

The lack of structure in the Stein Project, then, allows for more associative thinking (provided that the pedagogy of the course supports it), encouraging students to find their own answers, construct further questions, and offer new insights. Thus, a particular *kind* of critical thinking (analogical, relational) is being promoted. The Stein Storyspace, designed for a literature class, is much different from the highly structured psychology stacks, in which analysis, argument, and critique are the most highly valued critical-thinking skills. Methodology and approach necessarily change according to the program's function and the discipline involved.

Consideration of the user can go a long way toward building an environment in which students engage in the real work of the academy. It is sometimes helpful to think of users as real-life neighbors or professional colleagues rather than as children, either overpraising, condescending, or underchallenging them (common in skill-and-drill exercises). The language and images in the design can spark the kind of interactive, dialogic thinking advocated in these chapters. For instance, The Borges Quest Introduction (Figure 6.3) imagines that users "should be able to challenge Borges/Narrator/Menard by testing some of their claims." Such challenges are dialogic in that readers interact with the text, questioning the author, characters, and even the act of reading itself. This quest into critical thinking (through questioning and skepticism) need not be joyless, as "the private detective of authors" (Figure 6.4) illustrates. In the Stein Project, students are expected to become researchers and co-authors as *they* find their own connections between the boxes in Storyspace (i.e., Philosophy, Cubism, Stein, Modernism, Bibliography). They are instructed to create their own links and nodes in this constructive hypertext, sharing their discoveries with other users. Thus, the students become the experts, not just passive receptors of text, images, and sound.

Promoting expertise through active learning can be enhanced by navigation metaphors as well as by dialogic interaction and critical challenges. Navigation might fall under consideration or creativity, as the following example illustrates. Howard's fantasy quest, the Webhead project described in Chapter 11, uses the "Tree of Knowledge" as a navigation metaphor through the "magical realm of Professional Communi-

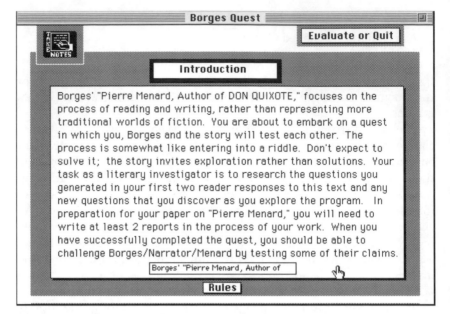

Figure 6.3. The Borges Quest—Introduction

cation wizards, dragons, and warriors." The users are invited to "carve [their] initials in the 'Tree of Knowledge.'" They are then cautioned to choose their paths wisely. The creativity of the directions bespeaks a pedagogical approach that is student centered and collegial. It implies that students will add to a body of knowledge and make decisions on their own (paths). Part of the motivation, according to Howard, was to keep students interested for a longer period of time, but another part may be to welcome them into a well-established discipline. That navigational metaphors also provide clarity and consistency is a point we make later in the chapter. While The Borges Quest and the Stein Project are pedagogically sound (largely because of creativity, curiosity, and consideration), they sometimes lack consistency, consideration, and clarity, which presents users with technological difficulties. Consideration and consistency prevent unnecessary frustration (for both designer and user) and increase the potential for learning. Inconsistencies in design can frustrate students, especially those who are inexperienced with computers. Note in Figure 6.3 (The Borges Quest) that the word "Introduction" is in a box similar to boxes for "Evaluate or Quit" and "Rules," both of which are clickable buttons. But the box enclosing "Introduction" is merely decorative, therefore potentially confusing to the user.

The "Take Notes" button, while clickable, probably should be outlined, like the other buttons. Note in Figure 6.4 that the "Take Notes" button is on the upper right-hand corner, whereas it occupies the upper left-hand corner in Figure 6.3. However, the cursor (which snaps its fingers when over clickable areas) was designed to correct for these inconsistencies and alleviate the need for extensive revision. Sometimes small computer screens make consistency difficult because icons cannot always fit in the appropriate places. In this case, the "Take Notes" button was added after Notepad Space was conceived as part of The Borges Quest; therefore, this button was impossible to include in the initial design. Changing the design in HyperCard might include creating new background buttons, fields, or screen patterns, necessitating a complicated, time-consuming procedure.

Inconsideration can also cause frustration for users. In the Stein Project (Figure 6.5), the links are not obvious, unless the user is familiar enough with Storyspace to know that pressing the apple and option keys simultaneously reveals each link. Additionally, the titles of text links are difficult to read because of their small size. Capitalizing them would help, especially with the smaller Macintosh screens. This problem can be eliminated by enlarging the screen, but in doing so, the overview is lost.

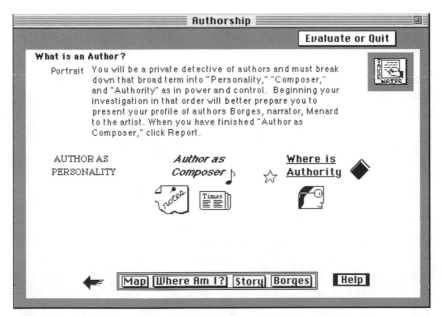

Figure 6.4. The Borges Quest—Author as Person

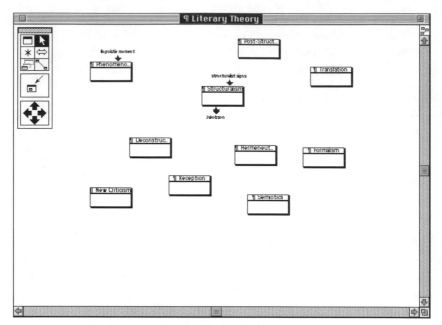

Figure 6.5. The Stein Project—View of Literary Theory

Despite these problems, The Borges Quest and the Stein Project were usable in class because instructors were there to guide students.

Correctness, Clarity, Consistency, and Coherence (In Multiple Classroom Applications)

For broader audiences, consistency is a major principle. When designing for more than one teacher, course, or group of courses, the application must function on its own. Therefore, correctness, clarity, consistency, and coherence become extremely important principles. Harrington and Condon's HyperCard stacks, developed for teachers of psychology at the University of Michigan, illustrate how and why these design principles are important to the work of the class. The stack instructs students in acquiring disciplinary knowledge in psychology: habits of mind, terminology (assertion, critique, and theoretical explanation), assumptions, and background knowledge. Correctness, or content accuracy, is crucial because it informs the computer application and, by extension, the heart of the course. This is not the easiest design principle to achieve, because in many disciplines there is no consensus as to what constitutes "correctness." Often there are regional differences or competing schools of thought even within a discipline. What counts as research, definitions of critical thinking, or good writing may vary within the broad field of psychology or its branches, such as experimental, behavioral, and theoretical psychology. An application's efficacy depends on a standard of correctness that will be accepted by a particular community.

Clarity and consistency are equally essential in helping students become practitioners of their fields. Because the stack's purpose is to guide learners through step-by-step procedures—by which one concept builds on the next—the software's structure must be linear and orderly. Consistency and clarity help *create* that structure, both pedagogically and technically.

A consistent and simple interface promotes efficient and effective learning; when the technical features (buttons, fields, etc.) are intuitively grasped, they enhance meaning. Furthermore, complex design takes more time, and time is a major factor in development and production. The psychology stack illustrates a user-friendly interface with clear navigational routes and procedural instructions. The card in Figure 6.6 contains complete explanations of all buttons and how to operate them. Note that in Figures 6.7 (a, b, and c) the name of the stack (Psy 170:

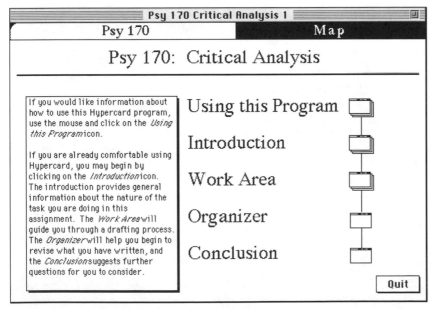

Figure 6.6. Psy 170—Introductory Screen

Critical Analysis) is always in the upper left-hand corner of the screen, the Menu Item "Work Area" (corresponding to the Map) is always in the upper right-hand corner, and the arrows are always above the composing field. The Work Area, which is called "Examining the Argument," is both pedagogically sound and well designed. The nine screens are clearly demarcated (Screen 1 of 9, 2 of 9, etc.) and move from Hypothesis through Methodology, Precision, Assertion, Critiquing Assertion, Empirical Evidence, Theoretical Explanation, and, finally, the student's own critique. Each term, such as *analysis*, is clearly defined, preparing students for the upcoming tasks, which are briefly but clearly explained.

As the psychology stacks illustrate, clarity is essential in helping students grasp and apply difficult concepts. Clarity refers to cognitive clarity, an intuitive understanding of the program's overall purpose and meaning. Cognitive clarity depends on a combination of structural clarity, verbal clarity, and visual clarity. However, the degree to which this last—but perhaps most important—principle is followed depends on the function of the application and whether it is for commercial or classroom use only. In any case, design flaws can have serious consequences. If you skimp on refinement, someone else will find the mistakes, and the sloppiness will come back to embarrass you, frustrate students, re-

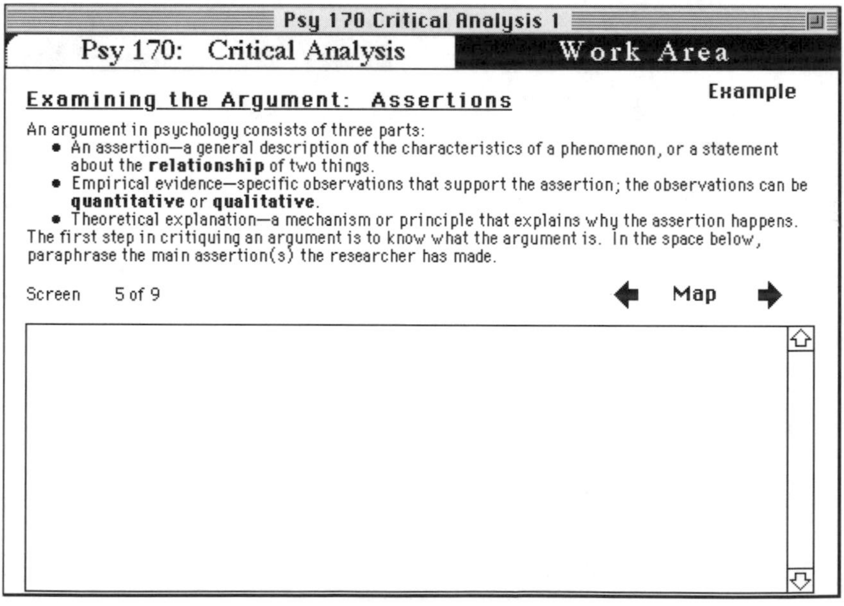

Figure 6.7a. Psy 170—Screen 5 of 9

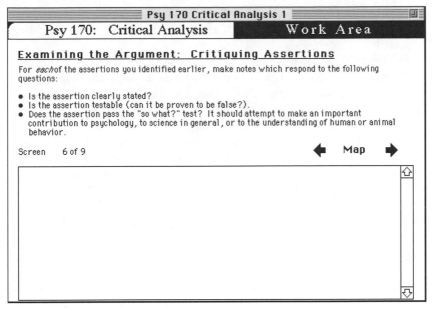

Figure 6.7b. Psy 170—Screen 6 of 9

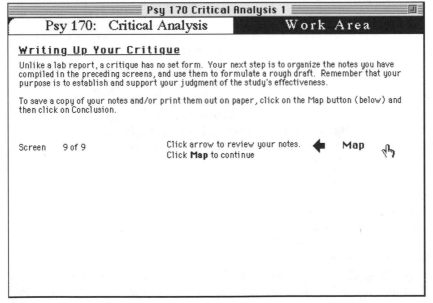

Figure 6.7c. Psy 170—Screen 9 of 9

duce sales, and alienate your publisher and other possible users. After you develop Web pages or HyperCard stacks, go through your application with a critical eye.

However, the real test of a computer application's viability occurs with first-time users. Field test or pilot your software with a small number of users similar to those in your target audience. They will find bugs and other problems the designer never imagined. Simulating the exact conditions will also save time and energy. Although The Borges Quest was created on a Macintosh, students would be using it on a university network. Transferring it to the network (a seemingly easy task) was enormously complicated and took weeks of work and collaboration with an expert. Planning for every possible glitch will be time well spent.

Structural clarity is essential in creating intuitive understanding; and structure depends on an underlying mental model. All such models should be pedagogically sound, representing key principles, habits of mind, and modes of discourse appropriate to the task and discipline. However justifiable the model is, the structure must be made clear to the users; that is, it should be fairly obvious in meaning and straightforward to operate. For instance, Figure 6.6 provides a kind of road map (overview) of the psychology stack; note that this screen (Map) instructs users about the various segments, each signaled by a link. The lines connecting them suggest a sequential order, demonstrating how psychologists work. The text (from Using the Program to Introduction to Conclusion) briefly explains the sequencing. Thus, it becomes clear from the outset that students will get information about and experience with performing a critical analysis as they work through these five areas.

Structural clarity also enhances intuitive understanding through overviews at various points. Good introductory menus, along with succinct prose and meaningful icons (see psych stack, Figure 6.6) can effectively and immediately illustrate a program's structure. When developers provide statements on what to expect, general sketches, and brief explanations, they not only improve usability but also increase learning.

Structural clarity depends not only on clear and intuitive navigation but on an organized focus. Ask yourself whether the paths in the application or Web pages are intuitive. In other words, do the navigational routes and icons demonstrate a focus and purpose? One of the best examples we found was the psychology stack for Psych 170. The text accompanying the menu (Figure 6.6) explains the connections between segments, thereby clarifying its focus. And the visual clues within segments (i.e., Critical Analysis, Work Area) remind the user of task and location. Focus is maintained at all points.

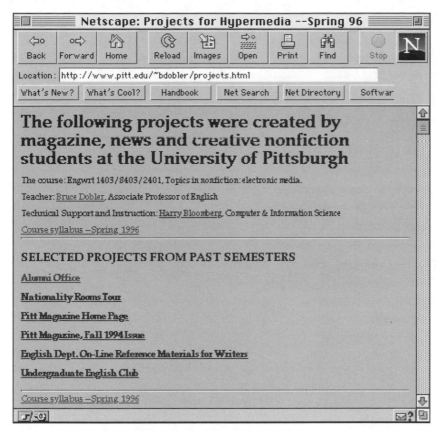

Figure 6.8. Web Page for EngWrt 1403/8403/2401

If structural clarity represents the macro level, verbal clarity represents the micro (sentence) level, which contributes to overall cognitive clarity. Following the rule of consideration, brevity enables more efficient reading, leading to greater productivity. For instance, in the psychology stack (Figure 6.7c), the three short sentences under Writing Up Your Critique are informative and instructional:

> Unlike a lab report, a critique has no set form. Your next step is to organize the notes you have compiled in the preceding screens, and use them to formulate a rough draft. Remember that your purpose is to establish and support your judgment of the study's effectiveness.

Verbal clarity demonstrates cognitive clarity, the program's tasks and goals.

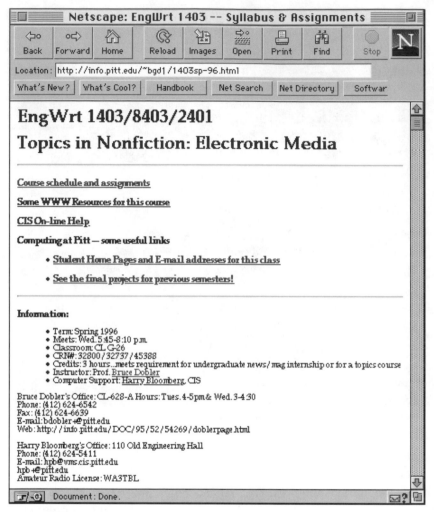

Figure 6.9a. Web Page for EngWrt 1403/8403/2401

When the design principles chosen are easily demonstrable, when they clarify the purpose, and when they interact well, then coherence is established. Coherence results when the user has an overall sense that things are as they should be, that the components logically, aesthetically, and emotionally fit together. Users are not left to wonder, "Why is this in here?" The psychology stack is coherent because users are not consciously aware of the technology or of the individual principles. It just seems right.

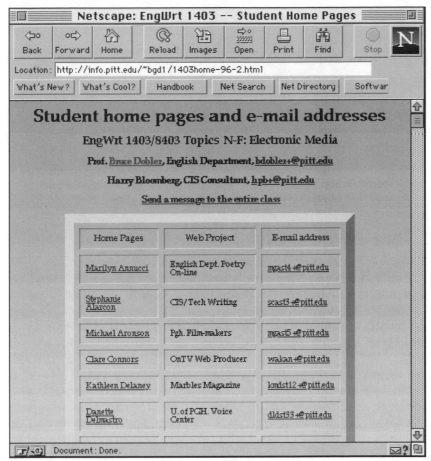

Figure 6.9b. Web Page for EngWrt 1403/8403/2401

Design Principles in World Wide Web Projects

World Wide Web homepages target a more general, larger, and some-times broader audience than do class or course applications. Some are designed for commercial markets (to sell products, to educate, to moti-vate) and are therefore more polished and complete, while others repre-sent projects in process (and may be incomplete). Many educators from middle school to university levels are beginning to use new Internet capabilities provided by Web sites.

Like any new technology, however, software too often is designed without regard for the fundamental design principles. For instance, cor-rectness on the WWW is being debated in academic circles. Some edu-

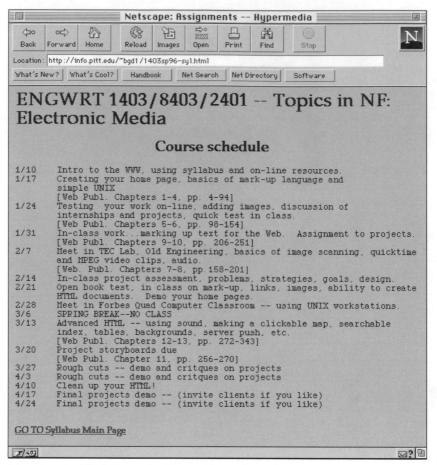

Figure 6.9c. Web Page for EngWrt 1403/8403/2401

cators have complained about an emerging aesthetic: lack of rules, over-emphasis of graphic presentation, randomness of linkages, inaccuracy of information, and failure to cite sources. Opening screens are often the most polished and complete, to attract the reader into a site. However, once hooked, you may find numerous links "under construction," grammatical errors, a chatty conversational tone that substitutes for intellectual depth, and incorrect information. For example, an online encyclopedia we read had an entry for Bill Gates, stating that he was a college dropout from Harvard. This claim, along with others, is blatantly untrue but probably accepted as fact by many WWW users who trust that online encyclopedias have rigorous standards. In other cases, what is promised is not delivered. An academic homepage on plays of the nineteenth century promises annotations, synopses, and information on authors, years of production, and social setting. But no annotations appear and the sociocultural material is largely absent. The author of the homepage obviously failed to consider the audience, who, in this case, would probably have already read these somewhat obscure plays and would be researching more esoteric information. Whether designing programs for use in the classroom or on the Internet, issues of correctness (audience, diction, grammar, usability, referencing, accuracy) should be seriously considered.

Another disappointment in our WWW exploration derived from a lack of pedagogical integrity. We found ourselves jumping from link to link over long periods of time, finding little information of real value. Although the graphics and other visuals can be enticing, as anyone cruising the WWW will verify, a larger purpose is not always perceptible. This lack suggests that educational goals have been sacrificed to curiosity and creativity, which, for our purposes, should be secondary considerations.

One notable exception is Bruce Dobler's homepage (designed by students in his Topics in Nonfiction course). Dobler's journalism course was more technologically demanding than some of the others we have discussed because his students, as budding journalists, had to create a product for the public and learn to program in HTML. (Some had little experience with computer use, let alone programming.) Thus, they had to consider more of the basic design principles.

Note the consideration (respect for time and usability) that Dobler and his student-designers exhibit in creating the graphical interface for a broader and potentially more commercial audience. The clickable areas are obvious (in HTML format, all links are underlined and highlighted), and the information is structured according to font size (Figures 6.8 and 6.9a, b, and c). Every new linked page has a large header at the top (Figures 6.9a, b, and c) declaring the subject content and the course, with smaller letters (though still quite large) for subheadings. Some inconsistencies in structure do occur, such as on the student homepage and e-mail address list, where the name of the course appears under the subject heading (Figure 6.9b). However, the designers may have intended the content of the page to take precedence over consistency. Usability is increased by providing manageable chunks of information on each screen. Each node covers from one to three screens, eliminating the need to scroll through long pieces of text; and the end of each node has a hot link, to return to the main menu. Thus, the possibility of getting lost or too deeply embedded is greatly minimized.

Another aspect of structure, visual clarity, also increases usability. Visual clarity occurs when overall screen design, individual icon designs, and text are aesthetically pleasing and functionally obvious. The Semester at Sea homepage (Figure 6.10) is a good example. The graphic—a collage of cultural images with a sea and clouds background—and text complement each other, the words "voyage of discovery" suggesting an intellectual exploration that is corroborated by "A floating university." In this case, creativity enhanced meaning, usefulness, and interest. The five lines of text (verbal clarity) whet the appetite, tempting possible voyagers both socially and intellectually, thus inspiring curiosity. The top part of the page provides brief information, while the lower part allows future voyagers opportunities to explore the possibilities.

In conceiving instructional projects designed for the WWW, designers should entertain certain questions. When and why should a project or program be posted on the WWW? Who is the potential audience and how might they find your document useful? How, for instance, would a student at another university or high school be able to learn from, build on, or revise the work presented? What is the purpose of the technology? In Dobler's course, the technology component was more time intensive and challenging than the co-teachers originally intended or expected. Was the content of the course compromised by the technological demands? What purpose does programming in HTML serve for journalists? To what extent is a course like Topics in Nonfiction a computer science course, and to what extent is it a journalism course? Attempting to answer these questions should produce stronger pedagogies, courses, and computer programs.

Having illustrated the seven design principles, we offer some basic rules for prospective and more experienced designers of instructional software. As our chapter has demonstrated, we cannot tell you which principles should take precedence over others or how they should interact. That can only be determined by the purpose, function, and pedagogical foundation of your application or project. With these qualifications in mind, the following are some general "rules" to consider. They are in no particular order (with the exception of coherence), sometimes overlap, and are offered as guidelines, not rigid prescriptions or formulas.

Correctness

Get reviewers from outside your discipline to assess correctness so that you can identify acceptable variations in content. For instance, psychologists may have a different notion of argument than philosophers. The

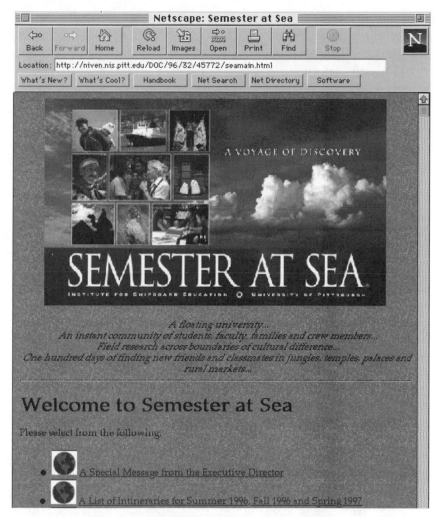

Figure 6.10. Semester at Sea Homepage

terms might be different; one discipline may prefer "claim" to "assertion." In medicine, terminology and methods of treatment can vary according to region. Even within the field of composition, some teachers might use terms of classical rhetoric (logos, ethos), while others may favor less formal language (evidence, support). Be sure that your information is accurate and well researched, whatever the audience or environment.

Creativity

Use creativity to enhance meaning, usefulness, and interest. In *Fire in the Crucible*, a fabulous book by John Briggs, not once does the author define his subject! Although a subject may be hard to define, it's easy to recognize when it isn't there. As we mentioned earlier, creativity may be less important in classroom applications than it is for published software, such as new forms of multimedia. However, the delight and excitement that an application generates can signify real innovation. Robert Winter's HyperCard stack, published by Voyager, inaugurated a new genre by analyzing Beethoven's *Ninth* with CD audio.

Consistency

Document the conventions you (the designer) decide to use, along with the rationale for making these choices. Doing so will make it easier to achieve internal consistency and minimize time needed for revision. If, for instance, you change your mind about the location of a button that is not part of the background, you may have to change it separately on thirty or more individual cards. Such revisions are essential in avoiding confusion and frustration for students who will spend unnecessary time searching for icons, instructions, and clues. Novice designers, anxious to begin creating stacks, backgrounds, buttons, and sound bytes, often sit down to the computer prematurely. It is best to consider every detail of interface design first; draw a sample screen on paper, testing out sizes, styles, colors, and locations. Thus, you will be revising as you design.

Clarity

Consider structural clarity from the outset by testing for informational objectives. Doing so will ensure pedagogical integrity. Ask yourself whether the objectives are being met at each point in the application. For instance, the original creator of The Borges Quest worked with a designer who continually asked her to articulate and justify what she wanted the students to accomplish in each segment. Is the structure making those objectives clear *to the user* and are they stated explicitly? Are they easily achievable? Because The Borges Quest was integral to the work of a composition course and preparatory for an actual assignment, fulfilling the objectives was crucial. As it turned out, those objectives called for an eventual rewriting of the course assignments (see Chapter 3). Make your writing (verbal clarity) more active, more engaging, and less wordy: (1) delete needless prepositions: from *The exhaust system of the car* to *The car's exhaust system*; (2) replace "to be" verbs: from

He is jogging to *He jogs* (3) avoid the passive voice: from *The paper was written by him* to *He wrote the paper* (4) avoid impersonal voice: from *Use of lower case is encouraged* to *Use lower case* and (5) avoid noun stacks: from *hematogenous bacteria transport system* to *bacteria carried by the blood.*

Consideration

Make sure that options displayed really do something: If they are inactive, gray them out or remove them (see Figure 6.3). Sometimes *what* they do can be confusing unless there are accompanying verbal cues. Icons should enhance meaning and function. For touch screens or mouse input, make the links as large as possible. Use color, size, and location to emphasize important information, not just as decoration. Be courteous in the persona you invoke: Do not use wisecracks if users make an error. Avoid stock phrases, such as "Very good. You seem to be catching on," without any basis for that claim. It is false praise and insulting. Minimize difficulties in listening and reading. If interviews in a multimedia application are difficult to hear or understand, provide transcripts. Alter the fonts for the words of each speaker. Make it easy to repeat important narration.

Likewise, make it easy for your readers to get around. Navigation metaphors (also representing structural clarity) provide an overview, in addition to easy access—getting in, moving around, and exiting. Maps are particularly useful in complex hypertexts, where users are likely to get lost or forget the task at hand. There are several screens of introduction for The Borges Quest (Figures 6.11a, b, and c) that explain the purpose of the application and how to use it. A navigational map (Figure 6.12), accessible from most screens in The Borges Quest, outlines the program's structure, though it does not explain it. Everything connected by lines (and the bottommost buttons) are links that enable quick and easy navigation through the application. Designing both introductory screens (to illustrate structural integrity) and navigational road maps would strengthen the Stein Project's functionability. However, because it is a constructive hypertext (continuously undergoing change), too much specificity is undesirable. A common technique for navigating through content-rich programs has been to use nested menus. But too often, this technique fails to give the user a sense of place or an idea of options. When nested too deeply, users can become lost or resent having to traverse up and down the menu structure to get to their destination. Ikonic Studio created a navigational structure for their Bandag kiosk that provides a fresh look at the classic problem of helping users who ask, "Where am I and how can I go somewhere else?"

Figure 6.11a. The Borges Quest—Introductory Screen #1

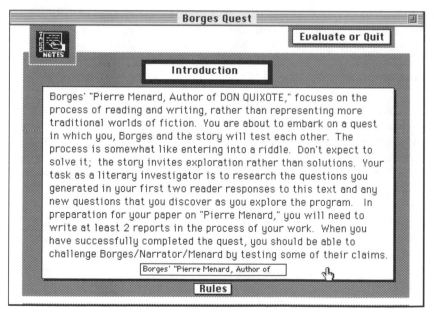

Figure 6.11b. The Borges Quest—Introductory Screen #2

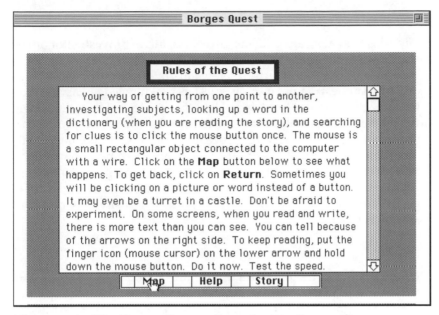

Figure 6.11c. The Borges Quest—Introductory Screen #3

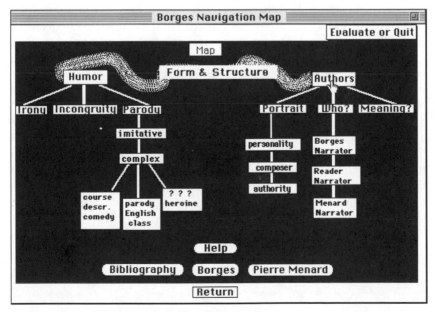

Figure 6.12. The Borges Quest—Map

Curiosity

Use curiosity as a pedagogical incentive. The literary investigator of The Borges Quest and the wizards, dragons, and warriors of the fantasy quest, create personas for users that intuitively illustrate both purpose and function. Fantasy quest defines users as questers for knowledge, carving their own insights into that "tree." Note, too, that the tree of knowledge will resonate for users on a number of levels as both a moral and educational imperative. However, exploiting curiosity for its own sake may create interest but be minimally useful for significant learning opportunities. Students enticed by a computer-game format (found in malls) may associate learning with passive transfer of information, rather than an interactive, dialogic *process*. Therefore, too much curiosity may be just as harmful as too little.

Coherence

Review all the principles and their interaction. Do they interact seamlessly and without provoking user awareness? Are they appropriate to the program's function and purpose? The best way to test for coherence is to pilot the software you have created. If it has been designed for stand-alone computers and then transferred to a network, be sure the transfer maintains the program's integrity. Testing will expose the bugs, which you can then eliminate before classroom or commercial use. Testing will also reveal any problems or confusions associated with a particular principle. Unfortunately, user frustration or confusion may mean restructuring or reconceiving function or purpose, but at least you will be able to isolate the causes. Testing for coherence enables the revision necessary for effective and productive instruction, the ultimate goal of educational software.

   Although these seven rules of design have proved useful for designers, they are not exhaustive; no list ever is. For instance, we have not discussed image design. In creating Web pages, you need to consider time constraints. Loading large and detailed images can take so long that the user loses patience and exits. For similar reasons, think about depth: using images and text, or *nesting* images. As we did when revising this chapter, you may want to consult a design expert for any issues you unwittingly disregarded. However, technology-enhancing critical inquiry is the fundamental "rule" and should precede all others.

III Writing as a Social Act

7 Computer-Mediated Communication: Making Nets Work for Writing Instruction

Fred Kemp
Texas Tech University

The commercial introduction of the microcomputer in the early 1980s gave some writing instructors the hope that what was wrong in the writing classroom could be fixed by presumably intelligent machines. During the intervening fifteen years, researchers have proposed six general computer-based instructional functions, each of which at one time or another has been promoted as what computers will principally "do" in a future of computer-dominated writing instruction. Recently, two of these functions or capabilities—computer-mediated communications (CMC), or networks, and hypertext—have become integral elements of the global supernetwork, the Internet, in ways that revive the promise of a technology-based universal learning. This essay seeks to provide an understanding of the instructional power of one of those functions— networked peer-to-peer communication. Along with a glimpse into how networking through the Internet may transform writing instruction, this essay offers a warning or two about what may be lost. The six proposed functions for computer-based instruction are that (1) computers could grade essays, (2) computers could provide self-paced drill and practice exercises, (3) computers could provide interactive invention heuristics, (4) computers could provide powerful word processing capability, (5) computers, using networks, could provide much greater student-to-student interaction, and (6) computers, using hypertext, with its ability to jump between portions of documents and documents themselves, could closely mirror the associative properties of the brain (whereby an external support system facilitates internal cognitive processes). All but these last two failed to deliver on their promise to influence writing instruction, and the decision is still out on networking and hypertext. Hopes, however, are once again on the rise. Much could be written on why automated graders, self-paced drill and practice, interactive heuristic "thought processors," and word processing itself have not affected instruction as much as once believed, but research indicates that the early excitement about, and fear of, "teaching machines" revealed both an unrealistically high appraisal of what computers could do and a disturbingly low appraisal of what human teachers (and writers) had been doing all along. The idea that computers could somehow glamorize instructional tasks that were inherently dull and unproductive arose out of an appallingly reductive view of our own students as primitives who could be bought into drudgery with a few pretty trinkets.

Because computers could not (as soon became obvious) employ natural language capability and therefore could not understand what students wrote, the dream of replacing graders and even teachers with machines, even for the presumed lowest-level student-teacher interactions, faded, and by the mid-1980s, some early enthusiasts were announcing the failure of computer-assisted writing instruction altogether. Yet the problem was, as always, not the lack of ability of the computers but rather the lack of imagination of those who would use them. The failed attempts to automate what teachers *presumably* do revealed the much greater complexity of what the mind and language are and what teachers *actually* do, and this encouraged skeptics, for a brief time, to reject the process-based tenets of the "new rhetoric" and return to the comforting view that teaching was an art, writing itself was ineffable, and any attempt to mediate the learning process with technology was a reductionist pipe dream.

But in 1985, Trent Batson at Gallaudet University established a form of computer-based writing instruction that bypassed the old problem of how smart or dumb computers really were and in some ways saved computer-based writing instruction from what was promising to be a period of debilitating retrenchment. At Gallaudet, which serves hearing-impaired students, Batson concluded that one of the problems with the writing of hearing-impaired students was that they communicated in their day-to-day discourse using ASL, American Sign Language, which only incidentally employed the English language as its base. Although hearing students were required to shift from oral to written English in their essays—admittedly a difficult task—the gap for hearing-impaired students between their everyday communication and writing was much greater: "when the typical deaf child encounters print, the child most often doesn't have the same potential for linking his previous communication experience with the symbol patterns on the page" (Batson 92). Batson decided to use computer networks, then in their infancy, and software that allowed a *synchronous* movement of electronic text from user to user as a means of allowing hearing-impaired students to communicate interactively in text, a sort of written conversation. In essence students sat at networked microcomputers and typed in comments that were then visible on every computer in the room.

By 1986 Batson realized that revitalizing written communication through networks could be valuable for *all* students of writing, not just those with hearing impairments.

> Very quickly it became apparent that the move to the network was not a simple shift from signed to written English; it led to a social shift as well. My role as teacher became very different once I was but a line on a screen and not the dominating presence at the front of the room. I also could see new energies emerging in our classroom interaction that had never occurred in my classes before. (99–100)

My colleagues and I at the University of Texas at Austin in 1987 picked up on his idea and applied networking to the collaborative learning theories of Kenneth Bruffee (Kemp, "Origins of ENFI"). Bruffee's distillation of ideas centering on the authority of discourse communities and the social construction of knowledge in a writing pedagogy (*Short Course in Writing*) seemed perfect for what the electronic distribution of student texts allowed. It was in Bruffee's 1986 *College English* article, "Social Construction, Language, and the Authority of Knowledge: A Bibliographical Essay," that we began to see how networks eroded the epistemological assumptions on which the traditional classroom was based, and how the epistemological assumptions privileged by networks dovetailed nicely with the challenges to classroom positivism, formalism, and imposed authority (current-traditionalism) that Bruffee described. The question of "authority" was central to issues of revitalizing classroom instruction. Sharon Crowley states emphatically that "current-traditional rhetoric maintains its hold on writing instruction because it is fully consonant with academic assumptions about the appropriate hierarchy of authority" (66). Networks, we realized, had the *potential* to decenter the classroom and redistribute authority in dramatic ways. By introducing us to Thomas Kuhn (*The Structure of Scientific Revolutions*), Bruffee also provided some frightened upstarts the courage to chip away at the Goliath of current-traditionalism that has long dominated writing instruction. Kuhn's discussion of paradigm shifts validated in our minds what we were seeing as the seismic shifts in classroom teaching presaged by computer-mediated communications.

The principal tenets of a network-based instruction were not new, at least to students of rhetoric and composition. Writing instruction theorists such as Jim Berlin, Richard Fulkerson, and Lester Faigley had earlier presented taxonomies of instructional emphases (based more or less on the literary critical taxonomy framed by M. H. Abrams in *The Mirror and the Lamp*) in which they all stressed a principal dichotomy between a fixed, formalist concept of what language is and hence how writing should be taught, and a fluid, rhetorical concept. This dichotomy is central to an understanding of the power of a network-based writing instruction.

Outside of Bruffee himself, the distinction has perhaps been most clearly articulated by Karen Burke LeFevre in *Invention as a Social Act* (1987). After quoting Bruffee, who underscores the importance of language as "the supreme means by which communities have created and continue to create knowledge by negotiating consensus and assent" (135), LeFevre acknowledges Thomas Kuhn as "among those who argue that knowledge is constructed by means of ongoing argument, and eventually, acceptance by a consensus of a community of thinkers" (136). "The inventing self," LeFevre says, "is thus socially constituted, and what is invented is judged according to its social contexts" (139). The knowledge community is a function of its social interaction and its ability to openly negotiate its meanings and values.

Networked computer-based writing instruction is based on a rhetorical or social dynamic in writing that, as proposed by LeFevre and Bruffee (and others), asserts that a genuine act of writing requires the open negotiation of issues in a classroom, and that presumes a reader who reads for information and effect, not simply to evaluate a performance, as a teacher does. The presumption on the part of the writer that his or her reader is reading merely to grade drains the writer of authorial independence and dilutes commitment to the writing act, causing in effect a breakdown in effort and the sorts of lazy, sterile writing that instructors are all too familiar with. Writing to peer readers, however, tends (over time and with the proper structure and intensity provided by computer-mediated communications) to restore a sense of engagement to the writing act, producing, in the memorable phrase of David Bartholomae (delivered in another context), the "sign of a student for whom something is happening" (16). Student writers often value the reactions of their peers over those of a professional reader—their teacher—and show more concern for their own text when writing for an audience they understand well. Effective writing, therefore, is not a "knowledge," in the sense of mathematics, that can be incrementalized and transmitted from knower to unknower as a hierarchy of principles or formulas, but rather a complex set of behaviors and highly individual comprehensions generated from intensive rhetorical activity.

The principal skill practiced in a computer-based networked classroom is the critical reading of student text, which is often flawed text.

Student readers learn not only to discover problems and areas for improvement in a text, but most important, they learn how to articulate their responses publicly. Over time, and as the result of much negotiation with peers through the network, student readers construct for themselves theories of effective and ineffective writing. As Joseph Petraglia, arguing against what he terms a "general writing skills instruction" (which I interpret as yet another term for current-traditional practices) has put it most clearly, "To the extent that rhetorical writing can be learned, it will only be so by students building individual models of how to be rhetorically effective and adapting those models to everyday situations where writing is called for and can serve a strategic purpose" ("Writing" 97). Because all student readers in a networked class are also student writers, they employ this emerging understanding as they revise their own papers. Motivated and thorough critical revising is, of course, at the heart of good writing.

But a major problem with group work and peer critiquing, as proposed by Bruffee, is managerial: distributing student texts and feedback, keeping groups on task, and keeping the always potentially disruptive psychological elements of group work to a minimum. By translating almost all peer interactions into electronic form—both informal "discussion" and the more formal student drafts themselves—the network largely bypasses the managerial problems of extensive group work and text sharing that arise in face-to-face settings. Because the interaction occurs through computer-mediated communication, the nature of the collaborative software ("groupware") and, above all, the tasks the instructor sets, have the ability to direct the students' efforts more thoroughly than is possible in oral class discussions and group work while, paradoxically, allowing the instructor to remove himself or herself from the role of classroom traffic cop.

A significant number of teachers complained in the early years of the networked classroom, and some still do, that the drastic reduction of face-to-face encounters in the networked class deprives the classroom dynamic of an important "human" ingredient. But it has been my experience, and those of most of my colleagues who seriously employ networked peer interaction, that while some aspects of personality are inhibited by the reduction of face-to-face activity, others are privileged through the networks. For instance, some groups or individuals normally intimidated in a largely oral instructional medium engage freely in class discourse, as Jerome Bump and Lester Faigley clearly show.

In an attempt to integrate theory and practice, the group in Austin developed an overview of computer-based instruction that recommended attention to four elements: (1) the proper equipment, (2) the proper software, (3) a coherent pedagogy (instructional theory), and (4) a group of people who can combine the previous three elements with energy, enthusiasm, and dogged persistence. We had discovered through experience that those who initiate computer-based instruction in their departments often concentrate on the equipment, give small attention to the software (usually choosing whatever popular form of word processing or desktop publishing software appeals to them), and ignore, often seriously, the pedagogy and the people who will use and manage the equipment and software, which generally creates what I have since called the "knowledge problem."

Of these four elements, what we lacked at the University of Texas in the mid-1980s was the software that would enable the written conversation over networks that Batson had pioneered. Batson's own work had been supported by a large grant that financed the development of special software, but the commercial version of that software was too expensive for our fledgling microlab, and the software contained instructionally unnecessary features and a troubling interface. Our efforts to link up with programmers at the university who might write local software for us failed, so three of us—Locke Carter, Paul Taylor, and I—laboriously applied our own rudimentary programming skills, first in BASIC and then in Turbo PASCAL, to produce software modules that would drive the computer-based classroom in ways that were consistent with our own research and experience as classroom teachers and with collaborative learning theories being developed by Wayne Butler and Valerie Balester, graduate students studying rhetoric. The result was a series of crude programs that were eventually more capably rewritten as a single piece of software marketed as "The Daedalus Integrated Writing Environment," or DIWE.

DIWE combines simple word processing, e-mail, and synchronous messaging with a menu-driven file management feature that allows students to turn in documents to a network and distribute them easily without fear of tampering or overwriting by other students. These capabilities of the software, and several adjunct writing heuristic and bibliography mechanisms are simple to use. The point is not so much what the software does but what the writing environment supports, and a major consideration is that the software should enable, not overwhelm, writing, reading, and peer responding. [1]

The educational software market eventually responded to an increasing enthusiasm for classroom CMC. In 1994 Norton expanded its Textra word processing software into Textra Connect, which employed functions of DIWE together with Textra's full-featured word processor, and in late 1995 Houghton Mifflin marketed software (CommonSpace) to compete with both DIWE and Connect. These products, along with the commercial version of the original ENFI software, Realtime Writer, several features of Aspects, and more generic groupware features being included in major word processing packages all support, in various ways, a "text-sharing pedagogy," or the ability of students in or out of a classroom to distribute their informal and formal writing to peer readers for extensive feedback. Comparisons of these programs, like comparisons between the Macintosh operating system and Microsoft Windows, often reveal little besides the predilections of various users; the differences pale in comparison to the similarities, which include synchronous messaging, e-mail, and document sharing.

The efforts of Batson and the Texas group to promote a network pedagogy helped produce in the early 1990s a resurgent interest in what was once called "computer-assisted instruction" (CAI) in composition, although professionals in the field generally came to refer to it as "computer-*based* instruction," having arrived at the realization that computer-mediated communications were transforming classroom instruction in the paradigmatic terms of Thomas Kuhn. Computers were no longer merely assisting precomputer instructional processes but rather providing a peer interactivity and a reading-writing arena that supported a new rhetorical base for instruction (or provided the old collaborative base with a new, enabling functionality). The "teaching-grading machine" idea that had so captured the imagination (in terms of both good and evil) early on had been replaced by the new notion that communication was the key to better writing instruction and that whatever facilitated peer-to-peer communication would improve writing instruction.

By the mid-1990s, the astonishing growth of the Internet provided a powerful push for CMC-based instruction and online group work, and the teaching community was suddenly faced with an exciting but bewildering range of techniques by which teachers could employ e-mail, e-mail discussion lists, real-time discussion (IRCs, MUDs, and MOOs), and information delivery systems (gophers and the World Wide Web) throughout the world. The tendency of instructors and administrators to tie a particular form of instruction to a specific piece of software was being belied by the new, universal networking capabilities of the Internet and the appearance of peer-to-peer collaborative pedagogy working across classroom, departmental, campus, and even national boundaries.

So what actually happens in a networked classroom? Although one can hardly present a "typical" picture of instruction that is anything *but* typical, I can describe a series of instructional tasks that some on my campus have employed over the past eight years in order to illustrate the sorts of assignments that lead to the benefits of using CMC and the Internet.

By 1996 the Computer-Based Writing Research Project at Texas Tech University, begun in 1988 and formalized in 1990, was supporting three Pentium and Performa classrooms of twenty-two to twenty-four computers each, all networked to a single local-area server and connected to the Internet. Some twenty-five instructors, mostly graduate students, were teaching full-time every semester in these rooms, serving about seven hundred to eight hundred students. Courses included composition, technical communication, literature, and creative writing. Accordingly, Texas Tech had gained considerable experience using classroom and wide-area networks for instruction, principally using DIWE. [2]

Although it would be difficult to describe in comprehensive terms all the computer-based networked tasks that teachers assign their students, in general the classes rely heavily on CMC and peer responding. Class discussions are conducted using synchronous messaging (as described previously), e-mail is sent between individuals to pursue topics further, drafts are shared online in a variety of ways, peer comments are mailed back to the writers, and both invention and responding are managed on the computer in structured and unstructured formats. Of the seventy-some instructors who had used these methods at Texas Tech through 1996, only two decided to return to the traditional classroom. What follows in the paragraphs below is a schedule of CMC-based tasks throughout an instructional unit.

At the beginning of an essay cycle (the series of student tasks that lead from prewriting to final draft), the instructor presents the class with a prompt to initiate an Interchange session (Interchange is DIWE's synchronous messaging feature). An example of such a prompt states that freshmen who live in the dorms should not be allowed to own cars. Immediately, a lively online discussion ensues, and the writer of the prompt is soundly vilified. But eventually (and this happens every time), someone posits that if freshmen didn't own cars, their studies would improve. A few others support that view. The exchange quickly evolves into a discussion of why people go to college in the first place, to play or to study. After thirty minutes or so, several conflicting points of view are supported, often by significant reasoning. It seems human nature cannot resist this sort of engagement; people discussing topics they are personally interested in will, largely on their own and especially when "protected" by the pseudo-anonymity of CMC, express contentious views. The nature of the contention encourages students to assert, support, and justify their opinions. First-time observers, sometimes teachers with many years of classroom experience, are often startled by what they characterize as the sheer "thinking" that takes place during an Interchange session.

After about thirty minutes, the instructor stops the session and asks the students to write on the word processor for ten minutes summarizing the gist of the discussion. These summaries are saved to Netmanager (DIWE's secure classroom database feature) and to the students' disks. The Interchange discussion is also saved to their disks. The students are asked to read the discussion at home or on the dorm computers and delete all but three of the most interesting points they themselves did not make. From these three points, they are to construct a thirty-line draft discussing whatever issue they have gleaned from the discussion. If they wish, they may cite their classmates in the draft.

The next class day the students read an online description of propositions (Bruffee's term for thesis statements) and are given fifteen minutes to construct adequate propositions for their own drafts. Then students e-mail their drafts to another member of the class, and the peer reader is asked to (1) comment on the quality of the proposition and (2) make general comments regarding the draft, such as how interesting it is and how it might be made more interesting. These comments are e-mailed back to the writer, who may then ask for clarification from the peer responder, either on e-mail or face to face. The instructor asks the students to revise the proposition and drafts according to feedback from the peer responder, building them to perhaps fifty lines of text.

On the third class day, the students load their second drafts into an Interchange session, almost instantly creating a classroom electronic anthology of drafts. The students spend twenty minutes skimming this anthology. (Students report that reviewing the drafts is extremely helpful in assessing their own skills and weaknesses in relation to the class.) The following comment from a student is typical:

> I hated the idea of other people reading my own writing at first. Then I realize[d] that they weren't much better than I was and that they made mistakes that I wouldn't make. I don't know why but I got a kick out of that. You [the instructor] say that reading other student papers makes us read our own differently and I really believe that now. Before [this class] I had never read anybody else's paper, and now I think I understand my own problems better.

Students are asked to freewrite about what they see as the major problems or strengths in regard to the class's writing and how their writing compares. The constant requirement to examine their own writing in terms of the class's writing encourages an awareness of writing itself and demystifies a process that many of them have been encouraged to see as purely mystical. The student quoted previously finished his evaluation by commenting, "Now I know that writing isn't just a matter of Fate," which I take as a significant realization that writing is an improvable skill—no small understanding for students who far too often assume that good or bad writing is "hard-wired" into their abilities and beyond their capacity to affect.

The students are asked to prepare a third draft for the next class period and are provided a description of various ways of supporting the essay proposition. On the fourth class day, students upload their third drafts into an Interchange session that has been broken up into groups of four students each. Each group reads the four drafts uploaded to its electronic space, and then members discuss how the writers managed to provide support for the propositions, similarities and differences in the writers' approaches, style, and so forth. The following student response illustrates this process:

> Both Jamie's and Howard's paper uses an item list to support the thesis and Robert used a chain of reasoning ["item list" and "chain of reasoning" are the instructor's terms for patterns of support]. But Howard, you should use a chain of reasoning because a thesis talking about space travel can't be supported that way. One thing has to lead to another but you just string out a bunch of ideas, not connected, . . . it's all kind of science fiction. Robert's way would fit better, I think. See how he "builds" his support and doesn't just say a bunch of unconnected things?

Such student analyses, delivered extemporaneously and online, are more effective than teacher feedback because the targeted texts are blended with interactive student commenting. The discussions are downloaded to the students' disks, and students are asked to review the discussions out of class and prepare a fourth draft of about seventy-five lines for the next class day, taking the comments of their group members into consideration.

On the fifth class day, the students turn in their drafts to Netmanager, and peers are asked to respond to the drafts using Respond, the DIWE feature that provides a structured revision heuristic, or a series of specific questions regarding the draft. Because the prompts can be written on-site, the instructor includes a number of specific queries regarding the proposition, the development of the proposition, managing support for the proposition, and so forth. (The Respond prompts increase in specificity and complexity throughout the semester, moving the students along a progressive understanding of the critical features of a student essay. I often use the Respond prompts as guides for grading my essays.) Each draft undergoes two Respond critiques, and the peer readers e-mail their Respond sessions (which include both prompts and responses) back to the writers and to Netmanager (so that the instructor can review and grade, if necessary, the quality of the peer readers' critiques).

Responding to student drafts is a learned behavior, as I well know from supervising sixty-five teaching assistants in Texas Tech's composition program. Even English graduate students often do poorly at first, so teachers should not be discouraged when first-year undergraduates struggle with the process and produce initially awkward results. But features like Respond provide the student responder with a "learning scaffold" or (an image I prefer) "training wheels" for the initial responding sessions, allowing progress to be measured and gradated. For instance, a prompt offered at the beginning of a semester received this response:

> PROMPT: Copy the proposition and judge its effectiveness.
> RESPONSE: The proposition is "So keep[ing] pets is good for a person's mental and physical well being." I like the thesis and it is arguable.

(One of the simple criteria I set for a good proposition or thesis is that it is a statement a reasonable person might disagree with.) I had asked students to provide at least four to six lines per response, and this student did not write four lines in responding to any of the six prompts. Eight weeks later, the same student responded to a slightly more difficult prompt with the following:

> PROMPT: Locate the proposition and critique how effective it is and how effectively the writer supports it.
> RESPONSE: You put down "telecommunications is ruining the agricultural base of America by allowing foreign ownership of industrial farms." This thesis makes me want to keep reading and even angers me a little, so it is good, but you describe how Japanese and Arabs own all this land and your data is good and well researched, but the telecommunications part is left out. There's one thing about global markets and satellites near the end of the paper, but almost nothing about telecommunications. You don't even describe what telecommunications is actually. The part about conference calls doesn't seem to me to be a definition of telecommunications. You need to put down a definition and then make it connect to agriculture some way.

There were twelve prompts in this later series of critiquing criteria, and all of the student's responses to them were equally detailed and almost as long. Practically all other students in this class produced commensurately longer and more detailed critiques, and I have found that the pattern generally holds true for all of my students who undergo the same process. The ability to expand the student's skill to read student texts critically lies at the heart of good writing instruction and for this, peer communication is essential.

For the last class day of the essay cycle, the writers are asked to prepare a final draft based on the critiques received, the directives of the instructor, and any relevant classroom discussions captured in Interchange. On this last day the final drafts are circulated to members of assigned groups for a rapid, last-ditch editing session in which peers can specifically point out surface errors.[3]

Those who support CMC-based instruction make strong claims that cause others to call for proof, but there is no proof that CMC provides better instruction than precomputer pedagogies, just as there is no proof that precomputer pedagogies provide any instruction at all. There is, in fact, no universally accepted substantiation for any writing pedagogy, for if there were, we would all be using it. Question of proof aside, however, there are still forces driving the transition to technology-based writing instruction that are stronger than the hallowed (if never validated) traditions of classroom instruction and the deep-seated mistrust of technology most teachers in the humanities feel. As one of my students trenchantly put it, society is "voting for technology in a big way." English teachers, with their undeniable love for the immutable truths of literature, have secretly and not-so-secretly prided themselves on escaping the vicissitudes of commercial and scientific pressures, but society's shift toward an information economy has inescapable implications: Unless we plan on transporting our students back to the nineteenth century on graduation, we must prepare them to use words in a rapidly expanding electronic environment. The Internet, especially, and the easily navigable World Wide Web, are rapidly becoming pervasive, exerting an influence on society at a speed never before seen by even the most transformative technologies. How does a networked collaborative pedagogy relate to the Internet?

Of the six computer-based functions that writing instructors have hypothesized as useful to their craft in the last fifteen years, the last two seem most faithful to the character of the Internet as it has evolved: networked collaborative instruction and hypertext-based instruction. Ironically, these two points of view, once seen as mildly antithetical among scholars, have both become integral to the Internet. The collaborative emphasis is demonstrated in e-mail discussion lists (managed by distribution software such as Listserv, Listproc, and Majordomo), and interactive discussion available in IRC (Internet Relay Chat) and MUD/MOO (multiple-user domains, object-oriented), two Internet features that provide synchronous messaging capability much like DIWE, Connect, CommonSpace, and other local-area programs but that allow real-time written conversation to extend throughout the world. The hypertext emphasis is dramatically displayed in the World Wide Web, a means of accessing information across the Internet in a simple interface charac-terized by Web browsers such as Mosaic and Netscape. Users merely click on highlighted terms that appear on their screens in order to quickly access further information located on computers anywhere in the world. Web browsers and Web servers have taken file access capabilities that have existed on the wide-area networks for decades and made them astonishingly easy to use.

Because of these capabilities on the Internet and their rapidly increas-ing ease of use, access to the Internet is exploding, within two years (1994–95) tripling in size to estimates of nearly 60 million users (Bournellis 47). The respected Nielsen ratings, in what *Time* magazine called "the first solid survey of the Internet," reported that 37 million Americans and Canadians were accessing the Internet by the end of 1995 (Dibbell 121). Statistics like these are important, for they show both how compel-ling CMC activities are to people outside instructional settings and how familiar the CMC process is becoming to increasing numbers of people. The argument, almost a given in the early 1980s, that computers and computer activities were intrinsically foreign to everyday human ac-tivities is being reversed, and we are finding more and more that, for the young, doing some daily activities *without* a computer seems strange.

The CMC activities that have been explored inside networked class-rooms over the last ten years at places like Texas Tech can be employed between classes, between campuses, and between countries. Written conversations, e-mail peer responses, publishing student writing to a peer readership—all can be done over networks using connections and computers that are proliferating at a mind-boggling rate because they are increasingly being valued by the society at large, not by the educa-tion community alone. The vast amount of this traffic being moved over the Internet by the 37 million Americans and Canadians is in writing, and a large proportion of that writing is being written interactively (Kemp, "Writing Dialogically"). In a number of ways, the expansion of the Internet is restoring to North America what another issue of *Time* (July 4, 1994) called "for millions of people, a living, breathing life of letters."

In other words, CMC is bringing millions of people into writing ev-ery day, and this in a society steeped in television, VCRs, radio, Nintendo, CDs, movies, and above all else, the telephone. CMC has made writing a "living, breathing" thing once more for people who had been seduced into a dependence on audio/video media, a dependence that no doubt has led more to the United States' declining writing skills than the short-comings of teachers and pedagogy. For our purposes, the popularity of the Internet is simply another indication of the inherent power of CMC to restore vitality to a form of expression—writing—that was in deep retreat, pushed into the fixed forms and purposeless exercises of classroom assignments.

What will happen to writing instruction when it takes to the Internet? For one thing, it will slowly lose its identity as "writing instruction." Just as word processing, following the example of the telephone and automobile, has moved from being a consciously considered process into the anonymity of being a fact of life, learning to write will be a part of writing itself, in a vastly richer writing and reading arena than now possible. Teachers will continue to make assignments, but the assignments will be directed toward a great, unknown readership out there, which, for the writer, will make all the difference. Classes from different campuses will link up and hold regular discussions online, share work, and argue principles. Students will encounter, and occasionally recoil from, the opinions of a readership they must learn to anticipate.

In the short run, pre-CMC practices will simply be extended onto the Internet and change slowly as the effects of CMC impact their current modes of operating. Writing centers, for instance, have begun to extend tutoring onto the Internet, becoming "online writing labs" (OWLs), as at Purdue, the University of Michigan, Texas Tech University, and other campuses. Students submit drafts through e-mail and tutors provide feedback. An even more adventurous process is called The Cyberspace Writing Center Consultation Project, supported by Roane State Community College and the University of Arkansas at Little Rock. Here tutors stay online in a synchronous writing environment (MOO), interacting with patrons who "drop in" at any time to talk about writing problems.

Likewise, classroom instruction is extending onto the Internet. One notable example occurred in the spring of 1993, when graduate courses at San Francisco State, the University of Texas at Austin, and Texas Tech conducted the "Interclass." The Interclass provided an e-mail discussion list for the students in the three courses. Because the courses were concerned with computers and writing, approximately ten scholars and researchers in computers and writing were invited to "present" a work-in-progress each week and then remain joined to the e-mail discussion list for that week, responding to student queries and comments, in effect creating a shared, online, living "text" for the three courses. The students were able not only to interact with well-known figures in the field (such as Cynthia Selfe, Trent Batson, Karen Schwalm, Michael Joyce, and Bill Condon), but they also engaged (sometimes heatedly) in discussions about the presentations and various points of view. The mix of students from the three campuses and the often competing agendas of the professors stimulated the colloquy in startling ways, contributing to a general feeling (admittedly not shared by all the students) that the intellectual fervor was compelling. One graduate student commented,

> The class was simply incredible. Never in my wildest dreams had I thought I would take a class where I was able to talk with (write with, actually) the famous people whose articles I was reading, and they treated me like my ideas were as important as their own (well, sort of). It's the first time I've ever thought I might some day actually be one of them.

Instructors at Texas Tech are experimenting with combinations of Internet features, including the use of Usenet newsgroups, class meetings held principally on the MOO, various uses of e-mail discussion and submissions of writing, and communication with other classes at other schools. At least nine sections of composition, literature, and technical communication were engaged in such Internet CMC activities in the spring of 1996, with more expected in the fall. One of the reasons these classes report·enthusiastic support from instructors and students is that the instructors who attempt such innovations at Texas Tech have considerable experience in local-area CMC and are usually cognizant of the perils and the preparations necessary; they know how to gauge their expectations to avoid the emotional swings that sometimes attend enthusiasm for CMC-based instruction.

Similar efforts are being conducted on campuses around the country in a technologically charged spirit of innovation that resists description in print. A principal online means of tapping into such activities in a timely fashion exists on the World Wide Web pages of the Alliance for Computers and Writing (http://english.ttu.edu/acw/). There, links can be made to the field's principal e-mail discussion lists, online journals, support organizations, OWLs, and a plethora of other sources describing K–12 and postsecondary uses of CMC. The social dynamic that drives writing engagement in CMC-based writing classes also drives professional efforts when participants in the discipline maintain continuous active contact with each other, electronically oblivious of time and space.

Although I remain, after ten years of struggling with the technology, an enthusiastic supporter of CMC-based writing instruction, I would be foolish not to recognize the downsides, and there are some serious ones. No change of the magnitude that I am suggesting in this essay occurs without severe individual costs. The most serious may be that fine teachers who have contributed decades to their profession will be unable to use computers and will find themselves shunted aside by social forces they find difficult to acknowledge. This same displacement is currently happening in every vocational setting in the United States, but teachers in the humanities have all too often blithely assumed that what *they* have to teach is protected from societal pressures, relying perhaps on the medieval perception of scholarship as purely defensive, something to protect behind monastery walls.

A few of these teachers will have been exceptional teachers who have thrived, as their students have thrived, on the sheer puissance of association. These are the teachers that we who have *become* teachers remember best and have wanted most to be like. To "decenter" the classrooms of these teachers is to deprive them of the very air they breathe and to deny their students an extraordinary experience. I would hope and would argue for administrators to recognize this dynamic and exempt such teachers from the collaborative processes described in this essay, but at the same time I understand how few in number they are and how we must not fall back on "golden age" notions of teaching as we try to provide a pedagogy for the learning of hundreds of thousands of students across North America and the globe. To ignore the diversity in human talent among teachers and mandate any particular form of instruction, even within a single facility, would be irresponsible.

There will be instructors who jump into computer-based processes simply as an escape hatch from teaching itself, thinking they see in CMC-based instruction a way to hide from their students. The danger for them is not realizing that, in order to succeed, the teachers using technology must be clever, hardworking, and ambitious. The computer-based writing classroom is a kind of learning kitchen where the heat is always on high. It is not (as often presumed) an automated assembly line on which the teacher can fade from responsibility and effort, but many teachers and many more administrators will revert to the old "teaching machine" concept and assume that computers will allow the dumbing down of teacher requirements, the increase of classroom sizes, and the shrinking of payrolls. This one issue is sure to fuel debate for decades to come, no doubt making some instructors long for the good old days when the classroom represented as fixed an activity as the pulpit.

Within many computer-based classrooms, there will be bad instruction, just as there is bad instruction in many noncomputer classrooms now, and often the technology will simply make things worse, perhaps glossing over improper training and lackadaisical effort the way that prettified laser-printed student papers can gloss over serious problems with the text. Administrators will see students clicking away at computers and assume that the technology is ensuring significant effort, an ironic reversal of the usual impression not long ago that a student at a computer was doing "nothing but typing a paper."

Many people see these problems as rationales for rejecting any intrusion of technology into the classroom. But the writing classroom is not an island separate from the society it serves and can no more preserve its own prerogatives in the face of overwhelming outside pressure than can any other element of society. Computer technology is not superfluous gimmickry that can be imposed or excluded based on individual likes and dislikes. Instructional fads come and go and the tough teacher can outlast most of them, but societal changes in information access and communication will require profound changes in the classroom and in the way most people learn. As always, the burden will rest on the classroom teacher to use the tools at hand to do the best for the students, and this requires anticipating and avoiding the pitfalls that will come with these changes.

Notes

1. For an extended description of DIWE, see Kemp's "The Daedalus Integrated Writing Environment."
2. A description of Texas Tech's computer-based research project may be obtained on the World Wide Web at http://english.ttu.edu/.
3. An online class that I taught may be examined through a Web browser at http://english.ttu.edu/courses/1302/kemp/sp96/.

Works Cited

Bartholomae, David. "What is Composition and (if you know what it is) Why Do We Teach It?" *Composition in the Twenty-First Century: Crisis and Change.* Ed. Lynn Z. Bloom, Donald A. Daiker, and Edward M. White. Carbondale: Southern Illinois University Press, 1996. 11–28.

Batson, Trent. "The Origins of ENFI." *Network-Based Classrooms: Promises and Realities.* Ed. Bertram C. Bruce, Joy Kreeft Peyton, and Trent Batson. Cambridge: Cambridge University Press, 1993.

Berlin, James. "Contemporary Composition: The Major Pedagogical Theories." *College English* 44 (1982): 765–77.

Bournellis, Cynthia. "Internet '95." *Internet World* November 1995. 47–52.

Bruffee, Kenneth A. *A Short Course in Writing.* 3rd Edition. Boston: Little, Brown and Company, 1985.

———. "Social Construction, Language, and the Authority of Knowledge: A Bibliographical Essay." *College English* 48 (1986): 773–96.

Bump, Jerome. "Radical Changes in Class Discussion Using Networked Computers." *Computers in the Humanities* 24 (1990): 49–65.

Crowley, Sharon. "Around 1971: Current-Traditional Rhetoric and Process Models of Composing." *Composition in the Twenty-First Century: Crisis and Change.* Ed. Lynn Z. Bloom, Donald A. Daiker, and Edward M. White. Carbondale: Southern Illinois University Press, 1996. 64–74.

Dibbell, Julian. "Nielsen Rates the Net." *Time* 13 November 1995: 121.

Faigley, Lester. "Subverting the Electronic Workbook: Teaching Writing Using Networked Computers." *The Writing Teacher as Researcher: Essays in the Theory and Practice of Class-Based Research.* Ed. Donald Daiker and Max Morenberg. Portsmouth, NH: Boynton/Cook, 1990.

Fulkerson, Richard. "Four Philosophies of Composition." *College Composition and Communication* 30 (1979): 343–48.

Kemp, Fred. "The Daedalus Integrated Writing Environment." *Educator's Tech Exchange* Winter (1993): 24–30.

———. "The Origins of ENFI, Network Theory, and Computer-Based Collaborative Writing Instruction at the University of Texas." *Network-Based Classrooms: Promises and Realities.* Ed. Bertram Bruce, Joy Kreeft Peyton, and Trent Batson. Cambridge: Cambridge University Press, 1993.

———. "Writing Dialogically: Bold Lessons From Electronic Text." *Reconceiving Writing, Rethinking Writing Instruction.* Ed. Joseph Petraglia. Mahwah, NJ: Lawrence Erlbaum, 1995. 179–94.

LeFevre, Karen Burke. *Invention as a Social Act.* Carbondale: Southern Illinois University Press, 1987.

Petraglia, Joseph. "Writing as an Unnatural Act." *Reconceiving Writing, Rethinking Writing Instruction.* Ed. Joseph Petraglia. Mahwah, NJ: Lawrence Erlbaum, 1995. 79–100.

8 Writing in the Matrix: Students Tapping the Living Database on the Computer Network

Michael Day
South Dakota School of Mines and Technology

Students in most writing classes produce papers for which the primary audience is the teacher and the primary purpose is to pass the course. Yet our study of rhetoric tells us that citizens need to be prepared to write for a wide variety of audiences in a wide variety of contexts. Further, students writing research papers often look no further than the books and journals in their own school library to gather source material. With the proliferation of the Internet, more and more students have access to what Howard Rheingold calls a "living database" of people grouped into virtual communities with similar interests. By first monitoring discussion groups on the network, analyzing the audience and discourse conventions used in these groups, then posting messages to the discussions, students can gain experience writing for real audiences that span the globe. Using the network in this manner allows them to become better writers in a real-world communication context.

Beyond Automated Databases

Like many teachers, I encourage my students to learn to tap the tremendous resources on the Internet through remote library log-in, gopher, FTP, and the World Wide Web. However, I recognize that there are many limitations to this approach. Because the Internet is a largely undocumented and changing collection of resources, students often find it difficult to locate and effectively use the resources they need. Sometimes they need to be able to ask questions in plain English. To allow my students to ask questions on the network that no automated software database could possibly answer, I have developed activities that tap the human element of the network by asking students to use e-mail and Usenet discussion groups.

In *The Virtual Community: Homesteading on the Electronic Frontier*, Howard Rheingold conceives of the network of interconnected human beings communicating in cyberspace as a kind of "grassroots groupmind" or "living database" (Rheingold 111, 115) (as opposed to automated databases that do not understand plain English). The living database is a network-based communication among minds that allows the formation of discourse communities not dependent on a physical place. Rheingold suggests that the network is allowing those connected through the network to reform society into social groupings based more on interest or professional fields than on geographic proximity. Many such discourse communities flourish in cyberspace, available to anyone with a network connection. Aware of the vast potential of the network, more and more educational institutions are making these connections available to students and teachers. I would like to outline a network-based activity that has worked well to give my students real-world audiences. Although I use this activity primarily with technical communications classes, it can be used in almost any writing class in which the students have some access to the Internet.

The Context and Problem

Most writing courses must meet a variety of needs of a diverse student body. I teach at a state technological university with approximately 2,400 students enrolled in degree programs ranging from electrical, mechanical, and civil engineering to our own interdisciplinary sciences program, which prepares students for a variety of careers in business, industry, science, and the medical services. Our students are intelligent and highly motivated, but what characterizes them more than anything else is the great variety of their needs in preparation for professional, technical, and business communication tasks. Indeed, neither the students nor their department heads can easily agree on what kinds of assignments will best meet their needs.

Further, we suffer from a rather pronounced geographical isolation. We are an eight-hour drive from Denver and ten hours from Minneapolis—rather distant from major university libraries and large concentrations of scholars. Colleges and universities on or near the coasts can stay up-to-date on the latest developments, but our geographical isolation sometimes results in our seeming provincial and behind the times in comparison with other institutions of higher education. Somehow we need to overcome this isolation, both for ourselves as professionals and for our students. We need to be in contact with other people, people who either think like we do, or whose ideas complement our thinking. Thus, enacting Rheingold's concept of the living database can help us overcome some of the isolation by providing that contact.

Another side effect of geographical isolation is the fact that our students have few chances to encounter other cultures and the wide diversity of opinions one might find on the coasts or near the big cities. Because we learn to understand ourselves better as writers, speakers, and thinkers if we can interact with people from other cultures and beliefs, those among us who teach a multicultural approach to composition want our students to gain some firsthand experience communicating with and gleaning ideas from people from different cultures. Many of our students will end up working in jobs and living in communities with much more diverse populations; thus, they need to develop awareness of and sensitivity to other cultures *now*, as part of their training in communication. Hopefully, they will become citizens of the world, better able to survive in an increasingly multicultural society.

Further, as most of us know from our scholarly reading, and as the rest of society is coming to know from reading article after article on the network in popular publications such as *Time* and *Newsweek*, the paradigm of communication is changing because of increased dependence on computer-mediated communication in business, industry, and even leisure. At many levels, electronic mail, the World Wide Web, and computer conferencing are changing what we define as writing, who we write for, how fast we expect a response, and how we archive our communications. From a pragmatic point of view, we know that more than ever, students need to explore and become accustomed to these new communication technologies because they will probably be using them in their future careers.

The Activity: Writing in the Matrix

To address these in my writing classes, I advocate a kind of network-based information literacy. Of course I encourage my students to learn how to search *automated* databases along with other library resources, but because I teach communications, I also emphasize our ability to connect to the *living* database of discussions and individuals conceived of by Howard Rheingold. To situate students in a relevant discourse community, I would like them to be able to write for and glean information from other human beings by communicating on the network through e-mail or real-time discussion. This entrance into a discourse community helps them better understand the range of real-world communication situations.

Because I want to help students write for a variety of audiences in a variety of contexts, I do not eliminate the more traditional writing and speaking assignments but instead endeavor to supplement them. How-

ever, in addition to assigning the research papers and essays, I ask what
I can add to enrich my students' understanding of discourse communities, of the notion of audience, and of the range of living databases available to them. Indeed, I ask just how I might teach my students to adapt
their communicative strategies for a variety of audiences, including those
accessible only on the network.

Many writing classes across the nation have already moved to the
computer classroom to do written group brainstorming.[1] These activities have much to offer in terms of practice writing for and with others,
but they involve only a local audience of those in the class. To access a
wider audience, they must turn to the network, the Internet,[2] that sometimes chaotic, sometimes treasure-trove of online information.

I chose to take my students online because of the success I have had
widening the range of colleagues I can contact and work with on the
Internet. I have found professional satisfaction and increased my own
knowledge and teaching repertoire by joining discussion groups on the
Internet. Because such a variety of professional conversations take place
on the network, I assumed that some of my class members should be
able to get involved, especially as all students at my school can get accounts on our Internet host. But having access and being able to use it
are different issues.

Because the school has no network literacy requirement, I find that I
must either train the students myself, using up valuable class time, or
ask them to attend library Internet orientations. So, either by myself or
with the library staff, I give the class two library orientations: a basic
session on electronic mail and UNIX functions for saving and arranging
files, and later an advanced session on gopher, FTP, hytelnet, World Wide
Web, and other network utilities. Once they get this far, I ask them to
demonstrate their e-mail capability by sending me a memo evaluating
their performance in a class activity.

Through their library orientation and our class discussions, my students learn how to find and join networked discussion groups such as
Bitnet lists, Internet discussion groups, and Usenet groups. They then
join at least one discussion group relevant to their field or interests. Many
of my students are majoring in mechanical engineering, electrical engineering, civil engineering, chemical engineering, and computer science.
They have joined lists for students and professionals in their respective
fields and developed contacts for jobs and research projects through those
lists. Our school has also created local Usenet discussion groups for various clubs and engineering societies, and a few classes have set up their
own Usenet groups. Students in my classes can receive credit for posts
to class groups as an alternative to journal entries, provided the discussion is sophisticated enough.[3]

I generally illustrate the idea of joining a professional or field-specific discourse community through networked discussion groups by outlining my experiences and involvement with several groups for professionals in the fields of rhetoric, communication, computers and writing, and English. Several years ago, friends and colleagues introduced me to groups such as MBU-L (MegaByte University), Purtopoi, CMC (computer-mediated communication), and Ortrad-L (oral tradition). My students learn how much my professional life has changed since I became part of the discussions in my field. Once an isolated individual with few colleagues with whom to talk, I now feel part of a community of scholars engaged in discussion to enlarge our field of knowledge. Further, I have met new colleagues with whom I have begun a series of collaborations on publications and conference presentations[4] that I might never have embarked on had I not encountered them on the network. I stress to my students that at its best, networked discussion can draw on the natural heuristic power of minds bumping raw ideas off each other, tweaking them a bit, and developing new thought structures in a synergistic manner. I hope that they, too, can be drawn into the conversation, writing as I do out of a desire to communicate with real people in a kind of virtual community.

After joining a group, each student begins by monitoring the discussion for a week or more in order to get a sense of the discourse conventions and expectations of the group. For the rhetoricians among us, this is a period of intense audience analysis, in which the students carefully examine every message from the group for evidence of shared discourse conventions, shared items of knowledge, and common rhetorical strategies. The students keep journals on what they find and discuss the conventions and strategies with each other in class. Only when they feel that they know the group and its habits and expectations well can they begin to post messages to its members. Some students elect to use the journal entries as a base from which to write a formal investigative report (directed to a professional in their field) on the value of participating in network discussion groups.

Because I usually make the networked discussion assignment elective (one of a number of choices), students know that they need to take time to investigate the discussion groups available and the quality of discussion by each group. After these preliminary investigations, we can talk about what makes a good source and why. How do we assess the credentials of those who post to groups and those who advise us? What positions do they hold, what research have they done, and what sources do they themselves cite? This can lead to more general discussion of source credibility, such as the difference between an article about extraterrestrial life in *Cosmopolitan* and one in *Science*. In this way, the students' network investigations help them better understand the different kinds of evidence, credentials, and rhetorical strategies that are useful for a variety of discursive communities and occasions.

After the monitoring and analysis period, students then draft a post (generally of less than a page because of the brevity required in e-mail) addressed to the group. It can be any sort of a post, but is typically related to a technical communications or other class project, and falls into one of the following categories.

Requesting Information

Students might be asking for information for their final projects, which are often proposals, manuals, literature reviews, or feasibility reports. One of my students needed government telephone numbers to find out about regulations for coding plastic containers for recycling, so he sent a request to the Recycling list. Within twenty-four hours, he had four responses with telephone numbers. A geology major posted questions about a test of deep earthquakes she was researching for her final project. One of the geologists involved in the testing answered her query in some detail. Yet another student had read an article by Marvin Minsky, renowned artificial intelligence expert at MIT's Media Lab. I was able to find the student an e-mail address for Dr. Minsky so that the student could ask questions related to his final literature review. Much to our amazement, Dr. Minsky replied (see Appendix A) with a very kind and informative message.

Answering Questions and Consulting for Others

Students might wish to answer the questions of other participants in a discussion group. My students were proud to be able to use their knowledge in their fields to help others with projects. This factor, perhaps more than any other, helped them assume the role of the concerned professional in all of their communications. They managed to break out of the tiresome routine of writing memo after memo for "practice" in an English class. They were also excited to be in contact with other professionals in their fields. For example, a geology major in my class was able to refer other geologists in a discussion group to sources and citations for their research, and he even set up a mineral sample exchange group with some of his Internet colleagues. He then took the obvious professional step in publishing an explanation of his exchange activities in a mineral newsletter. That article has since been reprinted in a South African mineral newsletter, and requests for help and trades have come from the Netherlands and many other corners of the world. He has said many times over that he feels that his network exchanges have paid off by allowing him to become professionally involved in his field (see Appendix B).

Gathering Facts and Opinions

Students might wish to gather multiple opinions on the feasibility of a project or to conduct a survey. One student was writing a proposal on upgrading our school's AutoCad software and needed information about what version of the software other schools used and for what purposes. He sent in his question to the AutoCad discussion list and received six responses over the next few days. Another student needed responses to a local survey on how the student technology fee should be spent and arranged to make the questionnaire available on one of the school's Usenet newsgroups. Currently, my students routinely collect information for class projects through questionnaires posted on our Internet host machine, where all users who log in can elect to fill them out (see Appendix C).

Conducting the Job Search

Students can also make job inquiries and contacts. I have my students investigate the Online Career Center[5] on gopher or the World Wide Web very early in the semester. Here they can research companies and jobs and even upload a résumé at no charge. Several students have been invited on plant trips and even been offered jobs through this process. But they must also be aware how crucial professional networking is to their potential for getting a job. Some students have been working on the network closely enough with their colleagues in business and industry to be invited to collaborate on conference presentations and publications. Network-based discussion involves students in field-specific projects that may lead to jobs and/or professional collaborations anywhere in the world.

Once the students have drafted their posts, they critique each others' posts on the network. First, the author of a message to an individual or discussion group sends his or her message to a classmate and asks for editing and revision help. The classmate then comments on the grammar, mechanics, tone, style, and technical content of the potential discussion group post, and sends it back in another e-mail message (see Appendix D). The original author revises the message according to the feedback she or he receives and sends it to the discussion group, with a copy to me. I ask for a copy of all my students' professional discussion group posts, along with other group postings that provide context for the messages, so that I can comment on and evaluate them.

However, the exercise is not yet totally paperless. I ask the author to create a printed discussion group portfolio, which includes the original posts, the group messages that provide the context for the posts, and the peer critique. In the best of worlds—had I fewer students and much more time—I would evaluate these portfolios on the computer. I feel that students would benefit from the neatness of the comments and the depth of comment I could make on the computer, given that I compose better on a keyboard. However, I am reluctant to add even more hours to the time I already spend with my tiring eyes glued to the computer screen, and I have not yet found an easy way of inserting marks in a student's text. Thus, I welcome paper for the ease with which I can move it, sort it, and make notes on it. Times may be changing, but hard copy does add a needed air of finality to what is essentially a snapshot of a work forever in progress.

The Gift Economy in Virtual Communities

Through the process outlined in the preceding section, my technical communications students are introduced to, asked to comment on, and become part of virtual communities. They learn the give and take of idea exchange in the living database, the feature of networked interaction that Howard Rheingold calls a "gift economy" (Rheingold 59). By participating in networked discussion and helping others, students not only build communication skills but also build valuable social capital. Rheingold describes a process by which networked collaborators exchange knowledge capital (information) for social capital (goodwill and respect from others) (Rheingold 62). What participants contribute to any group at any time may not be returned immediately, or by the same group. But with time they will find others helping them. Conversely, they might be so inspired by the help and feedback they are given that they go out of their way to help others. Although this may seem no different from the economy of idea exchange within any social grouping,[6] the network provides an easy way for distant participants with similar interests to share information and experiences. In sharing with others, they become part of the living database and learn something of the transactional nature of communication.

Sometimes, through reading and discussion, students find that they have questions for the authors of the articles they read, authors who are often recognized experts in their fields. Common sense might tell us that it would be a waste of time for an undergraduate to write to a renowned expert asking for clarification, but luckily not all students share our pessimism. I have frequently been approached by students requesting e-mail addresses for the authors of the articles they were researching. Although initially I was not hopeful about making contact, I used my network connections and social capital to get addresses for an artificial intelligence pioneer at MIT (see Appendix A) and a microbiologist investigating the HIV virus at Berkeley. A few weeks later, I was flabbergasted to learn that my students had sent e-mail to and received considerate, informative replies from these busy scholars. Without the possibility of the quick transmission and quick reply afforded by e-mail, how many of us would even think to write to the top people in a field to ask for help on a project due at semester's end? And yet, while we might never dream of *calling* such experts, e-mail is so unintrusive that many of us are emboldened to make requests of experts from whom we need information. If my students can make intelligent, well-written requests for information, they are learning some important strategies of communication based on their perceptions of audience expectations.

New Directions: Taking Discussion to Real-Time Environments

Participants in networked discussion groups sometimes get to a point in discussion or collaboration via e-mail when asynchronous communication just is not enough for the level of sustained interaction they need to pull off a project. When participants want to brainstorm or collaborate intensively, e-mail may seem too tedious or time consuming. In this case, a subset of an asynchronous networked discussion group may want to move on to real-time networked communication such as Internet Relay Chat (IRC) and multiple user real-time (MU*) environments. IRC is like CB or ham radio, except that everyone can talk at once and everything that is said appears in text. An MU* environment differs in that text may also be used to create descriptions of objects, characters, and rooms to give conversation a "setting" of sorts. These environments and their uses for scholarhip are described elsewhere (Day, Crump, and Rickly), but it should be noted that for some, IRC and MU* are logical extensions of e-mail and Usenet discussion groups; the synchronous, immediate, "fast and dirty" conversations of real-time complement the more considered prose of asynchronous discussions.[7]

Because of the reputation that IRC and MU* environments have among some faculty and computer systems administrators for being time and resource wasters, I have been reluctant to introduce these environments to my students. Yet, when the students themselves saw the value of working in an MU* environment and asked to try it, I could not refuse. In fall of 1994, I involved my classes in a collaborative work group project with technical communications classes in New York City, and in spring of 1995, we extended the project to include classes at the University of Southwestern Louisiana. My students were grouped with students in David Tillyer's classes at CUNY and John Ferstel's classes at USL, but not just as pen pals; they worked together on a collaborative report, negotiating every step of the process through e-mail. When some of the students expressed frustration at the time it was taking to make decisions via e-mail, I suggested MU* sessions to get work done quickly. Because MediaMOO is not for students, we were thankful for the offer from Daedalus Group Inc. to allow students to work in their MU* environment, Daedalus MOO. The students found communicating on the environment productive but also discovered that simply planning a time for all six of them (two from each school) to get together (especially with the two-hour time difference between Rapid City and New York City) was much more difficult than the act of getting work done on the MOO once they had mastered some of the commands and could talk freely.

I am encouraged by the students' productivity in the MU* environment and would like to give more students the opportunity to practice this synchronous form of writing in the matrix. However, I resist the urge to *require* my students to use synchronous communication. Just as we all have different personalities and work habits, so, too, do we adapt better to some writing and communication environments than others. One student may be flustered by the pressure of real-time written communication; another, typically silent in oral classroom discussion, may blossom without the social pressure of face-to-face interaction. I would like my students to try out these tools and be aware of what they have to offer, but above all I want them to be able to use the tools they are most comfortable with and that help them communicate effectively. Further, as Nancy Kaplan reminds us, "No tool can be innocent, free of ideological constructions. . . . Each tool brings into the classroom embedded conceptions of what exists, what is good or useful or profitable, and what is possible with its help" (27). We need to be aware that when we bring certain technologies into our classrooms, we may unwittingly be imposing our own values about how research, writing, and communication should take place. And despite all the benefits, there are a host of other reasons not to force students to use networked discussion groups, among them flaming (rude outbursts on the Internet, often based on misunderstanding), communication anxiety, and sensory overload (Hawisher 93). So I must recommend that these "writing in the matrix" activities be made optional. The activities are mainly to help students find groups and become comfortable with them. Still, I recommend asking classes of students who have networking capability at least to *try* tapping the living database once.

Evaluation

Because one of the goals of incorporating network-based communication into the classroom is to give students the opportunity to write for a variety of audiences outside the university, evaluation is always a thorny issue. If we add the grading hand of the teacher to the equation, the teacher becomes the primary audience, overshadowing, to some degree, the outside discussants. Many writing instructors who use electronic mail have suggested that it is best to leave assignments of this sort ungraded so that students can gain confidence in their abilities and know that they are truly writing to an outside audience. However, many of us have no choice in the matter of grades. Teachers may still be able to comment on e-mail portfolios but leave them ungraded, or they may be able to compromise with peer critiques, grade contracts, and self-evaluations. In every case, however, we need to place emphasis on the ethos-building evaluative eyes of the outside audience, not the grading hand of the classroom teacher.

Benefits and Limitations of Writing in the Matrix

What are the benefits and limitations of such an approach, an approach based on interactions between people and not with remote databases? First, this interaction is a kind of natural heuristic that spurs students to explore new ideas, both their own and others', and to build on those ideas. Second, in this "tapping of the living database" we have a new model of collaborative work in which great distances matter very little and scholars can work closely with the people who either think just like they do, or whose ideas complement theirs. In this way, we can form collaborative communities that overcome isolation and provincialism. Third, and very important, the experience gives students the sense of being situated in a field with other colleagues, who become real to them by virtue of the ideas they express. Many of our students would never have dreamed of approaching some of the experts in their fields, but the network affords them an easy way of making contact.

The discussion group activity provides an ideal focus for class discussions of the rhetorical concept of *ethos*. Students come to understand that if their contributions are to be accepted by the group and answered by its members, they must use rhetorical strategies to create the persona of a concerned and professional writer. They often do not get responses if they take on the "Gee, I'm just a poor inexperienced student doing a class assignment" attitude. They learn to use the language professionally and correctly to achieve a desired effect for a particular audience.

We recently found out how important that professional attitude can be. A professor of mechanical engineering from our school met a colleague at a conference in Florida who mentioned that he had seen our students' postings in some of the discussion groups and commented on how impressed he was with the content and quality of the messages our students were sending out. If the students take pride in their own knowledge and strive to be professional in their communications, it reflects well on the whole school. Thus, through the "writing in the matrix" activity, students come to understand the importance of professional presentation to the reputations of both individuals and organizations, and that understanding spurs them to improve their writing.

By breaking down traditional hierarchies between "expert" and "student," the possibilities for productive exchange among scholars at all levels are limitless. Yet we must also remember that, inevitably, not all expert and e-mail discussion group investigations pan out. Just because an author has an e-mail address does not mean that she or he will answer, and just because there is a listserv or Usenet group with a certain name does not guarantee that the group will be active or that the discussion will be worthwhile. In the past, I have had students complain that they subscribed to a discussion group such as IEEE-L and found little or no discussion. Another student seemed outraged that no one in the Usenet group alt.cows.moo.moo.moo could answer her technical questions on cattle feed.

The problems we face here are twofold. First, as active participants in networked discussion groups, we teachers may tend to romanticize the possibilities, leading students to develop unrealistic expectations for the quality and quantity of information they will receive. Second, we may talk about all the useful information we can get from others on the Net, but how reliable is this information? Who do we trust as a reliable, credible source, and why? To avoid unnecessarily disappointing students, and to help them understand the concepts of credibility and reliability of sources, we need to encourage classroom discussion of these potential problems before students even begin participating in networked conversations. Such discussions can help students focus a more critical eye not only on online sources, but also on informants and articles used in off-line primary and secondary research. In short, we help them see that online sources, like any others, must be subject to the same scrutiny lawyers give a witness in a court of law.

In the years since I began this project and the early drafts of this chapter, the Internet and its discussion groups have been growing at an astronomical pace. Now the would-be participants have a wide array of printed guides to online discussion groups to choose from at the bookstore, along with some handy online tools. For example, the Lists of Lists file is frequently updated and can be requested by e-mail from listserv@vm1.nodak.edu with the command "get LISTS OF LISTS" in the message body. But these days, by far the most comprehensive searches for discussion groups can be conducted on the World Wide Web, using tools such as Net Search and Net Directory. Many special interest and field-specific groups have Web pages, and you can often get information on how to join discussion groups from those Web pages.

If we claim to be teachers of writing and communication, we owe it to our students to help them get involved in professional and special-interest conversations so that they can gain valuable experience writing for specific audiences. And because more and more professionals will be using the network for primary and secondary research, we are doing our students a service by helping them become accustomed to and involved in these media. Finally, we have a way of allowing students to move on to wider audiences and to recognize their own communicative interdependence by tapping into the living database.

Notes

1. ENFI (electronic networks for interaction) is a real-time writing environment for the networked computer classroom, in which synchronous communications software allows teachers and students to explore, collaborate, and expand on ideas in class in writing. They see each other in the process of developing ideas; they write for each other and not just to the teacher. ENFI was pioneered by Trent Batson at Gallaudet University so that hearing-impaired students could have written discussions. Later, Batson and others discovered that the technology could provide an alternative idea-generating and discussion tool for all kinds of classes.

2. For those unfamiliar with the Internet and e-mail discussion groups, a brief explanation may be in order. The Internet originally came about as "ARPAnet" because the U.S. Department of Defense needed a fail-safe network for the transferral of information from computer to computer in case of emergency or war. Once the machines were connected, however, the inevitable occurred. Humans like to communicate, and they found the linked computers a perfect medium for passing messages. Soon those lucky enough to be connected to the government network were conversing about issues through electronic mail, and when the government opened the network to university researchers, beginning with the sciences, e-mail discussion blossomed. With the advent of Listservtype software, which takes a single message and posts it to a "list" of a few to a few thousand addresses, organized discussion groups came into being. There are a number of excellent printed resources with information about finding and subscribing to Listserv and Listproc discussion groups (look in the computer section of your bookstore), but your local Internet system adminstrator will probably be able to help you search for groups online. Active Listserv (Bitnet)

or Listproc (Internet) groups can rapidly fill your mailbox with messages, a factor that often causes networkers with very limited storage capacity to opt for Usenet discussions instead.

Usenet was born from Bulletin Board Services (BBS), which allowed subscribers to log in to read discussions on a variety of issues. Soon the BBS operators realized that they could facilitate wide-area discussions by transferring all the collected messages on one topic to other BBSs. These discussion groups, called newsgroups, allow readers from all over the world to read discussions without having those discussions take up any space in their accounts. Because Usenet discussions can be more chaotic and less polite than many Listserv and Listproc discussions, one has to choose groups with care. Contact your local Internet systems administrator for information about how to search and subscribe to Usenet newsgroups.

A random sampling of the thousands of Listserv and Listproc groups yields up groups from recycling to archeology and from vampires to chemical engineering. The choices are similar on Usenet, but Usenet seems to have many more recreational groups and miscellaneous groups for buying and selling goods and services. Both types, however, offer plenty of choices for our students.

3. By "sophisticated," I mean that the post is professional in every respect, from flawless or nearly flawless grammar and mechanics to a tone and content that nowhere demeans the writer by referring bluntly to the fact that he or she is a student in need of information. The ethos exhibited in the post should be collegial and demonstrate the fact that the writer has already consulted the obvious print and online sources.

4. See Spitzer 66–70 for an exploration of some benefits of professional collaboration on the network.

5. From gopher go to garnet.msen.com and choose the Msen Career Center. On the World Wide Web, the URL is http://www.occ.com/.

6. Consider, for example, the informal exchanges that go on at academic and professional conferences—yet how frequently can we travel to these conferences? Another comparison would be the Native American custom of gift exchange in potlatch. Or, in the words of Mauri Collins, "[We are part] of a global potlatch ... whoever gives away the most WINS (and acquires the most reciprocal debts!)"

7. In about 1991, some members of the computers and writing community who were active on the MegaByte University (MBU) networked discussion group decided to try IRC. IRC allowed them to meet weekly and sometimes even biweekly on a channel called #cw (for Computers and Writing) to discuss scholarly articles, plan events such as conference presentations, collaborate on articles, and, in general, exchange a great deal of information and ideas. In spring 1993, many of the group members saw the invitation to explore and use MediaMOO that was posted on MBU, and they registered themselves as characters there. They found that having rooms and text-objects they could move amongst and manipulate further augmented their ability to work collaboratively and share information. Now these teachers use MediaMOO for planned weekly meetings and to schedule work sessions regularly. They find the text-based writing environment ideally suited to a kind of collaboration based on the synergy that arises from the participants' willingness to explore and reflect on new ideas as they come up. They capture "thought coming into being" in text before the critical consciousness can quash it, a process that allows them to quickly build

rough-cut thought structures for later revision into more polished scholarly forms. In short, they think MediaMOO is a great tool for long-distance scholarly collaboration, often even more productive than face-to-face academic conferences.

MediaMOO is a virtual real-time environment for media researchers that exists as a database on a computer in MIT's Media Lab. See Rheingold, pp. 173–74, for an explanation of MediaMOO, and Chapters 5 and 6 in *The Virtual Community* in general for a fairly good introduction to IRC and MU* environments, respectively. Most of the text of this paragraph is taken verbatim from a virtual poster I have in my room—the panopticon—on MediaMOO. Guests and characters wandering through can type "read schol" to see the text and learn a little bit about what writing teachers discuss on MediaMOO.

Works Cited

Collins, Mauri. "RE: A Parallel Distributed Eliza." Message posted to Interpersonal Computing and Technology (IPCT-L@GUVM.CCF.GEORGETOWN. EDU) Sunday, 4 December 1994.

Day, Michael, Eric Crump, and Rebecca Rickly. "Creating a Virtual Academic Community: Scholarship and Community in Wide Area Multiple-User Synchronous Discussions." *Computer Networking and Scholarship in the 21st Century University.* Ed. Theresa M. Harrison and Timothy Stephen. New York: SUNY Press, 1996.

Hawisher, Gail. "Electronic Meetings of the Minds: Research, Electronic Conferences, and Composition Studies." *Re-Imagining Computers and Composition: Teaching and Research in the Virtual Age.* Ed. Gail E. Hawisher and Paul LeBlanc. Portsmouth, NH: Boynton/Cook, 1992. 81–101.

Kaplan, Nancy. "Ideology, Technology, and the Future of Writing Instruction." *Evolving Perspectives on Computers and Composition Studies: Questions for the 1990s.* Ed. Gail Hawisher and Cynthia Selfe. Urbana, IL: NCTE, 1991. 11–42.

Rheingold, Howard. *The Virtual Community: Homesteading on the Electronic Frontier.* New York: Addison Wesley, 1993.

Spitzer, Michael. "Local and Global Networking: Implications for the Future." *Computers and Writing: Theory, Research, Practice.* Ed. Deborah Holdstein and Cynthia Selfe. New York: Modern Language Association of America, 1990. 58–70.

APPENDIX A: Example of a Request for Information

Professor Marvin Minsky
Massachusetts Institute of Technology

Dear Professor Minsky:
As I mentioned in my letter last week, I would like to ask a few technical questions from the article "Will Robots Inherit the Earth?" I hope you can find time to give me some answers. You might find that some of these questions overlap, so just feel free to disregard those you feel overlap too much, or that you find irrelevant.

In the article you say "Eventually, using nanotechnology, we will entirely replace our brains." In this regard I would like to ask three questions:

(1) By this, do you mean that artificial intelligence (AI) and nanotechnology can make our brain useless (that our brain will meet the same fate in the future as our tonsils meet in some cases today)?

(2) Can you explain how you see the interrelationship, if any, between our brain and artificial intelligence in the future?

(3) How would this nanotechnology device interface with the biology of our bodies? Is it partially biological?

Your article mentions about the human life span and estimates its maximum to be about 115 years.

(1) Do you think that AI and nanotechnology can help fight autoimmune blindness and other biological problems that our body cannot repair by itself?

(2) Do you think we can develop equipment that has a life span close to ours, or don't you think of this (the life span of the equipment) as an issue?

Do you think mankind ever can develop a machine (Being / Mind Child) that "thinks" with the same flexibility our brains do?

Are there any articles/books on the subject you would like to recommend to students with interests in this field?

In the article you discuss many issues concerning the future use of nanotechnology and artificial intelligence. What do you feel is the most important issue you discuss in the article? Why?

Finally, I would like to ask a question not directly related to the article, but that is of great importance to me, as a young European (I'm from Norway). The first step on the moon was a great milestone for human-kind and maybe in particular for American government-sponsored basic research. But it also marks the turning point for this type of research.

Do you feel that there will ever be a possibility (political climate) to reestablish something like the Advanced Research Projects Agency (ARPA)? What would it take? Would the economic threat from Japan or from a united and stronger Europe (maybe, in the future, including Russia) be enough?

This concludes my questions. On behalf of my colleagues both at South Dakota School of Mines & Technology and City College of New York, I would like to thank you for being willing to correspond with me. I hope these questions did not take too much of your time, or cause you any inconvenience.

Thanks, sincerely
Borge Svardal
Electrical Engineering Student, SDSM&T

Date: Thu, 8 Dec 94 15:21:59 -0500
Mime-Version: 1.0
Content-Type: text/plain; charset="us-ascii"
To: bs6230@silver.sdsmt.edu, mday@silver.sdsmt.edu
From: minsky@media.mit.edu (Marvin Minsky)

>>In the article you say "Eventually, using nanotechnology, we will entirely replace our brains." In this regard I would like to ask three questions:

>>(1) By this, do you mean that artificial Intelligence (AI) and >nanotechnology can make our brain useless (that our brain will meet the same fate in the future as our tonsils meet in some cases today)?

I meant "ultimately" in the sense that our brains will turn out to be too small to be able to solve the problems that we'll eventually want to understand. So we'll expand them by artificial means until the original brains are relatively insignificant.

>(2) Can you explain how you see the interrelationship, if any, between our brain and artificial intelligence in the future?

I would hope that when we build better brains we'll know how they work. This will need better theories about both human and other kinds of psychology.

>(3) How would this nanotechnology device interface with the biology of our bodies? Is it partially biological?

It could be a long time before we know enough about how the brain works. In the meantime, we could begin to augment the brain by attaching new computers, via millions (or billions) of connections to our existing brains. This would require very small interconnection devices.
>
>Your article mentions the human life span and estimates its maximum to be about 115 years.
>
>(1) Do you think that AI and nanotechnology can help fight autoimmune blindness and other biological problems that our body cannot repair by itself?

Ultimately, cell repair and replacement should become feasible, but I see no way to estimate when.

>(2) Do you think we can develop equipment that has a life span close to ours, or don't you think of this (the life span of the equipment) as an issue?

Yes, not much of an issue. The critical thing is to use technologies that are easily maintainable—i.e., when something fails or wears out, replace it.
>
>Do you think mankind ever can develop a machine (Being/Mind Child) that "thinks" with the same flexibility our brains do?

Certainly. I don't think we're very flexible by trans-human standards.
>

>Are there any articles/books on the subject you would like to >recommend to students with interests in this field?

Well, my own book, "The Society of Mind," and Hans Moravec's far-out "Mind Children." He has a new book, but I don't have its title. Also Nanosystems, by Drexler—for students who want to learn more physics.

>In the article you discuss many issues concerning of the future use of nanotechnology and artificial intelligence. What do you feel is the most important issue you discuss in the article? Why?

I can't rank them. In my mind they form a coherent network.

>Do you feel that there will ever be a possibility (political climate) to>reestablish something like the Advanced Research Projects Agency (ARPA)? What would it take? Would the economic threat from Japan or from a united and stronger Europe (maybe, in the future, including Russia) be enough?

Good question—and very close to my heart because the support of AI in the 1960s was inspired by one of my friends and teachers, J.C.R. Licklider, who recently died, and two of my first student friends when I came to teach at MIT: Larry Roberts and Ivan Sutherland. So the "golden age" was actually, for me, very much like a family matter!

I don't know if it could happen now. It's just possible that the "new American politics" could do something interesting, because that Gingrich fellow is really interested in advanced things, despite his strange reputation; for example he is a space exploration advocate.

On the other side, I have a sense of a worldwide decline of critical thinking. American television is now dominated by all sorts of psychic pseudo-science;—fake psychics; bizarre "alternative medicine" ideas, including homeopaths; kidnapping by flying saucers; and now, amazingly, visitations by angels! I can't think of how there could be any popular movement toward rationality in the face of the press-dominated distribution of garbage.

>This concludes my questions. On behalf of my colleagues both at South Dakota School of Mines & Technology and City College of New York, I would like to thank you for being willing to correspond with me. I hope

these questions did not take too much of your time, or cause you any inconvenience.

I have fondness for Norway, but not enough contact. Been there twice, and from time to time I correspond with a former student, Lars Monrad-Krohn, who started more than one company involved with computers, AI, and education.

"Don't pay any attention to the critics. Don't even ignore them."
———— Sam Goldwyn

APPENDIX B: Examples of a Student Consulting on the Network

To: das6942@silver.sdsmt.edu
Subject: re: trading
Mime-Version: 1.0
Content-Type: text/plain; charset="us-ascii"
Date: Tue, 26 Sep 1995 16:19:13 -0700
From: (name and e-mail withheld by request)

Hi David,

I'd be interested in trading for some South Dakota minerals. What do you have? I have very nice samples of hanksite and pink halite from Searles Lake, Trona, CA and pyrite dollars from Illinois. Let me know if you are interested.

To: das6942@silver.sdsmt.edu
References: <199501172027.NAA47260@silver.sdsmt.edu>
Message-Id: <ABInF7luR3@minmuz.msk.su>
Organization: Fersman mineralogical museum
From: dmz <dmz@minmuz.msk.su>
Date: Wed, 18 Jan 95 14:32:34 +0300
X-Mailer: BML [MS/DOS Beauty Mail v.1.36]
Subject: Re: Trading minerals
Lines: 34

I am interested in trading some mineral samples with others. I have numerous extra samples from the pegmatites of the Black Hills of South Dakota. Such samples include schorl, triphylite, rose quartz, muscovite, etc.

If you or a friend would be interested, please contact me at the *e-mail* address below for a complete list.

Good hunting and I look forward to hearing from you.

David A.
Staskadas6942@silver.sdsmt.edu
South Dakota School of Mines and Technology

Hi, David !

I am interesting to see your complete list for trading.
We have in our museum had some experience in trading with South Dakota School of Mines and I think it would be good to continue. By the way, are you going to Tucson show? We are going to be there in Executive Inn (room 234)
Sincerely, Dimitri

Dimitri Belakovskiy
Curator of minerals dmz@minmuz.msk.su
FERSMAN MINERALOGICAL MUSEUM Phone: (095) 952-0067
Russian Academy of Science. Fax: (095) 952-4850
Russia, Moscow 117071
Leninski prospect 18-2

APPENDIX C: Example of a Student Questionnaire Administered on the Network

Impact of Web Page Resume Survey

We are researching the impact of resumes and personal portfolios on the web.

PLEASE CHECK ONE ANSWER FOR EACH OF THE FOLLOWING QUESTIONS.
1. How familiar are you with the web?
___Very __Somewhat __Not At All
2. How well do you know HTML?
__Very Well __Somewhat __Not At All

3. Do you have your own web pages? __Yes __No
4. If you do not have your own, would you like to?
__Yes __No
__Always __Sometimes __Never
5. How often do you use the web for job searches?
__Always __Sometimes __Never
6. How do you or would you use your pages?
__Business __Research/Education __Job Search/Resume
__Entertainment __Other
7. Which do you feel would be more effective in a job search?
__Web Page/Electronic Resumes __Paper Resumes
8. Would it be beneficial to post a resume on the web?
__Yes __No
9. Would you have a more detailed resume on the web than on paper?
10. Would you put your picture in your resume/personal pages?
11. Do you think that people you want to visit your web pages could find them easily?
__Yes __No
12. Would you be interested in information about publicizing web pages?
__Yes __No
13. Would you be interested in a guide on web page portfolios and resumes?
__Yes __No
14. Should personal web pages be reinstated at Tech?
__Yes __No

Thank you very much for filling out our survey. :-)

The results of our survey will be posted at
http://www.sdsmt.edu/~amv7624/survey.html by November 25, 1995
(Thanks to Amy Vander Vorst and David George)

APPENDIX D: Example of a Student Peer Editing Message

From vstoltz
Thu Mar 4 09:38:51 1993
Date: Thu, 4 Mar 1993 09:38:45 -0700
From: vstoltz (Vi Stoltz)
To: ljr5896
Subject: Peer Evaluation
Cc: Mday

Dear Becky,
I just received your letter for my evaluation. I just have a few suggestions that might make it easier to read (from my point of view).

In paragraph 1 you used the phrase "team working exploring." It may flow better if you say "team working to explore." In paragraph 1 and 2 both, you used the phrase "have been unable to find." If you would like to change one to "cannot locate", it may sound less repetitious.

In paragraph 2 in the last sentence you said, "It has either very sophisticated and complicated differential equations or it is . . .". Mechanically, I think it should be written as follows, "It is either very sophisticated and with complicated . . . . or it is . . ." (Incidentally, you need an "s" in sophisticated.) (You may wish to check with Dr. Day.)

Also, in paragraph 3, I believe there is another mechanical problem you may wish to check with Dr. Day. It starts "If you have any recommendations . . .. that (referring to recommendations) addresses . . ." If I remember my grammar correctly, it should read "that address" to keep them both in the plural tense.

In the third paragraph, I think a comma after junior-senior level would stress your point.

(Sorry for the unusual squiggles at the end of the above line.)

Becky, I hope this is some help to you, and I am not too critical.

Good luck on your project. Vi Stoltz, CPS

9 Conferencing in the Contact Zone

Theresa Henley Doerfler

Robert Davis
Eastern Oregon University

> Teacher-pupil language . . . tends to be described almost entirely
> from the point of view of the teacher and teaching, not from the
> point of view of pupils and pupiling . . . If a classroom is analyzed
> as a social world unified and homogenized with respect to the
> teacher, whatever students do other than what the teacher specifies
> is invisible or anomalous to the analysis.
>
> —Mary Louise Pratt, "Arts of the Contact Zone"

In this chapter, we discuss a project in which students and teachers from
three midwestern universities collaborated, using an asynchronous
conferencing software called Confer II. The teachers worked together—
in face-to-face, paper mail, e-mail, and Confer exchanges—to create a
first-year writing course focused on the theme of liberal education. The
students who enrolled in the course at the various sites worked in electronic collaborative writing groups, responding to a sequence of assignments on the theme of liberal education. One student from each school
was placed in a group and asked to complete a sequence of assignments:
a literacy profile; a "scavenger hunt" of university documents that define and discuss liberal education; a description of a panel discussion on
liberal education hosted by different participants at each site; and a collaborative, dialogic essay on liberal education. Interestingly, the course
itself became politicized, a contested site of liberal education. By describing some of our successes and failures, the possibilities and the limi-

We would like to thank our collaborators whose voices are not present in this document:
Bill Condon, from the University of Michigan, who graciously "hosted" this project in
more than one sense; David Jolliffe and Sarah Smith, from DePaul, who always asked the
right questions; Scott Dewitt, from Ohio State University at Marion, who has worked to
make computer-mediated communication a reality on his campus; and finally, the sixty
students who taught us how important communicating with one another can be.

tations of the technology, we raise important questions for teachers using distance education in their writing classrooms.

Neither the teachers' nor the students' texts can be understood from a single viewpoint. Therefore, we consider both the "teaching" and the "pupiling" that occurred during our long-distance collaboration—as teachers and researchers. Developing the course was a complex process for both teachers and students: creating and redefining their academic and professional roles online, facilitating collaboration, and negotiating the technology that made the collaboration possible.

In the process of designing a course that asked our students to write collaboratively over distance about issues of liberal education, we learned a great deal about the technology of distance learning. The teachers began to use the Confer software as a space in which to construct a shared syllabus—with expectations about what a syllabus should do. But we ended up sacrificing some of our ideas because the technology seemed limited. As the course progressed, however, we were able to release some of our "traditional" ideas about academic discourse, redefining it based on Confer technology. The students entering our courses created their own academic literacies by *using* Confer; the collaborative, electronic medium helped them define academic discourse and liberal education.

We do not claim that technology should always define discourse, but it was strangely appropriate for a course on liberal education: everything was called into question, no word was ever final, and no agreement was ever complete. Thus, the dialogue that Confer supports enabled critical thinking (reasoning, discussing, building consensus). Conversations read like scripts, with each utterance designating the speaker's name. Editing is possible only by mastering a complicated line editor—a difficult task. In Confer it is easier not to edit, to go back in search of perfection, but simply to move on.

At first, we saw some features of the technology as weaknesses, while our students came to see them as strengths. For example, before the course began, we imagined asking our students to produce a collaborative essay in Confer. Despite having used Confer ourselves, we did not realize that such a paper would be nearly impossible for our students—inexperienced with technology and with collaboration—to write. As the course progressed, we learned to look not only at the way our students wrote in Confer but also at the way they received and responded to the texts of others. Finally, a traditional essay would have been nearly impossible, and even undesirable, as the "product" of a distance education course. Instead, the conversation that emerged in Confer became the product of our course.

Background

The Confer project began as a failed grant proposal, originally written to involve ten universities around the country in an ambitious project involving electronic and face-to-face communication between participants. The proposed budget included travel money for teachers to plan the course and for students to meet one another. Part of the funding was allocated to follow up on the course. In retrospect we are not sure whether the face-to-face contact among participants in the unfunded "dream" course would be either necessary or desirable. Our students reported that the freedom they experienced in writing to a real, yet distant, audience was a highlight of the course.

The scaled-down version of the Confer course began after a lecture at Ohio State University, when a group of teachers at different schools agreed to link their classes electronically. We began to brainstorm how our students might work together online (without a budget for travel or course development). Our goal was to build a community while acknowledging individual differences. Because we all wanted our first-year students to begin defining and examining academic literacy, we agreed on the theme of liberal education. At this stage, Theresa Doerfler wrote in a course proposal:

> Students will be placed in collaborative groups with students in compatible disciplines from other universities. Each collaborative group will be composed of four students from different universities, who will work together to understand and define liberal education for the diverse needs of American college students today. Although the students will be communicating long-distance, they will all be working on the same class schedule and with the same syllabus.

She was working hard at this point to define academic similarities among the students and provide a common space where they could come together despite geographic and institutional differences.

At first we envisioned a shared syllabus among all the schools, and even a shared schedule of meeting times so that students could conference synchronously. For two reasons, it now seems ironic that we sought such consistency to overcome our geographic and cultural differences: first, because our ideals for the course collided with the reality of execution, and second, because we eventually revised course goals.

We exchanged e-mail about some initial ideas for the course, but because there were (at this point in the planning) six participants from four different schools, the exchanges seemed inefficient. So we decided to meet face to face in Ann Arbor, Michigan, to plan the course. During this July meeting, we made more progress in comparing divergent student populations and discussing our expectations than in drafting a syllabus.

We found ourselves limited by the calendars at our schools,[1] by our own professional schedules (some of us already had autumn teaching schedules before we began our summer planning), by the learning curve for the Confer software, and by the time allotted for planning the course. We also had very different ideas about what first-year writing should be. And, until we began using the Confer software, we had difficulty imagining how it might alter the teaching and learning in our classrooms.

The University of Michigan has the most diverse population of the four schools. Ohio State, drawing most of its students from Ohio, boasts less racial and ethnic diversity than either Michigan or the University of Illinois at Chicago. The Ohio State University at Marion has a population of students who are older than the average students on the Columbus campus and even less racially and ethnically diverse. The University of Illinois at Chicago draws many students from Chicago's ethnic neighborhoods and attracts many part-time and continuing students. We discovered that our teaching facilities were different, but more important, that our students had uneven access to technology on our campuses—a factor we needed to consider as we constructed our assignments.

Although we did not draft a syllabus during our face-to-face meeting, or even agree on a common set of readings, we left Ann Arbor with *Annie John* in hand and the tentative agreement to consider Jamaica Kincaid's novel as a point of convergence. The differences in syllabi, population, and schedules seemed overwhelming. In retrospect it seems ironic that our only point of agreement was a novel that was culturally and geographically remote from *all* of our experiences and had little to do with liberal education at a midwestern university. When we got home and started to work things through, we saw that the broad ideas (academic literacy, liberal education, the role of education, the university's mission) would drive the course. We hoped that differences in the ways students experienced these four areas would broaden their perspectives.

Finally, we began to negotiate the terms of our course online in Confer. At Ohio State, we were just beginning to use electronic mail in our offices and classrooms. Communicating electronically was new to us, and the Confer software was a bit more complicated than our primitive UNIX electronic mail software. Confer allows for asynchronous electronic conferencing from remote sites, creating spaces (scripts) in which different groups can work together. A user can sign onto a particular space and either read the whole script or browse through only the new postings (an easier task in Confer). Therefore, once a space gets used more than a couple of times, conversational threads are easily lost or abandoned. The Confer editor is clunky at best, and we never learned how to upload or download our work or how to print. At Ohio State, Confer was an exclusively electronic medium. In fact, for reasons we discovered about midway through the term, our students could use Confer only from the public lab where our class was held.

The Confer program has a distinct personality. When we teachers logged in for the first time (after several telephone calls to Ann Arbor for instructions), we came across Item 1 from The Management. The prompt read as follows:

> If you've gotten this far, the hard part is over—congratulations! At this point, your options are
>
> (R)espond, to type in something in response to this item;
> (F)orget, to tell the machine you never want to see this item again (DON'T TYPE F FOR FORGET!!); or
> (P)ass, if you don't want to respond to what you've just read.
>
> Why don't you type "R" for Respond and say a little something about how you feel about communicating with others in this electronic conference. How does it feel?
>
> When you finish your message, hit the RETURN key an extra time to let the machine know you're finished, and then type "D" for Done. Also, remember to hit RETURN at the end of each line you type (If you forget now and then, don't worry; we'll all be understanding about that, since we'll forget from time to time too).

The disembodied voice was friendly but directive. It congratulated users for gaining access. It gently suggested ("why don't you") that users write about how they *feel*. It issued friendly reminders. The voice even told us in advance how the group would work together. "We'll all be understanding."

Bill Condon, from the University of Michigan, who set up the conference and was already familiar with the software, took the initiative in the first post on August 3: "OK, so where is everyone? This is an auspicious beginning, eh . . . *GLOOM* I'm SO lonely!" (1:1).[2] There was professional pressure to type something, anything, in this massive blank space. On August 10, Scott Dewitt, from OSU Marion, logged on and wrote, "Ok, ok. So I logged onto Confer on 31 July, and no one was here. I was scared, you know, here in space, all alone. And now I get on, and I feel left out, like you all no [know] each other now" (2:5). Even for the teachers, there was a real fear of being excluded from electronic space. In asynchronous conferencing, unlike phone calls or face-to-face meetings, there is no immediate feedback, no nodding and smiling, just fragments of writing isolated in cyberspace. Therefore, a sense of conversation is lost.

Doerfler, who had a research stake in this project, got down to business in her first post: "Hi Bill . . . Perhaps we could start by discussing Annie John . . . I'm sure that the teachers all have many ideas for the way this course can be taught, so I guess I'll hang back a little until they all log in here" (1:2). She tried to get the others on task in the space designated for introductions. Robert Davis responded with, "Theresa—this isn't where we are supposed to talk about Annie John. This is where we are supposed to . . . talk about how it feels to be electronically communicating. I think it feels groovy Theresa—please exit confer and begin again" (1:3). David Jolliffe and Sarah Smith logged in together an hour later: "[We are] sitting at the terminal in the English Department at UIC experimenting with Telnet, Confer, and other groovy items" (1:4). They borrowed Davis's word "groovy" to express their reaction to the software. For pioneers in distance education, we were all remarkably tentative about how this space would be used and how we should express ourselves in it.

Because all of the responses in Confer were tagged with the participants' names, identity was crucial. When we logged in together, we felt the need to say so. For example, the first time they logged on, Jolliffe and Smith wrote, "This response says its coming from Sarah Smith, but actually it's coming from David Jolliffe and Sarah Smith together . . ." (1:4). The next time Jolliffe logged in solo, he wrote, "It's really me this time." Even though the Confer software did not allow us to log in anonymously, we felt the need to assert our identity online. Of course, we had an advantage (or disadvantage) over our students because we had established face-to-face identities with one another before the conference began.

As we began to negotiate the terms of the course, we found ourselves willing to give up some of our initial ideas, such as designing a shared syllabus. In fact, the course became much simpler from the perspective of teaching, administration, and research. Dewitt had to drop out of the project because his funding for a telecommunications hookup in his lab failed to come through. The rest of us finally agreed on a set of loosely designed assignments; students would work collaboratively during a five-week sequence on the topic of liberal education. Collaborative groups made up of one student from each school would post literacy profiles in the Confer space; go on scavenger hunts at their various institutions to discover places where their universities defined liberal education; participate in a panel discussion on liberal education with a student, a teacher, and an administrator; and write a paper on liberal education.

Finally, the calendar intervened. The course began in Chicago and in Ann Arbor before we finished negotiating the terms. As a result, our students did not share syllabi or assignments. Though the assignments were discussed and agreed on by the teachers, they were not co-written. For example, none of us knew how the others were presenting the literacy autobiography. And at this point, there was still an implicit assumption that in the end our students would produce traditional essays, using Confer only for brainstorming or discussion.

The Project

By agreeing on an open structure and few themes, we almost certainly committed a pedagogical crime, but we unconsciously opened ourselves to the possibilities created by Confer and the ways our students would work in it. At first some of our students were uncomfortable with the lack of structure. Group members did not necessarily approach the first assignment the same way, and as a result, students became confused about their teachers' and their groups' expectations. Eventually, however, and in most cases, students very quickly saw that a variety of approaches to a literacy autobiography could be advantageous. Students were able to broaden their perspectives simply by reading the work of others in the group, and they were able to direct their groups by discussing leadership roles.

In Confer the group was not present in the normal sense because members contributed at different times. The Confer program's script-making function created a discourse in which each utterance was labeled with one individual's name, identifying his or her contributions spaced over time.

At the same time, the group was never absent in Confer. Even the most private utterances appeared in a public space; each performance summoned an audience, each word its readers. For us, Confer collapsed public/private distinctions, favoring neither communal discourse nor individual viewpoints. Through a shared enterprise, Confer enabled each member to write individually and, in turn, help the group to advance. We saw also the interplay between public and private, communal and individual, in several aspects of our students' work: in recasting liberal education as multiculturalism; in the series of group projects that read like scripts; and in the traces of authorial presence—the ways in which students constructed themselves online.

Individual group members tended to construct themselves in Confer through communal markers. Again and again as we read the text, we saw students describing themselves in multicultural terms; they talked about their backgrounds, their class, their ethnicity, their race. Because our students came from various backgrounds and cultures, homes, and schools, they presented a unique mix of literacies. None of our students was the perfect example of the Mexican American first generation college student, nor the small-town European American, nor the middle-class African American. Instead, we had Cesar and Beth, Colleen and Dahron, Lama, Maria, and Dan—sixty individuals in all. They also cast themselves as students at their home institutions and as members of their respective composition classes. They bragged about their football teams and poked fun at their teachers. As the term went on, however, students identified themselves more distinctly as individuals and saw their collaborators as such. Students from different backgrounds—farm kids, athletes, students from different cultures and nations—began to find commonalities: a dislike for general education courses, a feeling of loneliness, a love of practical jokes. Difference became, for our students, a source of pleasure rather than a threat.

On the first day of the project, we noticed consternation and frustration, relief and surprise. The instructions for Telnetting from Ohio State into the Confer space were long and had to be followed perfectly. One slip, one missed keystroke, and a student would be expelled from the program. Overload was also a problem. On the first day, we noticed a pattern that would continue all term. Students had trouble getting the ports they needed to connect to Michigan, where Confer's virtual space is housed.

As teachers of first-year composition, we were concerned about asking our students (in their first two weeks at Ohio State) to enter the virtual community of Confer. We were afraid that they would be discouraged or decide that this project (or even college) was not for them. But most students hacked away, defeated neither by chance nor machine. They kept trying, encouraged by those around them, who were getting in one by one. Occasionally, a student went away angry, vowing to return later during open lab time, hoping the gods would not be so unkind. The overload pattern repeated itself, nearly every day. It became part of the mystique of Confer, part of the project's lore. Confer was a guarded space, an inner chamber, a private club, but it was also a space in which students increasingly made themselves at home.[3]

Much of the writing in Confer was done for the sake of writing. It was a way to leave an initial mark in an unfamiliar space. As they constructed themselves in a performance space, students began developing a sense of audience. Their first prompt was the same as the teachers'— expressing how it felt to communicate electronically. Because they were relative strangers, we thought our students might be cautious about interacting. And there was a great deal at stake: Group members were dependent on each other to succeed in the course. In her very first posting, a student named Jen wrote, "So far, I like talking on the computer. I want to see who else is here. Bye!" Two posts later, she expressed her impatience. "Does anyone know when we will talk to people at other schools?" Thus, Maria, struggling with the computer but aware that her message would be read by other students, wrote:

> D[DHi, this is Maria a student at uic[D[D[DUIC and I guess I like working with the computer, that's when I get in. Lately I've been having al[D lot of problems getting in, but I guess it's kind of exciting to talk to pw[Deoplr[De that you are never going to meet. Well, gotta go See[D[D[D[D[D[D[D[D! SA[Dee Y[D [Dya'! [Dpeace!

Maria set up a point of contact with her writing group. Her problems with Confer (she kept trying to use the delete key, which wouldn't work in Confer and only peppered "[Ds" through her posting) allowed others to lend support. Some were having similar difficulties, but others were able to offer solutions. Maria said that it was "exciting" to talk to people she was never going to meet. A sense of openness prevailed, and for the most part, students found it liberating to work with peers they knew only online.

Students used their first names to log into the Confer space, so gender was usually assumed. Many of our students chose to identify themselves according to race or class or ethnicity in their first postings. In his first posting, a student named Dan wrote, "I am a hispanic who has been through a lot of experiences that have an effect on what I want to do in life." Many students voluntarily provided the social and visual cues that were missing in Confer.

In the literacy profile, the first of the project assignments, students began to discuss themselves as learners. The relationship between home literacy and school literacy was a common theme. For some, the transition from home to school was easy; for others, it was more difficult. Dan wrote:

> Most of all I remember when I was a Freshman in high school, the humiliation my English teacher put me through in front of the entire class. . . . He told me that I should of went with someone to read my essay but who could have I told to read my essay. Besides at home I didn't have anyone who could of told me what was wrong with my essay. I always asked myself a question, why did he only criticized my writing, and not the other students?

Dan put himself in a vulnerable position by admitting his humiliation in an English class. He identified the conflict he felt between home and school literacy when he said that at home, he didn't have anyone who "could of told me what was wrong with my essay."

Sarah revealed her isolation as an immigrant through a series of questions. Her poignant profile described a Korean student struggling in the United States:

> Have you ever imagines yourself on an iceberg with thousands and thousands of penguins screaming their hearts out around you? If you have not, suppose you are left all alone there with nothing to do but learning penguins' language and fit into their world. Remind you, there is no way to go back home, and you do not know anything about living with penguins or better yet, communicating with them. . . Coming to the States and giving up all the academic potential I had in Korea was my own choice. Nobody said I had to, nobody said I was welcome to. I was too young, people said, to live alone in a foreign country where I did not even understand its language . . .

Sarah's profile built understanding through empathy. Readers could identify and empathize with her powerful image of a penguin's world.

Those who posted the first literacy profiles without comment or nod to the audience quickly became respondents. Jodi's second posting read, "Hi Dave! I liked a lot of the ideas you brought up in your entry. I especially liked what you had to say about coming to a large university. People do have a lot to offer one another." Angela's questions prompted Dan to reveal more about himself:

> I was born in Evanston IL, but at the age of 1 my parents moved to Mexico to a city called Nuevo Laredo. I'm sure that both of you have heard at least once about "The Rio Grande" This river divides Mexico and United States. Well Nuevo Laredo is located right at the border of Texas. . . .

A conversational style persisted throughout the project. Students made friendships, enriched their writing and thinking, and offered one another support. Sarah found a kindred spirit in Beth, a Korean American student from another school who had experienced similar stereotyping. Sarah and Beth were able to lend support to Colleen, who was from a small town and felt alone in college. With the voice of experience, Sarah assured Colleen that in a few months she would feel so comfortable that she would forget her discomfort about fitting in.

When the members of her group said they were worried about their writing, Jenny responded:

> Cesar and Jorge I also have the same problem as you guys. I just can not express all my thoughts on paper. Sometimes is the vocabularies problem I always have problem to write smoothly, because I often got stuck on the words which I know in Chinese but I don't know in English. I also have problem to put a good setence together. However, it really puts me in hale when there is a paper due. Cesar and Jorge how many hours do you have to spend on a one page

> single space paper? It sometimes take me more than 3 or more hours.
> Can you imagining. Oh! I forgot to tell you guys that to me your
> writing is relly sound good to me. . . .

Jorge wrote back:

> Jenny, this is Jorge. I read your essay and I find it very interesting.
> Your sentences do sound a little broken, but you write better than
> most people I know.I find your life very interesting, it must have
> been hard for you to do all that while in school.

The Confer project could have proven daunting: students were writing,
after all, in front of an audience of potential judges. However, group
members were supportive. When things went badly, the group was encouraging. When things went well, the group celebrated. Even a bit of
bragging was allowed. One day Cesar wrote, "I'm feeling so good today! I got another 'A' on my Math Exam. Boy, I can't feel any better than
this."

The support students gave one another was not confined simply to
Confer or to issues of schooling and literacy. As the project progressed,
group members continued to bond; digressions were permissible. There
was much talk about the weather, football, other classes, families, backgrounds, and majors. There were also a few entertaining episodes. In
Jenny, Jorge, and Cesar's group, descriptions of panel discussions and
scavenger hunt items sometimes were ignored as more pressing concerns arose. After Jenny said that her life was a bit mundane, Jorge told
her, "Jenny, your life isn't boring. All you have to do is just add a little
something out of the ordinary to it." His Halloween fantasy was to lie
on a sidewalk, have someone cover him with dirt, then stick out his
hand and moan when people passed by. He asked Jenny to share a wild
story. Sure enough, she responded in kind, relating an incident in which
she tricked someone into buying her dinner. The digressions in Confer
began to sound like the classroom chatter in a physical space, without
which group work would be strained and tedious.

The centripetal force of digression, however, was countered by the
tasks at hand. Often, this meant accounting for a variety of responses
and a diversity of methods and ideas. After reading her group's literacy
profiles, Lama put them into an interpretive frame:

> I really like your essays. I think we all had different interpretations
> of what [a] 'literacy profile.' [is.] My literacy profile's purpose was
> to tell you guys about what sparked my education most. Darhon,
> yours was more about what education meant to you. Elizabeth, yours
> focused more on your actual literary skills (reading and writing). I
> think it's interesting how we all took different aspects on this as-
> signment. This may be due to our different teachers. Well, I look

forward to talking to you guys later.

Lama was able to account for and accept the differences in her group's writing; her posting is an attempt to understand those differences productively. Angela wrote to her group, "Hey, I think your response was kind of cool, but now I have to do my teacher's stupid assignment." Her complaint might be seen as dismissing the assignment, or at least questioning its importance. However, it might also serve as clearing room, removing the teacher's influence so that she and her group members could begin to discover what they ought to be doing, what is not "stupid."

Courtney was more explicit about her group's need for independence:

> Well, your profile was quite interesting Jim. There's only one problem I think u our instructors are a little confused an gave us two totally different assignments . Now we are suck responding to each other at different levels. Oh well, as I understand it this program is going to be based on a conversation between the three of us on the computer.

Courtney dismissed the instructors, who were "confused," and came to her own understanding of the Confer project as a conversation. Perhaps the students realized sooner than the teachers that a traditional essay would be neither possible nor desirable as the product of this course. Together, their essays moved toward conversation.

After writing their literacy profiles, our students gathered scavenger hunt items: statements in which their university attempted to define itself or state its purpose (passages from course catalogs, excerpts from speeches by administrators, inscriptions from buildings). Students then attended a panel discussion (hosted at each school) on liberal education and asked questions of the panelists. They shared all their findings.

The next assignment, an essay on liberal education, was the capstone of the project. As the students prepared to write these essays, their collaboration grew more complex. They had to wade through and integrate their shared material, then figure out what they had learned in the context of the group. Group members had to bounce their ideas off one another, looking for areas of commonality and difference. They created a support system and found the common theme or framework necessary to define the group project.

The Confer program's "script-making" function made it impractical to expect a single-voiced group essay. However, most of our students did not see this as a problem. Confer allowed them to work individually, then respond to each others' drafts looking for commonality and difference. Colleen used her teacher's authority to frame her group's essay:

> Hi again guys! How's everything? ... I just discussed with my teacher
> what he exactly wants for us to do in our essay and he said it was
> basically up to us. He said we just needed to format some type of
> collaborate essay on what we have learned about liberal education.
> I think that the easiest way for us to do this would be for each of us
> to write our own essay and type them int[o] confer. We could use
> the information we have learned from each other, from class, and at
> our university. Then we could talk about what each other said and
> give our opinion.

Colleen defined a collaborative, dialogic essay for her group, the "easiest" thing to do in Confer and, finally, the most appropriate.

In their final essays, our students debated the value of liberal education, the proper method for obtaining it, and what it should entail. Some
stressed the importance of taking classes in a variety of disciplines. Others saw the need for exposure to different cultures and backgrounds.
Sarah wrote, "In today's society, I think classes dealing with racism and
other social problems should be included in liberal art educaion." Forrest
saw an intellectual as well as a social purpose for multiculturalism. He
applauded his university's "commitment to exposing its students to
multicultural view points" and asserted, "It seems no longer appropriate for a university in this country to see a liberal education as teaching
the classics of Western thought." The term *multiculturalism* became for
our students a way of defining some aspects of liberal education at their
various universities. But it was also a contested term. Fred raised one
point of contention:

> When you have a university as large as that or UM people tend to
> get lost. So they start clubs and organizations to get toknow people
> and find people with common interests, but one thing that I
> havenoticed is that a majority of these clubs are racial and ethnical
> clubs. Doesn't that kind of defeat the purpose of the whole
> multiculturism and racial ethnicticity? Maybe I am wrong, what do
> you two think?

John noted a similar dilemma:

> I said the social part of liberal education was good here at OSU be-
> cause there is such a huge mix of different kinds of people from
> different places around the world. The only problem with this is we
> find it difficult to communicate with each other.

Despite the painfully controversial nature of this debate, the Confer space
itself was remarkably peaceful. As we watched our students read and
write together online, we witnessed a working model of multicultural
America.

A student named Jeff saw the Confer project as a liberal education in
itself. In his course evaluation, he wrote:

> By working with others, I now have a more positive outlook on the whole issue of getting a decent liberal education. My initial thoughts were sort of narrow, but after some communication with students from different schools I got a chance to see all the benefits that come from building a solid, widebase in education ... I consider this whole collaborative project a gateway to my experiences in liberal education.

Like Jeff, the majority of our students seemed to feel that the Confer class was special, that they were doing something out of the ordinary in first-year composition. Representing their home institutions, students had to put their best selves forward. Many had never been online before the class began, but they formed friendships with group members based on electronic dialogue rather than on appearance. Our students consciously worked to broaden their perspectives and complicate their understandings. The course met our original expectations of student-centered, student-driven education.

Conclusions

Our students worked together in ways we had not imagined strangers could work together. Because their experiences with Confer allowed them—to a certain extent—to define academic discourse for themselves, they learned more than we taught them. Our primary task was to help our students work within the open framework we provided. We sorted through options and discussed group agendas, helping our students integrate their work into the larger project. The software gave the class and the conversation a collaborative, dialogic form. Our role as teachers was to revise our expectations—and those of our students—to suit the technologic capability.

In "Arts of the Contact Zone," Mary Louise Pratt notes that educators often talk about teaching, but lack the word "pupiling." Educational analyses tend to cast the teacher as the focal point and active party; the teacher determines the values and sets the direction of the classroom. When discussed, students are viewed as mirrors of the teacher. Good students reflect the teacher. Poor students do not. Pratt points out that even though the act of pupiling must occur, the term is missing in our analysis of classroom situations and in our students' vocabulary.

One possibility for first-year composition courses is to make the entrance into academia—the experience of pupiling—the focus of the course. The Confer course came close to approximating such an idea. In Confer, these sixty students, with unique backgrounds and course expectations, explored their status by attempting to understand themselves as students, to direct their own education, and to see what their universities could offer. In Confer, each student's individual experience was placed in the wider context provided by the collaborative group. The result was both an interaction of the heterogeneous social space of Pratt's "contact zone" and the formation of a provisional, virtual community. In Confer, students began to recognize themselves in others. The experience of pupiling drew people together from different backgrounds and perspectives. The students were caught up in an academic culture and a larger society that is itself in transition. The Confer groups became both a means of transformation and a support structure to guide students through that transformation.

Confer enabled us as instructors to revise our understandings of pupiling, teaching, and textuality. Conditioned by prolonged exposure to print, and by experience with collaborative groups preparing printed texts, we came to Confer expecting our students to produce "papers." Our way of reading and evaluating student writing was based on the single-voiced, single-subject, nondigressive text. In Confer, however, it was not possible for our students to produce such a text. As instructors we had to reconceive our criteria, learn to value more than single utterances or final products. In the end, we judged not only the complexity and thoughtfulness of students' ideas about the issues at hand, but also the ways in which they interacted with their collaborators—what they did, or failed to do, to help their groups create conversations rich in content, inclusive in form, and friendly in tone.

As we anticipate future projects with students working in virtual space, we can apply several things we learned from using Confer. First, the interplay of difference and commonality can be an important component in successful online group work. The students involved in the Confer project had some things in common: All attended large, public universities and all had at least reasonably good access to computers. However, there were also major cultural and intellectual differences among the students. We found that our students were able to bridge cultural differences and talk to one another easily, but were able to reach only the most tentative closure on intellectual questions. Future projects might join institutions with a greater or lesser degree of similarity, or connect different classes or sections within the same university. In each case, however, we believe that the interplay between commonality and difference can be the dynamic by which the project operates and the creative tension that allows it to thrive.

Second, having a stated purpose or theme for the online interaction is productive. Although writing online is fun, and a sense of play can co-exist with the "real" work, students should understand that they are online for a serious purpose. In the case of Confer, the word *project* was useful. It seemed to help students conceive of their work as a special endeavor that would continue for some time, rather than a series of un-related online exercises. Students came to class each day with a purpose in mind, but they also knew that the project was ongoing, and that they did not have to do everything at once.

The theme of liberal education worked well for us, especially when the students began to explore issues of multicultural education. Survey-ing the current academic scene, students were able to talk about the na-ture and purpose of education, which they recognized as changeable. As we have rethought the course, we have seen that the "liberal educa-tion/multicultural education" theme, coupled with the loose assignment structure and the Confer technology, helped us to create a class that was in large measure student driven.

Third, we learned what we thought we already knew: The medium is the message and all technology is both enabling and limiting. An effec-tively designed online project will incorporate technology that allows and even encourages the sort of work the project calls for. The work that we initially expected from the Confer project was not the sort of work for which Confer was designed, nor was it the sort of work best suited for the collaborative enterprise we had established and the open struc-ture and broad theme we had selected. Fortunately, the content of the course, the limits and capabilities of the technology, and the work and attitude of our students helped us to reconceive our expectations. In the future, we hope to design a project in which technology, content, and teacher expectations are integrated from the start.

Notes

1. While Ohio State is on a trimester system, with the autumn quarter going from the third week of September until the first week of December, the Univer-sity of Michigan and the University of Illinois at Chicago both use semester systems, which begin at the end of August and go through the second week of December.

2. The numbers in parentheses refer to the thread and message numbers in a discussion thread. Thus, the first message of the first thread is archived as (1:1).

3. For project participants at Ohio State, the feeling that accessing Confer was an underground activity was highlighted by the following event: About midway through the Confer section of the course, we asked one of the Ohio State tech support staff for help with a question we had about Confer. He told us that what we were doing—telnetting to a remote host from our classroom lab—was not only, supposedly, impossible (due to a network security apparatus that was apparently not working in our lab) but also a violation of Ohio State's sys-

tem rules. He promised that it would take a couple more weeks before he would
be able to report us—enough time for us to finish the Confer section of the course.
We did not receive the technical support we needed, but we did continue to
engage in our subversive activities. Every moment we worried that an official
technowizard would pull the plug on our project, cutting off our connection
with the outside world. Thankfully, we made it through the project.

Work Cited

Pratt, Mary Louise. "Arts of the Contact Zone." *Profession 91*. New York: MLA,
    1991. 33–40.

10 Rhetorical Paths and Cyber-Fields: ENFI, Hypertext, and Bakhtin

Trent Batson
Seton Hall University

As Fred Kemp explained in Chapter 7, ENFI (electronic networks for interaction), introduced the idea of using local-area computer networks to teach writing in a real-time, online environment. The idea of networked classrooms took hold in many English departments around the country, and, subsequently, computer discussion tools such as Daedalus Interchange were developed. Though I developed the ENFI[1] concept, along with Dr. Joy Peyton of the Center for Applied Linguistics in Washington, D.C., I had never fully understood the rhetorical and dialogical connections between networking and hypertext until I taught a graduate class at George Mason University.

The Unsettling Impact of Computers on Teaching and Learning

As we adopt computers for more and more of our work on campuses (teaching, learning, communicating, researching, archiving, presenting, and decision making), we often find ourselves searching for new analogies or metaphors to understand their impact. How can we understand the social and psychological dimensions in cyberspace that often seem so different from those we are accustomed to in the physical world? How, in particular, can we best understand what it means to teach and learn in an environment as radically different from the traditional classroom as a computer-networked writing classroom, where group discussion often occurs on a computer screen rather than in verbal exchanges? In traditional classrooms, only one person can speak at a time because simultaneous utterances would result in an incomprehensible cacophony. But, when using the computer network, all can "speak" at the same time, allowing the computer to create the discursive "turn taking" based on the order in which the written messages are submitted. The messages scroll up the screen, one after the other, creating the illusion that each has been written in response to the last, even though in most cases the writing has been simultaneous, or nearly so. Because all participants write concurrently, it is impossible to "stay ahead" of this written conversation—no one has the "floor," no one controls the discussion; indeed, there is not even a shared conversational "present." It is like looking at stars and knowing that none of them is really where they appear to be because the light has taken years to arrive at our eyes (indeed, the stars may have blown up millions of years ago, leaving nothing but empty space where we "see" a star), and realizing that the concept of a shared "now" is more complex than we thought. This experience on the computer network can be disturbing, upsetting our usual understanding of human conversation.

Because it is so different in many ways from a traditional classroom, the networked classroom has left many of us grasping for ways to understand all the forces at play. Though many good theoretical descriptions have been advanced over the years, I do not believe we have yet discovered an ideal way to represent this new rhetorical context. But one way to understand the dynamics of the networked classroom is by seeing it in Bakhtinian terms, as the contributors of this volume have recognized. This new rhetorical environment, in fact, could have arisen out of Bakhtin's imagination. His vision of the dialogic nature of language in novels—its simultaneously unifying and decentralizing tendencies and its tendency toward stratification of discourse—has appeared much more clearly than ever in the networked classroom.

For those who sense this "Bakhtinian moment," the networked classroom can be an epiphany. We already know from the experience of a few pioneers in computer-based education that networked classrooms and hypertext can alter the teaching of writing in radical ways. How radical and in what ways teaching will be altered are slowly being determined.

Still, it is a big step from a classroom in which most discourse is controlled by the voice of the teacher to this apparent free-for-all in the networked classroom, or from the traditional linear essay, in which argument is directed by logic, to hypertext, in which argument only emerges after the reader traverses the text a few times, as one does with poetry. How do writing teachers find bridges from the familiar terrain of the current traditional classroom to carry them to this brave new world? A couple of such theoretical connections are collaborative writing theory for the network-based classroom and postmodern theory for hypertext literature. At the same time, as helpful as these connections are for initial understanding of the new writing spaces, they lead us to understand the new in terms of the old. They do not provide a new perspec-

tive arising more purely out of an understanding of the rhetorical dynamics in cyberspace. We are still using theory derived from print culture to understand the dynamics of a decidedly nonprint environment.
We need to leave behind the well-worn rhetorical paths and explore the
bright new cyber-fields.

The Case Study

In the Rhetoric of Electronic Text, a graduate course at George Mason
University, students found new ways to understand these cyber-fields.
They used the ENFI-inspired program called Interchange, the most commonly used software in the network-based writing classroom. Teachers
using Interchange generally consider the written discussion as simply
another form of the traditional oral class discussion. Unlike oral discussions, however, network exchanges disperse and fragment conversation.
Because all students can respond simultaneously to multiple threads of
conversation, dialogue moves erratically as messages scroll by on the
screen. What I respond to *now* might have been written several minutes
ago. In the meantime, others may have posted their responses to two
other messages that were moving in different directions. The congru-
ence we normally experience—someone says something and then hears
an immediate response—does not generally occur with Interchange or
with other similar technologies because the disunifying forces that generally underlie an utterance are magnified. Nonetheless, it does not take
much time before it actually feels natural to participate in three conversational threads simultaneously.

The critical skill for a teacher in such a situation is not "teaching,"
which generally means leading the discussion, but facilitating all student interactions, influencing those interactions, modeling thinking, and
providing a scaffold of phrases, words, and interesting ideas. Good facilitating requires paying less attention to the points the teacher wants
to cover and more attention to group process, which I cannot resist saying is probably what teachers should have been doing all along. To understand how this group process can function using ENFI, I turn now to
the graduate class.

The First ENFI Session

The course at George Mason had eighteen students, only one of whom
had seen computer-network group discussion software before. This first
ENFI session occurred near the beginning of the semester, before the

class had much experience with any form of electronic text other than word processing. These six comments by five different students are derived from various parts of the discussion, which continued for ninety minutes and consisted of about twenty pages when printed; all are reproduced verbatim:

> So, I've just had the familiar feeling of being completely lost in front of a computer . . . again. Perhaps by the end of this course, I will feel this way less frequently.

> Is anyone else being driven crazy by computers?

> We are simulating what monkeys would produce if they were let loose on a keyboard for a 1000 years.

> if order isnt important i guess capitals and punctuation arent either maybe you could do a research project on teaching composition without them

> Is this what every class is going to be like?

> God help me, I think I might like this class.

Unlike traditional classroom discourse, most of these exchanges consist of one or two sentences. Students also bring into class a kind of language play that seldom finds its way into face-to-face class discussions. They talk about food, sports, or popular figures, make jokes, and play self-consciously with language. In my many years of teaching in the network-based classroom (I was the first one to do so, in 1985), I have seen this pattern dozens of times, as students explore this novel discursive environment. The pattern is as follows: (1) *confusion*—"So, I have just had the familiar feeling of being completely lost in front of a computer . . . again. Perhaps by the end of this course, I will feel this way less frequently"; (2) *frustration*—"Is anyone else being driven crazy by computers?"; (3) *sarcasm*—"We are simulating what monkeys would produce if they were let loose on a keyboard for a 1000 years"; (4) *exaggeration of language conventions*—"if order isnt important i guess capitals and punctuation arent either maybe you could do a research project on teaching composition without them"; (5) *doubt whether this kind of discourse is legitimate in the academy*—"Is this what every class is going to be like?"; and (6) *grudging acceptance*—"God help me. I think I might like this class."

During this first session, it seemed that the group missed the traditional teacher-leader, the authorial discourse that Bakhtin argues unifies social heteroglossia. According to Bakhtin, the "unitary language" of authorial (or teacherly) discourse is always "opposed to the realities of heteroglossia" (270). When this discourse is absent or minimized, students lose their sense of boundaries until they begin to acclimate to the new social order; in the meantime, the disunifying forces become exaggerated. Thus, our discussion did not achieve much coherence as the students experimented with the new form of interaction. Their comments were tentative (the frequent jokes revealed their discomfort). Their topics of discussion and concern with the linguistic differences between the new form and the old unmasked the different strata that always inform heteroglossia but are not always visible. Bakhtin explains that "At any given moment of its evolution, language is stratified not only into linguistic dialects in the strict sense of the word . . . but also . . . into languages that are socio-ideological; languages of social groups, 'professional' and 'generic' languages, languages of generations and so forth" (271–72). With the appearance of unexpected languages, the students were self-consciously watching themselves write rather than writing to communicate. But because this was the usual pattern for groups new to ENFI, I was not concerned.

The Second ENFI Session

Just two weeks later, we had our second ENFI session. By this time, the class had started the unit on hypertext and had more experience with electronic text. We used Storyspace, a hypertext authoring tool, and, by this ENFI session, most of the students were comfortable writing text in little boxes scattered around their screen with lines (or links) between the boxes (see Chapter 2).

Because the students now had more experience in this second form of electronic writing and because I gave them a specific course-related topic to respond to, our second ENFI session was less playful and more focused. Some semblance of authorial discourse had returned. All comments quoted below were in response to a question I posted at the beginning of the ENFI session: "Now that you've read some of the Landow book [George Landow's *Hypertext*], and we've had an oral discussion [about the book], what are some of your thoughts about how hypertext may change the way you write?

> I think hypertext is more likely to change the way I read than the way I write. While I don't have access to a hypertext editor normally, I do use things like multimedia encyclopedias that use linkages and some nonlinear reading protocols.

> How do you sustain argument in non-sequential writing? Lots of examples and hope the reader "sees things" the way you do?

The "theme" of your writing in hypertext is contained in overall meta-text, i.e., all of the various nodes viewed together. So the argument must somehow be contained in this metatext.

Some of my thought, especially my memory, is already nonlinear, so hypertext might allow these things to be recorded when they would be unreadable without external links.

toss out notions of "complete" in the hypertext world. it does not happen

I have always been interested in biography and I think [the] comment on how . . . memory works might bring an interesting approach to the writing of biography in a hypertext format. Memory certainly operates under the influence of random events, an odor, a song, a place. Why shouldn't biography be allowed the same kind of wanderings?

So what do I do?!! I have so many links I want to make because I see such strong relationships between the writings, but I will never finish. It is like Murphy's Fifth Law (there is always one more bug). I would rather have several reasonably developed paths than a million footprints going off in infinite directions.

The odd thing—to me—was that the class was talking about hypertext through ENFI; they were talking about one form of electronic text through another form. Inevitably, the two—hypertext and ENFI—became confused in the minds of some of the students during that evening's class. This was an important insight, perhaps one of the most important discoveries I had yet made about electronic text. Read the following comments:

it scares me to think of people spending more time communicating through the keyboard than face to face. healthy, happy human beings need to use their voice box and interact with one another. the expressions and tone one uses in communicating can be as valuable as the message itself and this aspect is lost in hypertext. [Note that this is not really true, because hypertext is not a medium for people to communicate with, so the comments could only be referring to ENFI or some other form of computer-mediated communication.]

Those who cannot communicate in hypertext will become extinct by natural docuverse selection. Long live hyper-Darwin! [Again, one does not communicate in hypertext, at least not as one does in e-mail or ENFI.]

I don't think hypertext depersonalizes human beings. In fact, I think it allows us to let our hair down . . . Sure people do a lot of talking face to face, but they keep themselves hidden behind the walls. This form allows those walls to come down. Sure we sacrifice the 'look them in the eye technique', but we learn more than we ever would

by trying to get people to open up. [Clearly, this student thought of
hypertext as ENFI.]

Though only a few students explicitly showed they had combined
hypertext and ENFI in their minds, interestingly enough, no one corrected these few students.

Because both electronic texts—the individually crafted hypertext web
and the group-created ENFI conversation—have multiple voices, and
because participants need to follow multiple paths or threads in both,
hypertext and ENFI began to blend in the minds of my students. The
circle of people in the ENFI lab became the circle of ideas in a hypertext
document. This point is worth exploring because the elision suggests
that the students were making a crucial connection between internal
multivocality—the multilinear associative way in which our minds
work—and group multivocality. That the students made this connection unwittingly seems significant, suggesting to me that the two discourse experiences had prompted an instinctive and compelling understanding of language that was similar to Bakhtin's description. As Galin
and Latchaw point out in Chapter 1, Bakhtin explains that "dialogue
may be external (between two different people) or internal (between an
earlier and a later self)" (427). This instinctive association between the
swirl of voices "out there" and "in here" (in the head) got me thinking
about how we process communication and what kinds of communicative worlds we set up.

What Bakhtin struggled to express—a sense of the constantly evolving, multivocal nature of language—was also finding expression in the
"confusion" my students showed between hypertext and ENFI. This
was Bakhtin come to life. The students are not so much confused, he
would say, as they are struggling to gain a common knowledge base for
meaningful utterances.

However, whether brilliant or confused, after little more than thirty
minutes of this discussion about hypertext, and while I was still pon-
dering this Bakhtinian moment, the students grew restive. What I had
thought was a highly successful, focused, and productive discussion
began to fall apart. Because writing is slower than talking, the students
began to feel harnessed, slowed, dragged down:

> see, that's what I mean! we're all in such a @#$%!^ hurry to get our
> message out that we all sense of content [sic]—ALL WE DO IS GET
> A MESSAGE OUT, ANY MESSAGE!

> Does anyone have the urge to turn around and start a conversation
> instead of hacking it out on these keyboards? What about the people
> who feel like they are at their best when they talk things out or par-

> ticipate in a heated argument. The thought of spending my day
> 'talking' in this mode leaves me cold. It is fun for 45 minutes but . . .
> I don't know what I'm getting at. Different key strokes for different
> folks, I guess.
>
> I have a very strong urge to talk to the person next to me or behind
> me but at the same time that competes with my urge to see what's
> been added here and who's following what 'text.'

What they said aloud to me—in speech, so we have no record of these
comments to include here—was more assertive. Many said they did not
see the point of wasting time interacting through a computer network;
they got the point: They understood real-time conferencing and could
we now just get on with the class. Although others liked ENFI, I sympa-
thized with the poor and frustrated typists. So we continued our
hypertext unit in the traditional teacher-led seminar familiar to most
graduate students. During the next month, we sat around a seminar
table with no computers in the room and talked, or we used a classroom
with a computer at the front so that students could project their hypertext
webs on a screen and explain their projects. I was disappointed that we
could not use ENFI more because this was a course in electronic text
and a major form of electronic text had just been rejected. What I did not
know was that this period of "retreat" was extremely productive for the
class. And we did not retreat totally: We continued to e-mail each other
actively, which seemed to solidify the students' imaginative shift to the
digital world.

The Third ENFI Session

By the time we had our third ENFI session, four weeks later, everyone
had completed their hypertext authoring projects and had participated
in the regular class e-mail conference between classes. This third and
final ENFI session of the semester was more successful than the second:
It reflected growing ease and comfort with electronic text. The messages
were neither short and empty, as were the first ones, nor essentially pa-
per-based paragraphs transposed to an electronic format, as were those
from the second ENFI session on hypertext. The messages in the third
ENFI session reflected the growing computer conferencing skills many
in the class had developed.

All responded to this prompt: "Discuss the final project: content and
organizing ideas."

> so . . . does anybody have any ideas?
>
> Is anyone else hungry. We could have a pizza here in 30 minutes.

This brainstorming is scary stuff.

Before I start thinking seriously, I need to know what a moo is—other than the sound a western md. cow makes

a moo is an onomatopoeia usually associated with certain bovine creatures, also the sound my mother-in-law makes when bellying up to the feed trough. [Note: A MOO is a multi-user dimension, object-oriented, an Internet real-time discussion tool—ENFI at a distance—that can create "objects" like stage objects to enhance the sense of space in virtual space.]

Hi guys, I have no idea what to say about the final project. I guess I was kind of picturing it as something that would compare and contrast the conventions of electronic and printed text.

Well, I am really interested in the idea of personas in CMC [computer-mediated communication]. The idea that you are someone else ... brave ... or witty ... or just different tone you take on a different medium.

Is [a class member] there? Maybe we can talk about your idea about e-mail humor.

I think it is time for that standoff I have been waiting for. One thing I think the final report should do is somehow pit all you hypertextualists against us linearians (see, Trent. Everyone is not averse to using long words in this form of communication). I would be interested in knowing, after all this is over, how many people REALLY feel this is the way of the future and how many simply see it as another tool to make an already cumbersome job more difficult.

I am quiet because I think it is more important to be a listener, not because I am schizo (you are, too—no, I'm not—shut up—up yours).

I'm now ready to get involved in the discussion: obviously I'm interested in the educational component of whatever topic we choose

I like green peppers and onions and draft killians with my pizza"

I agree with [a class member]—perhaps focusing on work-place impact or some other practical aspect. (vague enough?)

"What do you define practical as?

Who said Killians. Stop that. We're supposed to be concentrating (frozen mug) here. You can't think about beer (cool, refreshing ...) during class!

Yes, it may be cumbersome ... but, if it is a tool that encourages (ooh, ahh ...big word) participation from a higher number of group members, aren't the ideas that are produced somehow ' OWNED' by everyone to a higher degree ... thus affecting commitment to the organization, respect of ideas of others, ... just better feelings all around...CMC seems to facilitate f2f communication...to enhance it." [f2f = face-to-face]

Here's what i'm interested in—taking your (collective) views on 'this stuff' e.g. e-communication and looking at how your ideas have changed (*if* they've changed) over the last few months takers?

(Did you see the looks on those two [a couple of students who wandered into the lab not realizing we were having a class and who were chased out] . . . kinda like, Is this a class? Is it in session?—I think the public's perception of these technologies is interesting.)

The participants continued in this manner. *This* conversation was working: it flowed, all the students were engaged, language play pervaded the comments, and it was fun. New issues were continually introduced; as time went on, the interest grew rather than waned, as opposed to the second ENFI session. The students seemed to have mastered the discourse features of this rhetorical space, the construction of persona and audience, and the ambiance of this medium.

Look at what they were doing here: (1) not only sustaining the main topic thread but also interweaving "underlife" elements (pizza and beer) by using subordinate clauses or parentheses, and even satirizing the underlife thread—"Stop that. We're supposed to be concentrating (frozen mug) . . ."; (2) identifying the person for whom the message was intended, which they had learned was essential in this discourse space— "I agree with . . . "; (3) mixing in stylistics typical of print text—"but, if it is a tool that encourages"—with speechlike elements—"(ooh, ahh . . . big word)"; (4) maintaining coherence in three conversational threads by including cohesion features to show which thread or threads the current message is connected to (the pizza thread, the long word thread, the final project thread); (5) reflecting a tone of ease, pleasure, comfort, and understanding; (6) producing appropriate text chunks for the medium (large enough for an idea unit, short enough to maintain the flow); (7) adopting e-textual features such as ellipses and dashes; putting metacomments in parentheses; (8) getting right to the point in each message; and (9) significantly, not expecting the teacher to lead the discussion. During this session all participants took responsibility for making the conversation cohere. All were serving as conversation managers, not just the teacher. This was a marked improvement since our previous (second) ENFI session, which had been painful after the initial paragraph-length position statements about hypertext. Yet a month later, this session was sparkling, productive, appropriate, and enjoyable. What had happened?

We had come to know each other better. We had used e-mail. We had, each of us, developed an electronic persona that made the electronic medium not a denial but a celebration of our humanity. And we had all had more practice writing electronic text. Yet what emerged from our oral discussion, and what seemed most evident to all, was that the class now felt comfortable in this peculiar, hybrid, multivocal rhetorical situation. In our discussion, we acknowledged that individual writing in hypertext was the most important reason for the surprising turnaround in the class's acceptance and enjoyment of the ENFI session on that evening. What had seemed like confusion was in reality the Bakhtinian moment. The students had, in fact, begun to be aware of the ongoing "conversation" in their own heads and were beginning to understand that writing is as much dialogic as expository, declamatory, exploratory, or any other traditional rhetorical classification. Through their experiences with ENFI, with e-mail, and with hypertext, along with our "normal" classroom discourse, students seemed freed from the belief that they had to produce a unitary voice speaking to a standard, fixed, academic audience. They found other means of unifying their discourse at the same time that the many voices in their own heads—playful, alive, intellectual, assertive—engaged with the many voices on the network—each giving life to the other—and the many, many connections led to a happy evening of discovery. The frustration of the second ENFI session had become a celebration during this third session.

The Mental Steps the Students Took

The mental processes necessary for my students to make these psychological shifts into these new forms of writing and thinking are worth exploring. Though our e-mail experience undoubtedly played a role, I will examine only hypertext in the following analysis:

From: **To:**

•*dependence on linearity* ———> *acceptance of associational linking*
(The students wrote hypertext using Storyspace, in which the text units are laid out like mind-mapping chunks, graphically splayed out in the space; through this experience, they had to make sense of their own multiple associations and validate the nonlogical, multilinear nature of their own thinking.)
•*associational linking* ———> *acceptance of multiple textual paths*
(Once they accepted the multilinear nature of their own thinking, students could accept that text can be read in multiple ways, through many paths.)
•*multiple paths* ———> *many (individual) voices*
(If thinking is multilinear, and text can be read in multiple ways, then perhaps one's own thoughts can be organized multilinearly. When they

authenticated the nonlogical elements in their texts, they seemed to free the nonlogical elements in their heads.)

•*many (individual) voices* ———> *multivocality (voices of many individuals)*

(When students allow that there can be multiple voices in one's own text and thus in one's own head—rather than a single authorial voice—it is not so hard to live with the many voices of others in a group-written discussion—rather than a single teacherly voice.)

•*multivocality* ———> *alternate means of maintaining coherence*

(Finally, once students were comfortable with the many voices in text, in their own minds, and in groups, then dependence on linearity (for coherence) is less critical. Students are then free to look for alternate strategies to create coherence.)

The movement from inside the head to outside, from individual composing to collaboration, occurred in the new imaginative spaces made possible by the technology. The effort was basically toward acceptance of multiplicity, from linear thinking to associational, which legitimized multiple paths both in the head and in text. From there, it is not so hard to accept the many voices in an ENFI environment.

Rhetorical Paths and Cyber-Fields

Let's look at this in another way. Text on paper is usually linear, although we have developed conventions such as footnotes, marginalia, and boxes to break out of this mold. Some magazines seem to be striving hard to become as hypertextual as possible. But, even given these efforts to break out of the confines of paper and print, academic writing has tended to be linear because it generally follows certain set discourse patterns, sustaining an "appropriate" register (as I am doing in this chapter), and imposing a logical order so that the succession of ideas is congruent. We can think of this writing process as a path through a field.

But what if the text is not viewed as a path but instead as the field itself? What if your experience as a reader is like wandering around the field, seeing the field from many different perspectives, going in circles instead of a line? What if you are not led through the landscape but just let loose in it? What if a conversation or a discussion is not a line but a field, where you seem to move recursively among conversational threads?

Whether the precise steps listed above actually occur in adjusting to electronic writing spaces, writers need to sense multiple elements at work in a field of text. Writers have long worked in the field of text *in their heads*, sorting through the various ideas and images and phrases as they write, creating one path in that field. But dealing with a field of voices out there on the screen is a new skill. It is one thing to have a field of possibilities in your head, out of which you select a logical sequence, that becomes your essay, but it is another to have that field of possibilities itself *become* a text.

What seems to have happened in my class was that working in hypertextual space made the students more comfortable with multiple elements in composing space. These multiple elements could be their own internal voices or the many voices of their classmates. Students became more comfortable working in a textual field rather than along a textual path.

Groups Achieving Coherence without a Leader

What is this field? How can it exist? How does a textual field organize itself? We have tended to think of text as either an individual creation or a collaborative effort led by an individual. But, then, we have only begun to recognize that coherence can develop from the actions of independent agents. As Mitch Resnick explains in *Turtles, Termites, and Traffic Jams: Explorations in Massively Parallel Microworlds*, for example, it is easy for an observer to assume that a flock of birds follows the lead of a single leader bird.

> A flock of birds sweeps across the sky. Like a well-choreographed dance troupe, the birds veer to the left in unison. Then suddenly, they all dart to the right and swoop down toward the ground. Each movement seems perfectly coordinated. The flock as a whole is as graceful—more graceful—than any of the birds within it.
>
> How do birds keep their movements so orderly, so synchronized? Most people assume that birds play a game of follow-the-leader: the bird at the front of the flock leads, and the others follow. But that's not so. In fact, most bird flocks don't have leaders at all. There is no special "leader-bird." Rather, the flock is an example of what some people call "self-organization." Each bird in the flock follows a set of simple rules, reacting to the movements of the birds nearby it. Orderly flock patterns arise from these simple, local interactions. None of the birds has a sense of the overall flock pattern. The bird in the front is not a leader in any meaningful sense—it just happens to end up there. The flock is organized without an organizer, coordinated without a coordinator. (3)

As Resnick goes on to explain, there are many examples of this kind of self-organizing principle. "In all these systems, patterns are determined not by some centralized authority but by local interactions among decentralized components." People behave in a similar way, he points out, in such situations as heavy traffic on the interstate, or when attempting to applaud in unison:

> Sometimes, at concerts or sporting events, thousands of spectators join together in rhythmic, synchronized clapping. There is no conductor leading them. How do they coordinate their applause? Here's one way to think about what happens. Initially, when everyone starts clapping, the applause is totally unorganized. Even people clapping at the same tempo are wildly out of phase with one another. But, through some random fluctuation, a small subset of people happen to clap at the same tempo, in phase with one another. That rhythm stands out, just a little, in the clapping noise. People in the audience sense this emerging rhythm and adjust their own clapping to join it. Thus the emerging rhythm becomes a little stronger, and even more people conform to it. Eventually, nearly everyone in the audience is clapping in a synchronized rhythm. Amazingly, the whole process takes just a few seconds, even with thousands of people participating. (138)

We teachers tend to believe we must be in charge almost every moment during class time for productive learning to take place. Even those of us who have moved toward collaborative learning feel the need to monitor the groups, keep them "on task," and generally ride herd during the whole process of collaboration. Learning has come to be identified overwhelmingly with teacher influence. But the evidence that Resnick presents about self-organization suggests that teachers might be missing chances for student groups to find their own organizing principles, particularly regarding group work in the network-based classroom. As Paul Taylor of the Daedalus Group has suggested in his work,[2] groups tend to move toward coherence in their ENFI sessions. This should not be too surprising because an ENFI session is in many ways like other situations we experience when people are using their voices instead of keyboards to communicate. A hostess at a party in her home can wander from cluster to cluster of guests, make an appropriate comment, and, in just a few minutes, judge whether the party is going well. What is new about ENFI, and other CMC events, is that they are in writing rather than in speech.

In fact, our seeming discomfort with CMC may be more a result of the nature of print than of our own nature. It may be that we, in fact, have no inherent problem understanding multivocality with the reduced presence of authorial discourse but instead have little practice understanding it in writing. The experience of my students, with whom we have visited in this chapter, suggests this is true.

But How Do I Teach in a Cyber-Field?

Although we may know that bird flocks and crowds of people do not need a teacher to lead them in order to achieve order, how does that translate to the classroom? How do we make use of this analysis to better teach writing? If in fact network discussion tools and hypertext interact to create a new rhetorical space in which the Bakhtinian vision becomes reality, how can we teach writing given long-held or traditional expectations? How can we still take advantage of the new learning opportunities? And what happens to "academic writing"?

Though the ability to develop arguments, write descriptions, or adhere to other traditional rhetorical forms will remain a requirement for any writer, we cannot ignore the new writing spaces. E-mail, the World Wide Web, electronic meeting rooms, companywide "intranets," and various kinds of computer conferencing are becoming as important in some organizations as more traditional work forms. Also, the opportunities for exciting new prewriting exercises, new collaborative groupings, and new connections with text are there before us in the network-based classroom. We need to think not only about the new kinds of writing students will be doing, or are doing, but also about the new opportunities for teaching writing.

Not Just in the Academy: Cyberspace in Corporate America

Information technology not only provides better ways to see and develop certain rhetorical skills, but it also allows groups to work together more efficiently, saving time in reaching decisions and arriving at consensus. Business and government have thus developed electronic meeting rooms to take advantage of these opportunities. Thus, students can broaden their views of writing in a networked classroom and learn more about new collaborative patterns that are likely to exist in the work world once they leave college. In corporate and governmental settings, we do not hear about Bakhtin in reference to electronic meeting rooms or the groupware used in them, but these rooms are every bit as much a new cyber-field as ENFI.[3]

Groups meet in electronic meeting rooms to speed up their processing of ideas. Just as we have seen in an ENFI session, everyone in such a room can make comments at once, so many more ideas get produced in a short period of time. Also, because no one needs permission to make a comment, the discussion forum seems more egalitarian. A higher percentage of the group participates more fully than in a meeting in which one voice takes charge. Thus, the quality of the deliberation is higher because all participants contribute ideas. In a traditional meeting, ideas expressed in powerful, confident voices often carry the day, but this does not automatically happen in an electronic meeting room, where the "voice" is in writing, not speech, and differences in volume or pitch are absent. In other words, the male voice does not automatically have an advantage. Generally, the discussion is influenced as much by the quality of the idea as by the mode of expression. All of these factors convince many companies and government agencies that they can do a better job by supplementing regular meetings with electronic ones.

In many of these electronic meeting rooms, a set of software tools called a group decision-support system (GDSS) is used. Let's imagine ourselves meeting in one of these rooms. Usually, the computers—maybe twenty or thirty—are arranged in a horseshoe shape, with participants sitting around the outside of the horseshoe and the facilitator at the front, visible to all. All computers are networked, of course, and a video projector is set up at the front to allow certain views of the group interaction on the network to be projected during the session. Generally, a working group meets in the electronic meeting room to use the GDSS. The leader of the team is just one of the participants during this session; the facilitator is a professional group facilitator who understands the GDSS software and thus can adapt it to the purposes of the meeting that day.

The software has many modules, allowing the group to work in many different modes, from group brainstorming to identifying and prioritizing the ideas generated, so the facilitator has to decide which modules to use and in which sequence so as to best suit the purposes of the group that day.

Let's imagine we start with electronic brainstorming. This software is like "inkshedding" with paper and pen. If we were in fact inkshedding, we would all start with pieces of paper, write down an idea about our topic, then pass the papers on to another person in the room, who would add his or her idea, either in response to the first idea on the paper or a new one. This process of passing the papers might go on for five or six turns, until all papers have become full. Using the software, the same process occurs, and, as with the paper, each participant sees only a few of the comments of others.

Next, we move on to idea organization. On the computer, we scroll through *all* of the comments made during brainstorming, drag and draw the best comments up to the top of the dialogue, then reduce them to one line. Continuing the process, the group then submits their favorite one or two ideas, which they have reduced to one line, to the whole group. Then the group verbally edits and reduces the list of, say, twenty-five one-liners—now projected onto the projector screen at the front of the room—to maybe ten topics. The group can even vote on prioritizing the final ten: The computer registers their votes and displays the results in an instant. From these ten topics, the group can then write collaboratively, each seeing what the others are writing about each topic.

The GDSS process uses cyberspace to speed up decisions or to build consensus. Its purpose is not to expand rhetorical awareness, yet this software set could be used in a writing class just as well as any of the ENFI software. Participants in a GDSS work in a synchronous, multivocal environment, just as my students did. The GDSS software is more directive, less free-form, and less overwhelming for the first visit. But it is interesting to note that the academy and corporations have been exploring synchronous technologies to simultaneously expand and intensify their work.

We are used to writing conventions—the metaphor of the rhetorical path is essential to good writing; only one person at a time is supposed to speak; good thinking equals a logical path; authoritative writing is a unitary voice that maintains a consistent register; order can be achieved only through authority. Through traditional writing conventions, hierarchy is imposed in the classroom and in all business meetings and is even imposed as a scheme to understand text. When all of these writing conventions are called into question through experiences with software writing environments, they do not seem so immutable. But moving away from the solid ground of traditional writing conventions to a more Bakhtinian view of order, authority, and writing is profoundly disturbing. This new view is not linear, not hierarchical, not unitary; it is multiple, interactive, in flux, always becoming, and certainly not linear. The experience of communicating through voice and paper has led us toward the linear and hierarchical, but the experience of communicating through information technologies leads us to the multiple and associational. This new world is horizontal; the current world is vertical. The challenge for writing teachers is to make the shift from the current world to the new world while still working within the expectations of the current world. The nature of writing—indeed of all knowledge creation—is no longer the same, but most do not yet know it.

The Final Word

I'll let one of the students from the class at George Mason have the last word. Listen to David (now in a graduate program at Georgia Tech). He reflects on the adventures he and his peers had out in cyberspace. He refers to his collaboration with several other students to produce this final paper:

I read our e-mail and I try to place myself—where was I when I read it? What was I thinking then? What was going on? How are things different now?

And you know what? It is too much. There's way too much here to keep track of. The experiences are now too big to talk about, there are 500 messages! 500! I can't place all of it, it runs out of the frame and into whatever space exists between here and there (so interested in what happens in that space . . .), but space enough to take the experience and invert it, twist it just enough so that it still *feels*, but different, just different enough to notice. And slip.

It is an experience without reference, or more properly, without *referent*. Signifiers are signifying properly, but they refer now only to themselves, the true po-mo test passed with flying letters, headers *and* subject lines. To say again: in reallife we write about what we experience; in CMC we write and we simultaneously experience our writing. The writing *is* the experience, the ground that changes only by CMC form, *connecting the figure against a ground of writing*.

And so it goes, the endless loop of signification to derive meaning to remember to experience to *re-experience*.

Until all we have left are the words.

Not words, but wings.

. . . . . .
I'm just a guide here, one voice today among many . . . How much of me did I keep? How much did I give away? . . . In finding our voice I'm losing mine. . . .

Voices colliding in the wash, moments of unease in the worlds of CMC come together (if only for an instant).

David senses the unease, the disparities, the loss of traditional boundaries we all used to share as he explores the dimensions of these new rhetorical spaces. We are leaving the well-worn paths and venturing into new fields of awareness and discovery. We are re-creating both our ways of writing and our selves. We hardly have the terminology to talk about our experience. We grope for analogies.

Notes

1. ENFI, electronic networks for interaction, began at Gallaudet University in Washington, D.C., as a way, through computer networks, to make English more lively for my hearing-impaired students. In the early 1980s, I had been searching for a way to replicate, through computers, the rich interactive language play that people with normal hearing engage in to make language learning palatable and possible. When Joy Peyton and I first started working with the

ENFI idea, because we saw it as a hearing-impaired-education initiative, we had different terms for the acronym, including "English natural form instruction," in honor of the more natural way that hearing-impaired students could experience English, interactively and conversationally, in a group. The networked classroom depends on network software that supports group real-time conferencing: The software used most often is Interchange, a tool that grew out of our original work with the networked classroom, which has subsequently (owing in part to the genius and drive of the Daedalus Group) established the networked classroom as the dominant implementation of information technology for the teaching of writing at the college level.

2. Paul has worked for several years with chaos theory and its application to the networked classroom. As one of the original designers of the Interchange software program, he has a strong interest in the nature of the discourse that occurs in an interchange.

3. The comments here are based on a three-year funded project studying computer-based group decision-support systems (Project Common Ground, 1990–1993, funded by IBM and Gallaudet University).

Works Cited

Bakhtin, Mikhail. *The Dialogic Imagination: Four Essays by M. M. Bakhtin*. Trans. Caryl Emerson and Michael Holquist. Ed. Michael Holquist. Austin: University of Texas Press, 1981.

Landow, George. *Hypertext: The Convergence of Contemporary Critical Theory and Technology*. Baltimore: Johns Hopkins, 1992.

Resnick, Mitch. *Turtles, Termites, and Traffic Jams: Explorations in Massively Parallel Microworlds*. Cambridge, MA: MIT, 1994.

11 Four Designs for Electronic Writing Projects

Tharon W. Howard
Clemson University

It is rare to find an educator today who has not at least heard of the Internet and its potential to radically change the nature of our classrooms. And yet, for all the press the Internet has received, few composition teachers have actually had an opportunity to *teach* on the Internet. Until fairly recently, the Internet's funding and operation were controlled by the National Science Foundation (NSF). Consequently, the Net has been populated primarily by university students and educators from disciplines in science and technology, and, generally speaking, if writing teachers were not employed at a large, research-oriented university, they did not have the opportunity to take their students online in order to experiment with wide-area networks in their writing classrooms. So, while there is a great deal of interest in teaching writing in networked environments, there are relatively few examples of actual writing projects that have attempted to integrate these new technologies into composition pedagogy.

Fortunately, I have had the luck to teach in institutions that did have the resources necessary to offer its students and teachers unencumbered access to the Internet. As a result, whenever a new software package hit the Internet, I have been able to experiment with it in my writing classrooms. This chapter describes four electronic writing projects conducted between 1988 and 1995 that used four different wide-area networking technologies: (1) simple, one-to-one electronic mail exchanges with simple e-mail programs, (2) one-to-many e-mail distribution lists with Listserv, (3) networkwide file distribution services with gopher servers, and (4) global electronic publishing systems using World Wide Web servers. Yet, while technology was certainly an important factor in each of these projects, this chapter really is not intended to be a celebration of these four tools, nor are the projects I describe intended to serve as models of how to teach using these tools. Instead, what I hope to show is how several of my colleagues and I experimented with these instructional technologies in our teaching, what sorts of things worked, and (perhaps more importantly) what sorts of things did not work. Hence, the discussion of each project is broken down into four areas: (1) an assignment description, (2) the technological requirements for the project, (3) what students learned from the project, and (4) what problems were encountered in the project.

Project One: Electronic Pen Pals

Assignment Description

This project took place several years ago between students in one of my technical writing classes at Purdue University in Lafayette, Indiana, and students in a business writing course taught by Bill Karis at Clarkson University in Potsdam, New York.[1] Because Karis and I shared the belief that preparing students for writing in the workplace meant teaching collaborative writing skills, students in both of our classes were asked to role-play in a realistic scenario that would require them to collaborate via e-mail. My students were asked to imagine that they worked in the technical consulting department of an international firm that specialized in developing small, entrepreneurial businesses. Karis's students were to play the role of entrepreneurs who needed to write a business plan and proposal aimed at getting a loan from the Small Business Administration (SBA). In both classes, students collaborated with one to two classmates, so that two to three of Karis's students worked with two to three of my students via electronic mail messages.

Karis's students were required to research businesses in the Potsdam, New York, area to come up with an idea for a small business that would fill a market niche and to develop a proposal for the business. In order to allow my students to play the role of technical consultants, they were provided with documentation from the SBA on how to write loan applications and were asked to do research on how to write business proposals. Once our students had received the documentation and done the research necessary for them to play their respective roles in the scenario, Karis's students were instructed to e-mail my students an outline of their business concepts and a request for technical assistance; my students were instructed to respond by sending back a report explaining how to prepare an SBA proposal. Using the information in these reports, Karis's students drafted proposals that were e-mailed back to my students for critique. My students were then asked to analyze the draft proposals and to write recommendation reports back to Karis's students aimed at improving the proposals. Karis's students received grades for their final proposals; my students received grades for their recommendation reports.

Hardware, Software, and Technical Requirements

The technological requirements for this kind of simple, one-to-one e-mail exchange project are minimal, and a similar project could be done if both instructors have Internet e-mail access at their respective institutions or on commercial services such as CompuServe or America Online. In our project, however, not only did Karis and I have Internet e-mail access, but all of our students had also been issued a personal e-mail account from both institutions and thus were able to send messages directly to each other without the instructors' assistance.

Some Concepts Students Learned

In order for students to complete a collaborative writing project successfully, each member of the project team needs to share an understanding of where the group is in the process, what tasks remain to be done, and who is responsible for completing the tasks by specific dates. And, while this is as true of face-to-face projects as it is of electronic collaborations, the nature of the online environment highlights the need for a clearly articulated and detailed project management plan. Networked writing projects strip away many of the tacit, contextual cues that students take for granted in traditional classrooms, thereby forcing students to state goals and assumptions that normally remain implicit and unconscious in traditional classrooms. For example, assumptions about how long a semester lasts or the disciplinary backgrounds of other students in a class simply cannot be made in networked collaborations; students are not able to take for granted that every member of the project team knows that tasks must be completed before spring break, which may be scheduled at different times from one school to another. Indeed, they cannot even assume that everyone on the team agrees with a point that one of them might have made because nodding heads do not appear in e-mail messages. This loss of context meant that almost every aspect of our project's process had to be articulated and negotiated among students on each collaborative team. This loss also meant that because my students had to explain and defend their project plans and writing processes to each other, they learned more about the skills involved in and the importance of project management than I could ever have taught them in the traditional lecture/presentation classroom format.

In addition to project management, my students also made unexpected discoveries about graphics and page design. Today's students represent a generation that has grown up with the computer revolution. Indeed, most of my students are not even aware of any revolution, and they find desktop publishing technology as ubiquitous and unremarkable as the typewriter once was. They have grown accustomed to systems that allow them to select from a wide variety of font types and sizes or that allow them to paste graphics into their texts with a few clicks. Making such students cognizant of the importance of page design is often difficult because, for them, changing the format of a page is like breathing—in other words, it is just something they do without thinking. Of course, it is precisely because students do not think about it that they often do it badly.

One happy accident that came out of this project was that my technical writing students learned a great deal about how much they depend on page design and formatting in their writing because they could not use it in e-mail. Before we started collaborating with Karis's students, my class had just finished a segment on writing résumés and cover letters in which one of my major foci was the importance of page design in résumé writing. Switching to a medium in which they could not use italics or boldface, change their font size, or even center text very easily had the unexpected effect of driving home everything I had tried to teach them about formatting résumés.

Perhaps the single most important and pervasive reason I have found for continuing to teach writing on wide-area networks is the way it teaches students the importance of audience awareness. During their academic careers, students have learned that most writing in traditional classroom settings is not an act of communication; rather, because they write to audiences that already know more about their subjects than they do, they learn to "perform" rather than communicate. However, networked projects like the one Karis and I did make writing a significant act of communication again. Of course, students in my class knew they were writing for a grade that I would give them, but they quickly learned that they were also writing for people who desperately needed the information they had about how to apply for SBA loans. The Clarkson students required the information the Purdue students had in order to perform well in Karis's class, and as a result, they held the Purdue students accountable for not explaining content clearly and for not anticipating and responding to their needs. I found that the "grading" performed by the Clarkson students had a far greater (and I hope a more lasting) impact on my students' sense of audience awareness than any letter grade or marginal comment I might have made.

The shock of getting a response from a group of Clarkson students suggesting to my students that their peers found their writing inadequate was epiphanic for many of them. More important, when my students realized that the Clarkson students had formed personal impressions about them because of their writing, they were motivated in ways no teacher can replicate. Once my students realized that Karis's students thought that they were "lazy," "stupid," or "ignorant" when they sent them writing that failed to communicate effectively, they were blasted out of their "perform-for-the-teacher" stupor and compelled (in some cases for the first time in their entire academic careers) actually to use writing to communicate.

Problems/Issues Encountered

Every time I decide to take a class online, I am always surprised (and dismayed) by the tremendous amount of advance planning and work that has to go into the projects. I find it ironic that so many school administrators are motivated to shove technology into classrooms because they think it will make teachers more "productive." In my experience, planning a networked collaboration is a black hole that sucks up huge amounts of time and yet is never adequately filled. This project was certainly no exception. Karis and I invested a great deal of time in planning the project, and yet we still ran into difficulties that, in hindsight, we might have avoided with *more* planning.

One of the first items that has to be established in any successful networked collaboration is that the instructors must have compatible pedagogical goals and they must make them explicit. In this project, the degree to which this was a successful collaboration was due to the fact that Karis and I did share compatible goals. We have known each other for years, and we routinely meet, both on the Net and at national conferences, to discuss writing pedagogy. And yet, even though we knew we shared a similar commitment to teaching collaborative problem solving in real-world scenarios, we still found that we had to spend a great deal of time negotiating in detail the exact goals we wanted to achieve in this project. Indeed, we went through three different scenarios and almost three months' worth of e-mail exchanges before Karis came up with the concept that allowed *both* of our classes to achieve our pedagogical goals. I have been involved in projects in which the teachers did not share their goals, and those projects had to be canceled because they were disasters.

Even though we did what seemed a thorough job of planning our goals for this project, we experienced a fair amount of difficulty because I had not realized that we would need to plan to the hour when students would exchange messages. We knew and had provided our students with information about when the project was to begin and end, as well as the dates for the major milestones along the way. Even so, students simply were not able to manage the more detailed aspects of their exchanges without the instructors' intervention. I had hoped that, by making the students responsible for this level of project management, they would learn more about the collaborative process, and in fact, they did learn about project management. But instead of learning it while the project was ongoing, they learned it after the fact because they did not do it well. And because they recognized and learned from their mistakes *post facto*, my students failed to tell Karis's students what information they needed and when they needed it in order to produce their respective reports. Thus, my students' writing suffered.

The main point I want to make here is that instructors have to let students know *exactly* when they have to send e-mail messages to peers at other schools and when they can expect to receive responses from their collaborators. For a networked collaboration like this to work, the instructors must share not only a detailed understanding of their respective pedagogical goals, but they must also share a detailed step-by-step timetable for the project from the very beginning.

One aspect of this project that most appealed to me was that it required students to use writing to communicate critical information to an interested audience. In order to write effective recommendation reports, my students needed to understand the business plans that Karis's students had put together, and conversely, in order to write effective loan applications, Karis's students needed to understand the information my students gave them about how to obtain SBA loans. Each group was dependent on the writing of the other for success. In retrospect this mutual dependency turned out to be a double-edged sword, for while it certainly made the writing more meaningful for some of the students, serious problems emerged in those groups in which either motivation or writing ability was lacking.

In one case, the Purdue students simply could not understand the business plan that one of the Clarkson groups had proposed because the authors of the plan had made unfounded assumptions about their audience. The Purdue students did not know that, when Clarkson students talked about marketing "Ben and Jerry's products," what they were planning was a Ben and Jerry's ice cream franchise. (At the time, the popularity of that product was a northeastern phenomenon that had not yet caught on in Indiana.) As a result of their inability to understand the Clarkson students' business plans, the recommendation reports the Purdue students wrote failed to adequately address the Clarkson students' needs. Indeed, many of my students did a very poor job of providing SBA information to Karis's students. Because I assigned them the task of writing reports on getting SBA loans, many of them treated the reports they sent to Karis's students in the same way they would treat an academic research paper for a history course. In other words, they wrote *about* the SBA instead of explaining *how to get* an SBA loan. However, because the Clarkson students needed to understand SBA loan application procedures in order to write the proposals that Karis was going to grade, simply telling them the history of the SBA was setting them up for failure. Ultimately, Karis and I had to give up on my students' reports, and Karis gave his students the information they needed during one of his class meetings.

Looking back, I would have to say that many of the problems that resulted from this project occurred because I overestimated my students' writing abilities and motivation. In fact, this has been a common problem in many of the online collaborations in which I have participated. In order to make the writing real, we have to make students dependent on each other; yet, if we make one student's grade totally contingent on the motivation and writing ability of another student, we may be setting the stage for a disaster. The designs for online collaborations must, therefore, include ways to make students dependent on each other for information they can reliably provide, and care should be taken so that instructors do not overestimate their students' capabilities.

Another issue that often comes up in any collaborative project, whether face-to-face or electronic, is the problem of deciding how members of a team are going to collaborate. Indeed, as I have already mentioned, my students learned a great deal about project management because the collaborative nature of this project required that they articulate and negotiate all of their assumptions about their goals and understanding of the steps in the project's process. However, all of the negotiating that goes on in a collaboration can backfire if the participants do not have a good grasp of how they are going to resolve disagreements that develop or how to decide when enough brainstorming and discussion has taken place. In this project, there were several occasions on which students ran into these collaborative "logjams" and would have benefited from explicit instruction in how to manage conflicts. Students needed instruction in systems such as Roger's Rules that would have allowed them to bring their online discussions to a closure and make substantive progress toward their ultimate goals.

In traditional classroom formats, when students need correction and guidance, there is little doubt about who has the authority to offer direction (Balester, Halasek, and Peterson, 34); however, in an electronic exchange between two classes at different institutions, the authority we teachers take for granted in traditional classrooms is seriously problematic. In this particular case, Karis and I discovered that we were "pulling our punches" out of a concern about potentially offending the other instructor. I found, for example, that I had no difficulty letting my students know when I thought they were off-track in one of their messages, and yet, if I observed a similar problem in messages from Karis's students, I would refrain from responding for fear of offending Karis or of sending "his" students off in a direction with which he would disagree. Eventually, when we became frustrated with the amount of time we were having to spend negotiating about what I wanted a group of Karis's students to do or what Karis thought a group of my students needed to do, it became clear to us that our failure to establish grounds for shared authority was interfering with the efficient conduct of the project. We decided that we should treat both classes as "our students"; in effect, we gave each other permission to teach our respective classes.

As mentioned previously, one of the major stumbling blocks in this project was due to the fact that my students did a relatively poor job of providing the Clarkson students with critical information about the SBA loan application process. I believe that part of the reason the students did not do a better job of providing this information is that their messages at this stage of the project were not graded. I had assumed that students would be motivated to write well, first, because they were communicating with real people at another institution who needed the information, and second, because they would realize that the good work at the beginning of the process would pay dividends later on when their messages were graded. Both of these assumptions were incorrect. I have learned from this and other similar online projects that students are not motivated to use wide-area networks just because the technology is new and interesting or because they can use it to talk to people all over the world. They like the novelty and the connectivity, but they still do not respond well if they are asked to use networks without receiving a grade for doing so. Consequently, now when I set up these types of projects, I make sure that my students know the exact dates that I expect them to send e-mail messages and that their grades will be directly affected by the messages they send.

Project Two: Class-to-Class Design

Assignment Description

Unlike the project just described, in which students worked in small groups and exchanged messages directly, this project used an e-mail conferencing software package (called Listserv) that allowed an individual student to send an e-mail message to a single e-mail address and then have the message redistributed to every student in both classes. In effect, every time a student sent an e-mail message, everybody received a copy. The project took place in 1989 between James Benenson's English language classes at a small technological university in the suburbs of Paris, France, and my Electronic Publishing class at Purdue. Benenson's students were collaboratively producing a manual for American transfer students on "Life in France" (the whole class wrote one manual). In order to learn about what American students would need to know for such a manual, the students in both classes were to conduct an online discussion (primarily in English) about differences between American and French educational systems and cultures. The French students would then produce their manual based on the differences discovered, and the American students would then make revision suggestions for the manual. American students were required to send two messages a week to the group; their messages were collected in an electronic portfolio, and the portfolio received a grade.

Hardware, Software, and Technical Requirements

Unlike the one-to-one e-mail exchange described in the previous section, the system requirements for a many-to-many conference are high, and most teachers will need to seek the assistance of their institution's computer support staff or computer center. The minimum hardware requirements are a UNIX or VMS workstation connected to the Internet. You will also need Listproc, Listserv, or Majordomo software in order to run your conferences, and all the students and faculty involved will require individual e-mail accounts.

Some Concepts Students Learned

My students were extremely surprised to learn how different the French educational system and culture is from American education and culture. I cannot speak for Benenson's students because, though he and I have collaborated on a number of networked projects, we know each other only electronically; however, most of my students thought they knew a great deal about the French and that there were relatively few differences between French and American cultures. As they began discussing their day-to-day educational experiences, however, they were startled at the depth of the differences between the two systems.

My students generally assumed that anyone who wanted to go to college and had the money to pay for it could do so. They were surprised, therefore, when the French students began describing the different levels of colleges and universities in the French system and the tracking system used to place students in them. For students at a land-grant institution with a liberal admission policy for state residents, the system the French students described seemed (as one of my students put it) "somehow un-American." Another difference my students found startling was the commitment that the French students had to their educational careers. For many of my students, the main college activities were partying and surfing the Net; classes were secondary—or at least that was the way students were supposed to talk about them. When the French students began describing their dedication and commitment to their course work, and when a couple of them commented that the American students did not seem to share this attitude toward education, the American students felt uncomfortable. Of course, as a teacher I have to confess that I enjoyed their discomfort.

One of the more subtle and yet important things that my students learned as a result of this exchange was how to adjust their diction and syntax to meet the needs of non-native speakers of English. In traditional composition classrooms, we often try to teach students how to adjust to the reading level and social register of their audiences, but this is difficult to accomplish in a traditional format. Because of the oral and dialogic nature of e-mail discussions, however, I found that my students learned to adjust their writing to their French audiences almost instinctively and without my heavy-handed intervention.

When Benenson and I began planning the project, I believed that what his students were writing was a manual for American foreign exchange students, and both my students and I assumed from the term *manual* that we would be getting a step-by-step set of procedures for such things as how to find housing, how to exchange currency, how to locate good cuisine, how to register for school and classes, and so forth. Throughout the entire planning process, and in spite of the extended conversations we had with the French students about what they were writing, we assumed this was the kind of manual we would receive. Not until we got the first draft of the actual text did we discover that the procedural "manual" was actually a fictional narrative about a typical day in the life of a French student. This experience slammed home for us the importance of background, cultural context, and language in interpreting the world around us and how much our "realities" are linguistic and social constructs.

Problems/Issues Encountered

Although students really seemed to enjoy the conversation about their respective cultures and educational systems, once the French students began the drafting of the manual, the American students lost interest in the project. Because the Americans did not feel any sense of ownership in the manual, their critiques and revision suggestions were halfhearted. For these kinds of collaborations to be successful, students need to feel a

sense of ownership and responsibility for the final document being produced.

Another serious problem with any cross-institutional collaboration
is differences in schedules. In the case of international collaborations,
this problem gets even worse. By the time the French students' semester
was getting underway, our semester was almost over. As a result, the
American students lacked the time and motivation to give the project
their full attention because they were preparing for finals and writing
final reports.

One of the major differences between an electronic pen pal collaboration, like the first project described, and a class-to-class discussion is the
volume of e-mail that students have to read and respond to. In this particular project, there were more than forty-five students involved in a
single discussion, and all twenty-three of my students were required to
send two messages a week. Students complained not only about having
to read so much e-mail but also that there were not enough topics to go
around. This problem was exacerbated by the fact that though my students did not have any choice about sending mail, Benenson did not
require his students to send messages. Thus, whenever a French student posted a message, all the American students wanted to respond to
it but complained that after two or three responses, there wasn't a lot
left to say. And because not all of the French students were participating, there weren't a lot of messages to reply to in the first place. As a
result of this experience, I have learned that either both instructors should
require that their students post the same number of messages per week
to a conference or neither should require students to post.

Another potentially negative effect of requiring my students to post
to the list when the French students did not was that the American students heard a lot about American issues and less about life in France—
which was what they most wanted to discuss. Consequently, my students felt they were investing a great deal of time reading about topics
with which they were already familiar, topics that, from their perspective, seemed trivial.

One of the more interesting complaints students made during this
project was that I did not respond often enough to their e-mail. I found
this particularly interesting because one of the main reasons I teach online
is to deemphasize my role in the classroom. As is often pointed out, in
an electronic class discussion, the teacher's voice is but one among many,
making it difficult for the teacher to dominate the classroom (Faigley
191). However, as Gail Hawisher and Cynthia Selfe have also observed
in their experiments with networked collaborations, students often resist our attempts to fade into the background. Students consider it their

job to "psyche out" the professor, and when the teacher's voice gets lost in the polyphony of an electronic mail conference, the students feel confused and frustrated by the lack of guidance.

An unfortunate—though not altogether unusual—incident during the course of this project was that one of my students lost his Internet access privileges because he was harassing other people on the Net by sending them sexually explicit e-mail messages. Beyond the obviously distasteful nature of this behavior, the student's loss of Internet access presented me with a serious logistical problem; in order to participate in the class project, he needed to be able to send and receive e-mail messages. At that time, I did not have a policy for this sort of situation, and consequently, I had to develop essentially a whole different set of projects for this one student so he could complete the course. Ever since this experience, I have made it a policy that students who lose their network access privileges due to ethical or legal violations of network policies automatically fail the course or the particular assignment (Howard 6).

I have already mentioned how American students complained that there weren't enough messages from French students to "go around," and how the opportunity to respond to a message from a French student was seen as a valuable commodity. Even more valuable, however, were those occasions when French students responded to an American student's message. In the "microeconomy" of this particular e-mail conference, American students regarded a French response to their individual e-mail messages as golden. Unfortunately, there is a certain amount of competition in any economic system, and in this case, the competition became gendered when male students began complaining that female students were receiving more responses to their messages than they were. I find this particularly interesting because one of the claims often made in support of electronic conferencing is that the discursive practices are more egalitarian since race, gender, class, physical appearance, dress, and other aspects of the physical context are missing in cyberspace. But these male students' responses suggest that there is at least a residue of traditional discursive practices in e-mail conferences.

Project Three: Writing for GopherSpace Design Assignment

Assignment Description

This assignment was given to Professor Dixie Goswami's Writing for International Readers students in 1993. Like the projects previously discussed, this assignment focused on using writing to address a real need, in this case, the need to publish current information about resources in the Languages and International Trade (L&IT) program at Clemson University. Because the L&IT program was a relatively young and inter-disciplinary program, students from a variety of backgrounds and na-tionalities needed information about such diverse topics as how to keep their visas current, how to file tax forms, which faculty on campus had international business experience in a student's target language, what study-abroad or international internship opportunities were currently available, and so on.

In short, faculty and administrators in the L&IT program saw a need for a handbook and up-to-date database that L&IT students could ac-cess twenty-four hours a day and use throughout their academic ca-reers in the program. Putting this information on a gopher server seemed to be the perfect solution because: (1) the electronic distribution system did not have high printing and mailing costs; (2) it could be updated quite easily so that new internship or study-abroad opportunities could be announced at any time; (3) L&IT students and faculty could access the information at any time by connecting to the campus computing system through a modem or a network connection; and (4) its Internet accessibility meant that L&IT students studying abroad could continue to keep in touch with developments in the program. Furthermore, hav-ing students research, design, and write documents for the gopher server as part of the Writing for International Readers course also seemed like an excellent class project because: (1) most students in the course were L&IT majors who already wanted to know the information they would be gathering; (2) students would be further motivated because they knew that they were actually using writing to communicate to a *real* audience; (3) the Internet's worldwide distribution meant that students had to take the needs of international readers into consideration; (4) students would have easy access to all of the information they needed to research in order to "write" the gopher server because this was a local project; and (5) students would gain familiarity with a medium that was and is rap-idly emerging as a primary means of international communication.

Because the entire class was working collaboratively to produce the gopher server, the project needed to be broken down into phases over the course of the fifteen-week semester. Initially, Goswami gave the class the overall project assignment and then brought in a group of "experts" to provide the requisite background information. As one of these ex-perts, my involvement in the project was to introduce students to the electronic publishing potential of "gopherspace," to teach them how to use gophers during the research phase of the project, to help them un-derstand how gophers are designed and maintained, and to help them work out the logistics of creating text files in the correct format and then saving them in a file and directory structure consistent with the gopher server's requirements. Other experts included students, faculty, and administrators in the L&IT program who helped students determine the content and organizational structure for the gopherspace the students were creating. Once students understood what a gopher server was and, generally speaking, what the goals were for the server, they began to do needs-assessment research in order to determine what sort of information prospective students, students already enrolled in the program, and faculty in the program expected to find on the server. They studied their intended audiences in order to establish both what information their audiences needed and how their audiences sought that information. They also studied the organizational designs of other gopher servers around the world in order to collect data they needed for their own server and to better understand how "electronic readers" use and interpret texts in this new medium.

Using the information collected during the needs-assessment phase, Goswami had the students identify broad content areas that the server would need to cover. As a whole group, the students collaboratively roughed out a general organizational design for the gopher server, using a hierarchically arranged branching tree structure as their model. The single group then broke into smaller collaborative groups that focused on collecting more information about their particular "branch" or content area through interviews, questionnaires, database searches, and other research techniques. Once the data were collected, the groups created a directory structure for their particular branch of the server, wrote the documents contained in it, and submitted diskettes containing the files and the directory structure for transfer onto the server itself.[2] The students then conducted usability tests on the completed server by observing how L&IT students actually used the system they had created. Finally, the students developed a formal oral presentation on the entire project in which they described the overall process they had used and what they had learned from the project to university administrators, L&IT faculty, and the experts who had participated in the project. This final reporting phase of the project was critical to the success of the project's design because it allowed the students not only to take pride in their accomplishments but also to step back and analyze the project management process they had used to complete the writing.

Hardware, Software, and Technical Requirements

One of the reasons gopher servers have been so successful on the Internet is that they do not require much to operate and public domain software is available for UNIX, Windows NT, DOS/Windows, Macintosh, or other popular operating systems. In this project, we used a Mac PowerPC 7100 16/340/CD with Ethernet connection and an external 1.2 GB hard drive. The software we used was MacTCP 1.0 and GopherSurfer software.[3] Students also needed access to basic word processors in order to create the text files that were stored on the server.

Some Concepts Students Learned

Because my role in this project was often limited to that of observer, I was not always privy to students' comments; however, one of the most impressive elements of Goswami's design for this project was the way she had students critique each aspect of the collaborative writing process. Composition teachers know that often one of the most difficult concepts to teach students is that writing is a complex process that involves far more than simply encoding thoughts on paper. Goswami's design forced students to give up this product-oriented approach to writing and encouraged them to develop a metalinguistic understanding of the complex, recursive steps involved in a successful writing process. It forced them to examine how invention, research, and audience analysis, for example, directly influenced the writing they produced. Thus, as one student observed in her final presentation, she wished they had done a more thorough job on the gopher server, but ultimately she thought that really did not matter because they had learned a writing process they could use in their future business careers.

Organizational structure is addressed in every writing classroom. It is rare to find a teacher who does not use outlines or skeletons or some other visual representation technique to teach students about organization. However, when we teach students about organization, we are often not very effective in helping our students understand *why*, from a rhetorical perspective, they need to organize their writing. Consequently, though we may require our students to make outlines of their essays, the students do not actually use them when they write because they do not understand why they are needed.

Teaching students to write for gopherspace addresses this problem because, basically, a gopher is little more than a high-level outline, with either text or subcategories embedded underneath each topic listed on the outline. For example, if gopher users came to the L&IT gopher server and selected "Information for International Students and Visitors at Clemson University" from the opening screen, they would see the menu shown in Figure 11.1.

Now, if you look at Figure 11.1 as an outline for an essay on information that international students need to know, it is fairly unremarkable. The fundamental difference here, however, is that unlike an outline for

```
┌─────────────────────────────────────────────────────────────────┐
│ Information for International Students and Visitors at Clemson University │
│                                                                   │
│ —>1.  Campus Organizations/                                       │
│    2.  Families and Family Services/                              │
│    3.  Important Requirements/                                    │
│    4.  Living in South Carolina/                                  │
│    5.  OIPS - Office of International Programs and Services/       │
│    6.  University Services/                                       │
│                                                                   │
│                                                                   │
│ Press ? for Help, q to Quit, u to go up a menu        Page: 1/1   │
└─────────────────────────────────────────────────────────────────┘
```

Figure 11.1. A Sample Menu from L&IT Gopher

a traditional paper, this "outline" is *rhetorical* because it is intended to *be used by a reader*. Gopherspace clarifies the rhetorical purpose of organizational structure for students (particularly if you ask them to perform usability tests on the gopher, as was done in this project). Students recognize that, if users are going to locate the useful pieces of information, they must be able to navigate through the "outline." In other words, though in a traditional classroom we often talk about the logical presentation of information and an essay's "flow," students often have a hard time with this concept because it is abstract. But in gopherspace, hierarchical arrangement and logical subordination are not abstractions; they are the *sine qua non* of a successful gopher server. Students understand that the implied relationships among the words they select for gopher menus have a significant rhetorical impact on the reader. And once they have grasped this concept in gopherspace, they have an easier time understanding how it applies to traditional print-based writing.

In an important early study on computers and composition entitled "Seeing It on the Screen Isn't Really Seeing It," Christina Haas describes how computer writers often find it difficult to revise their texts on the screen, preferring instead to work from printed copy. Haas's study suggests that the reading behaviors of electronic readers differ significantly from those of print readers, and she hypothesizes that screen size and the limitations of human memory may, at least in part, cause these differences (25). The typical computer monitor will not display nearly as much text as the traditional 8.5" x 11" sheet of paper, and once an electronic reader has seen more than two screens full of text, "the size of the text makes it difficult to hold an accurate representation in memory" (25). Haas argues that size constraints make it easier to misread electronic texts. These same limitations might also explain why electronic readers are extremely uncomfortable with long, dense passages of text.

In this project, students learned quickly that, in order to be successful gopherspace writers, they would have to eschew the long, detailed analyses that had served them well in their history and traditional composition classes. Instead, they had to learn to adapt their writing for electronic readers. They learned to break their topics down into "chunks" that could be covered in no more than two screens full of text. They also learned to use short paragraphs and to provide plenty of white space on the screen in order to encourage readers to continue reading. In sum, they learned to adapt the traditional writing style they had learned in other courses to the new constraints of their medium and the needs of their readers.

It has become a cliché these days to talk about "getting lost in cyberspace," but the phenomenon is real, and students writing for gopherspace must learn to contend with it. The problem with gopherspace (and the World Wide Web, for that matter) is that it is extremely difficult for readers to maintain an understanding of context, which they need in order to interpret effectively what they are reading. Gophers make it possible for writers to link their text to any other gopher anywhere in the world without the reader ever being aware that the linkage has been made. Consequently, if the authors of the text are not careful to provide context, readers can impose an inappropriate context on the writing. For example, in an early draft of the L&IT gopher, one menu option was simply titled "Faculty." Now, normally one would expect that, because this option was accessible from Clemson's L&IT gopher, the faculty listed were Clemson faculty. However, it turned out that this menu option was actually a link to Vanderbilt University, and because Vanderbilt had not provided any context for their faculty pages, if readers did not read carefully, they would never know they were not actually getting information about Clemson faculty. These kinds of misprisions, resulting from the authors' failure to provide an interpretive context that would aid the reader, were commonplace; consequently, students learned a great deal about the role of context in the ways that readers interpret texts and the importance of providing a context in writing in order to assist the reader.

Problems/Issues Encountered

One of the more frustrating problems I had during this project was getting students to use filenaming conventions and directory structures appropriate for transfer to the gopher server. Unfortunately, the computers we had to use as our gopher servers were located in a restricted-access facility, so the students could not actually put their files directly on the system themselves. Instead, students were supposed to provide us with Macintosh formatted diskettes that had the text files stored in the correct folders or subfolders for their particular branch of the gopher server. We could then simply copy the contents of the students' diskettes straight onto the server's hard drive, and because the platform we had planned to use was also supposed to be a Mac, we would not have to worry about filenames or the directory structure because copying from a Mac-formatted diskette to a Mac hard drive would retain all of the original names and subfolders.

Unfortunately, for most of the project we were not able to use a Mac as the server, and even when we were, it was never as easy to get files onto the system as it was supposed to be. Initially, we had to use a DEC Alpha running an OSF/1 operating system as the gopher server, which meant that we had to manually recreate all of the students' subdirectories from their Mac-formatted diskettes, then transfer each individual file across the network to the correct subdirectory we had just created on the DEC Alpha, and, finally, change the ownerships and access permissions OSF/1 uses to maintain security on the system. This turned out to be a huge undertaking and a logistical nightmare, but the whole thing became even more complicated when we realized that we had not figured out a system for students to revise their files. Once the server was operating and students saw what their work actually looked like on the gopher, they began to find problems that they wanted to fix. However, because they could not get access to the files directly, they had to write memos telling us how they wanted us to rename subdirectories or replace text files with new text files they gave us. But because the students had no idea how the OSF/1 operating system worked, and because they did not have a map of the subdirectory structure for the server, they ended up telling us, for example, to rename a particular file that was located eight or ten levels down in the directory structure, where we just plain couldn't find it. The result was that we became frustrated with the students' inability to provide accurate and sufficiently detailed information that would allow us to make the changes they wanted, and the students became annoyed and frustrated because we kept sending them messages telling them that they had not given us the information we needed to make their changes. Indeed, the level of frustration on both sides was so high that I resolved never to do another project like this if students could not directly access their own files on the server.

In order to display text properly on virtually any type of platform, gopher servers require that text files be saved in ASCII (American Standard Code for Information Interchange) format, and it is rare to find a word processor today that cannot save files in an ASCII format. At the beginning of the project, I thought that the ubiquitous nature of ASCII was a plus because it meant that students could use whatever software they were accustomed to, and the faculty would not have to take time away from class discussions of project content to teach technology. But there are subtle differences in the ways word processors save ASCII files that "gear heads" like myself tend to overlook because we have tacit strategies for dealing with them. In retrospect I now see that my technological arrogance generated all sorts of difficulties for students because it meant that I failed to provide them with adequate instruction in how to save properly formatted ASCII files.

One of the first problems students encountered was that, though many word processors can save files in ASCII format, they do not call it ASCII. For example, Microsoft Word, Claris Works, MacWrite, and several other packages use the terms "Text Only" and "Text Only with Line Breaks" for ASCII. And, in addition to the obvious problem of using a different name for ASCII, there is a big difference between a "Text Only" ASCII file and a "Text Only with Line Breaks" ASCII file. Even if students knew that "Text Only" was an ASCII format, they would not get the desired results when the file was put on the gopher server. Gopher software needs a line break at the end of each line of text so that it knows where it is supposed to stop printing each line of text on a screen. Without line breaks, the gopher software tried to display an entire paragraph of text on a single line, and as a result, the students' text ran off the right-hand side of the screen where it could not be read.

The problems did not stop with the "Text Only" versus "Text Only with Line Breaks" distinction, either. Even if students correctly saved their files as "Text Only with Line Breaks," they still ran into trouble if their word processors used smart quotes, smart apostrophes, em dashes, or other characters not defined in the ASCII character set, because the gopher software did not know how to display these characters. But the biggest problem by far was when students produced their text in a proportionally spaced font such as Arial instead of a nonproportionally spaced font such as Courier. The reason this was a problem can be illustrated by comparing the following two lines:

Now is the time for all good citizens to come to the aid of their country.

```
Now is the time for all good citizens to come
to the aid of their country.
```

Obviously, the line printed in the Arial font is much shorter, even though both fonts are nominally the same size—10 point. Now when students saved files as "Text Only with Line Breaks," the word processor automatically inserted a line break at the ends of the existing lines, so that, in the case of the first line, a line break would have been inserted at the end of "country." On the second line, however, two line breaks would have been inserted, one before the second "to" and the other at the end of "country." This seemingly trivial difference turned out to have serious consequences. When readers tried to access the file from the gopher server, in many cases their software would display the text in a nonproportionally spaced font such as Courier, and so the line would run off the right-hand side of the screen.

These kinds of trivial yet vexing technological problems seriously disrupted the project because they drew students' attention away from the larger, conceptual issues of the course and forced us to teach the technology instead of the writing process. In order to make the technology more transparent and less distracting, it is important to have all students use the same software and hardware (as much as possible) so that teachers can reliably anticipate problems students will encounter and can provide instructional materials that will push the problems into the background where they belong.

In the previous section on what students learned in this project, I discussed how students learned to adjust their writing to the needs of electronic readers, who tend not to read long passages of electronic text, and how this encouraged students to develop a wider repertoire of voices. However, there was a flip side to the students' recognition that they needed to keep their texts short, preferably not more than one screen full. Basically, the two problems that emerged were, first, that the short length of the files and the amount of content that needed to be covered encouraged the students to have far too many menu levels, with too many options on each menu in the server. Second, trying to keep the length of the text short led some students to use a writing style that was heavy on nominalization and short on the prosaic descriptions an international student would need in order to understand the material.

To understand why the number of menus and available options on each menu was a problem, consider the following scenario. Let us assume that you were an international student who wanted to learn more about the computing facilities available to you if you enrolled in the L&IT program at Clemson. If you started at the top level of the Clemson University gopher server, you would first have to select "Academic Departments," which would take you to another menu. From there you would have to select "College of Liberal Arts," which would give you yet another menu, from which you would have to select "International Resources" in order to arrive at the opening screen for the L&IT gopher server shown in Figure 11.2.

```
┌─────────────────────────────────────────────────────────────────────┐
│ International Resources                                                │
│                                                                       │
│ —> 1. 00 About This Gopher                                            │
│     2. Bibliographies and Other Internet Sources For International Educat../│
│     3. Clemson Affiliates with International Experience/              │
│     4. Directory of Administrative offices and Staff/                 │
│     5. ESL Directory/                                                 │
│     6. INS International Student Employment Regulations (gopher.vt.edu)/│
│     7. Information for International Students and Visitors at Clemson Uni../│
│     8. International Directory of Faculty/                            │
│     9. International Employment Resources Gopher/                     │
│    10. International Internships and Study Abroad Programs/           │
│    11. International News and Information (Skidmore)/                 │
│    12. OIES - Office of International Education & Services (Iowa U.)/  │
│    13. Office of International Prog, NAFSA (U. of Col., Ft. Collins)/  │
│    14. Office of International Services (Vanderbilt)/                 │
│    15. The Language and International Trade Major at Clemson University/│
│                                                                       │
│                                                                       │
│ Press ? for Help, q to Quit, u to go up a menu          Page: 1/1    │
└─────────────────────────────────────────────────────────────────────┘
```

Figure 11.2. L&IT Gopher Server Opening Screen

Now, from the fifteen options available to you on this screen, you would need to select "Information for International Students and Visitors at Clemson," which would give you another six options (see Figure 11.1 for details). Having already gone through five levels of menus without having read a single text file, you would next need to select "University Services" in order to get yet another menu, this one with twenty-one different options, one of which, at long last, is "Computer Facilities." Finally, seven levels deep into the gopher server, your perseverance is rewarded with the text file shown in Figure 11.3 below. If you are like most people, at this point you are probably saying to yourself, "I went through all that for this? I wanted to know if I would have access to Pagemaker on a fast PC, but instead all I learned was the names of buildings I have never seen and phone numbers I can't use since there's no area code given."

Of course, to be fair, it has to be pointed out that the students were not unaware of these kinds of problems. Because they did usability testing on the server, they learned that readers were often disappointed when they had to go through a long series of menus to get information that did not satisfactorily answer their specific questions. They even complained that there was not much they could do about the gopher interface and that the technology was designed as a database intended to serve up discrete chunks of information.

The problem for writing teachers, then, is whether to hold students responsible for failing to produce texts that measure up to standards intended for print when they are using technological tools that work against those standards. As Nancy Kaplan has pointed out, "Each tool brings into the classroom embedded conceptions of what exists, what is good or useful or profitable, and what is possible with its help. Teaching agendas, however, are already informed by ideologies" (27), and when those ideologies are informed by old technologies, we as teachers have to first recognize the conflict and then find new methods (such as usability) as standards by which we assess students' writing.

Project Four: Webheads Design

Assignment Description

The Webheads were professional communication graduate students who enrolled in a course called "Researching and Designing Online Documents and Electronic Publishing" that I taught in the spring of 1995. The students good-naturedly came to call themselves "Webheads" because their major assignment for the semester asked them to collaboratively research, design, produce, and usability test an electronic brochure for Clemson's Master of Arts in Professional Communication program, which they published on the World Wide Web.[4]

The Division of Computing and Information Technology (DCIT) is located in the Computing Facilities in R.F. Poole Agricultural Center basement (656-4307, 3494).

DCIT supports student coursework and research through a network of on-campus computers. This network consists of an MVS mainframe with 128 megabytes of main memory and several VAX computers. Three VAXes, along with intelligent disk and tape controllers, from what is known as a VAX cluster running the VAX/VMS operating system. Another VAX computer running the Ultrix operating system is also available.

User Locations:
Remote sites containing a variety of microcomputers, terminals and peripheral equipment are maintained in Martin, Daniel, Lee, Lowry, Kinard, Brackett and Sirrine halls; Hunter Chemistry Laboratory, Cooper Library, and Poole Computer Center.

Figure 11.3. L&IT Gopher Computer Facilities Information

The Webheads project was broken down into six phases. The first was the problem definition and needs-assessment phase, in which the students[5] determined that primary audiences for the brochure were people seeking enrollment in the program and students and faculty already in the program who needed specific details about the program. During this phase, students conducted interviews with the target audiences in order to determine what kind of information they required. The second phase involved teaching the students to tag text in HTML, the formatting language used to produce World Wide Web pages. As students were learning HTML, they were also studying other Web sites in order to develop an understanding of the interface designs that other Web authors were using. Specifically, students read Brenda Laurel's book *Computers as Theatre* to develop a theoretical framework that allowed them to see how interface designs are driven by metaphors (for example, the desktop metaphor used in the Macintosh operating system [Selfe and Selfe, 486]). Once students understood their audiences' needs and had developed an understanding of what could be accomplished with Web pages, they entered the third phase—collecting the information that would go into our Web pages. The fourth phase entailed actually deciding which metaphors and navigation systems would structure our pages and then actually creating the Web pages. Finally, the fifth and sixth phases involved usability testing of the Web pages and revising the pages based on the results of our testing.

Hardware, Software, and Technical Requirements

Like gopher servers, one of the strengths of the World Wide Web is that a Web server will run in every popular operating system. In this project, our main server was the same Mac PowerPC 7100 with Ethernet connection and 1.2 GB hard drive that we used as the gopher server in the gopherspace design project. We also used a DEC Alpha workstation running OSF/1 and HTTPD whenever we needed to create interactive forms; this was not really necessary, but because I did not know AppleScript very well, I could not write the necessary code for the Mac. As for Mac software, we used MacTCP 2.1 (required to connect to the Internet), MacHTTP 2.0 (the Web server software for Macs), HTML SuperEdit (a program that automated the HTML tagging process for the students), and Webmap 1.0 (which allowed us to create clickable maps in our pages).[5] In addition to all of these shareware packages, we also found that we needed access to a flatbed color scanner and Adobe PhotoShop for graphics development.

Some Concepts Students Learned

It is important to bear in mind that the students who were taking this course were graduate students in professional communication and that most of them were there because they wanted to prepare themselves for careers in industry. They recognized that to be competitive today, it is not enough to say you have been trained as a technical writer. As Pat Sullivan has pointed out in her excellent article, "Taking Control of the Page," the desktop publishing revolution of the 1980s means that professional communicators can no longer afford just to be good writers and editors; they also have to demonstrate typographical, page layout, print management, and graphic design skills to be successful (51–52). And now that a new revolution has begun, one that promises to replace desktop publishing with multimedia authoring and CD-ROM publishing, professional communicators must add interface design to the list of skills required to be competitive.

Authoring Web pages turns out to be the perfect opportunity for students to develop all of these skills because the World Wide Web is the first true electronic publishing and distribution system on the Internet. Unlike the technologies discussed in the previous projects, the Web allows authors to produce publications in which they can change a font's size and type, display graphical images, play audio or video clips, and create hypertextual links to other Web pages anywhere on the Net. It is also surprisingly easy to learn, particularly as there are now a number of HTML editors available. Indeed, creating Web pages is no more difficult than formatting text with a word processor, and there are already large numbers of elementary school children with their own Web pages.

Because Web pages allow authors to control the layout of the page, the size and type of fonts used, and the placement of graphical elements on the page, HTML authoring requires many of the same skills found in desktop publishing. However, there is a fundamental difference—Web pages are hypertextual in nature and intended to be read solely on a computer screen. In other words, because Web pages are accessible only through the computer, effective HTML authoring not only requires desktop publishing skills but also an understanding of interface design techniques.

In the Webheads project, the principal goal of the course was to teach master's candidates in the professional communication program a theory of interface design they could use to produce all kinds of hypermedia and online documents, and the primary theory we used was based on Laurel's observation that "designing human-computer experience is not about building a better desktop. It is about creating imaginary worlds that have a special relationship to reality—worlds in which we can extend, amplify, and enrich our own capacities to think, feel, and act" (32–33). Consequently, we focused on metaphors because interface designers use them as conceptual maps to provide users with familiar landscapes. Thus, in our electronic brochure we spent a considerable amount of time pursuing different kinds of metaphors that would allow our users to navigate through the content we wanted them to read.

Based on our needs-assessment research, we knew that users of our pages wanted to know about such things as admission requirements, financial aid, foreign language requirements, faculty backgrounds, required courses, and so on. As interface designers, our challenge was to come up with a metaphor that would allow us to develop a navigation system to guide our readers through these different content areas in a way that would be both easy to understand and engaging. We considered a number of different metaphors and themes for this purpose. One popular option was to involve users in a parody of *Monty Python and the Holy Grail*. The idea here was that the users would be asked to play the role of a character in the movie and would move from page to page, roughly following the movie's plot, learning information about the MAPC program as they went. Similar approaches were suggested for *Adventures of Huckleberry Finn* and *Star Wars*. A visual metaphor was suggested, using Clemson's tiger paw as a map. Each of the toes of the paw was labeled with the different content area, and users could click on whichever toe most interested them.

Ultimately, we chose both visual and thematic metaphors for the pages. We decided to use the visual metaphor of the tiger paw for people who wanted to locate specific pieces of information about the program very quickly. However, for the casual Web browser who was only looking at the pages out of idle curiosity, we decided to use a thematic metaphor based on a fantasy quest. The idea here was that, by making the Web pages into a kind of game in which users went on a quest through the MAPC Castle in search of the Tree of Knowledge, we would encourage the casual user to stay in the pages longer. See Figure 11.4 for the first page of the fantasy quest.

In his book *The Electronic Word*, one of Richard Lanham's central theses is that using technologies in composition classrooms encourages students to "look AT texts" rather than "THROUGH" them (5). In a literate culture where the traditions of print have become reified, Lanham argues, students tend to look through the text, or rather to "look on ideas as in themselves they really are, unmediated by language" (74). In other

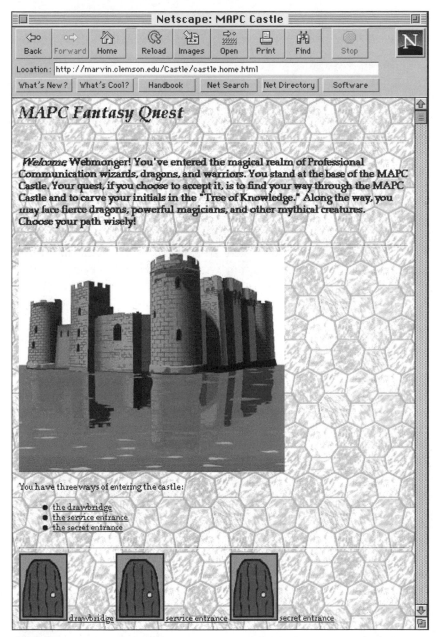

Figure 11.4. The Fantasy Quest

words, students fail to see how they are manipulated by language and how, as Marshall McLuhan long ago observed, the medium massages the message.

Particularly because of its focus on the use of metaphor and interface design, this project encouraged students to look carefully *at* texts. The newness of the World Wide Web medium defamiliarized text for the students and caused them to focus on its rhetoric.

Problems/Issues Encountered

In most of the collaborative projects I have assigned, there have always been a few students who did not pull their weight and who allowed other members of their group to complete their work for them. In this project, however, the students complained whenever any of the other students completed some portion of the project without *everyone* having been involved. The students were so excited by the medium and the project that they felt cheated if they were not involved in every aspect of it and became quite angry when they thought someone was doing "more than their fair share." Though it was sometimes uncomfortable, this was one of the nicest problems I have had in a collaborative project.

Because one of the most attractive features of the World Wide Web is that it allows HTML authors to include graphics in their pages, it should come as no surprise that everybody wants to have lots of graphics in their Web pages. Unfortunately, if you are not an artist, it can be difficult to find all of the graphical images you would like, and you may be tempted to scan images of photographs and artwork from published books and magazines. This was certainly the case for the Webheads. We had more than seventy Web pages in our electronic brochure, and almost every one of them required at least one graphical image. Consequently, we had to be on guard constantly to make sure that we did not obtain graphics that would violate any copyrights.

Another problematic area with the Webheads project concerned incorporating photographic images of female students and faculty in the MAPC program online. There are an estimated thirty-five million people using the Internet, with more coming online every day, and not all of these users are nice people. Because our Web pages could be accessed by virtually anyone on the Internet, several of us—particularly female graduate students and faculty—were concerned about how these pages might be used, as our original plans called for a collection of Web pages that would serve as "electronic résumés" and that would have photographs of individual students and faculty in the program as well as information about how to contact them. However, because I have had some unfortunate experiences with sexual harassment and electronic "stalkers" on the Net over the years (see Howard), we decided not to use people's photographs without first sensitizing students to this problem. We also discouraged students from putting their home phone numbers and postal addresses on their personal Web pages.

Finally, we had a problem with the ways in which other students and faculty in the department characterized what we were doing. We all want our colleagues to recognize and respect the work that we do because, no matter where you work, success depends on the goodwill of colleagues and administrators. In this project, however, some of my colleagues in the English department were a bit perplexed by what we were doing. For many of them, discussions about "networking," "interface design," and "HTML tagging" just did not sound as though they had a lot to do with the study of language and literature. Indeed, I think some of them, from their perspectives outside the class, thought that what we were doing really belonged in the Computer Science Department. However, had they been privy to our in-class discussions about the ways in which metaphors shape interpretive experiences and the ways in which a textual encounter is a dramatic, rhetorical event, I think they would have seen the connection. Indeed, when I described what we were doing to a Shakespearean colleague in the department, he remarked that Shakespeare would have been very much at home in our class. Still, as Lisa Gerrard has also pointed out, "many faculty members in English departments view computer-assisted instruction with indifference, disdain, or outright hostility" (5), so, if we are going to use technology successfully in our classrooms, one of the first things we have to do is find ways to bridge the gap between print-based pedagogy and electronic pedagogy. At the very least, we have to ask our colleagues to come in and observe our classes so they do not form impressions of our work on the basis of stereotypes and partial information. We have to state the value of projects like these as clearly and bluntly as possible; in this course, for example, three of the students had lined up positions in industry doing HTML tagging and usability testing before the course was completed. Administrators love to hear that our students got positions at IBM because of a course, and though it is sometimes repugnant to "toot your own horn," we have to make these kinds of successes known if we are going to get the resources and commitment necessary to bring technology into our classrooms.

Conclusion

Looking back on these four projects, it would be nice to offer some pearls of wisdom that educators could use in any context requiring the integration of technology and writing pedagogy; however, I suspect those "pearls" would really be little more than sweeping generalizations. Still, I would have to say that the process of designing and executing these projects probably reflects many of the typical stages other teachers in the computers and writing community have gone through over the past five years. Like most teachers, I started with simple e-mail pen pal exchanges and then moved to more complex technologies, but in the process, I found my pedagogical designs also had to change.

Technology is not the neutral tool many would have us think; it shapes what and why we teach, sometimes in unexpected ways. You can use a hammer to pound a screw into a piece of wood, but a screwdriver might provide a better result. Technological tools are not that much different. Different networking tools encourage different writing behaviors from students and require teachers to adjust their project designs accordingly. Asking students to write a traditional essay for a "general audience" in networked environments is essentially asking students to work against the technology. Networks are designed to put people in touch with people, and, as a result, they work best in writing classrooms when the writing assignments are firmly rooted in project-based learning. In all four designs, for example, what worked was having students write for "real" audiences with "real" purposes. The technology made it possible for the students to see that their writing was first and foremost an act of *communication* that took place in a particular context with a particular group of readers. Yet, while this is the greatest strength of the technology, it is also the case that, the more a project's design forces students to ignore the real needs of their audiences on the Net, the more the technology will work against the students and the teacher. In the exchange between the French and American students, for example, my failure to provide a realistic reason for communicating with each other on the Net was responsible for many of the problems we experienced. When we were communicating simply to use the technology, we had difficulties. Instead, the project should have been designed the other way around, so that we were using the technology because we needed to communicate.

Looking back, then, I would have to say that the single most important conclusion I have come to is that the technology of the Net is a compelling rhetorical force in the composition classroom. When it is tied to role-playing scenarios and project-based learning opportunities, the Net can be a powerful pedagogical tool for teaching writing. Used in this way, there is no better means for teaching students that writing is first and foremost a public act of communication with consequences for writers, readers, and their communities. Yet, when teachers ignore the rhetorical situations and contingencies the Net creates, when they try to use technology for technology's sake, when they try to simply relocate traditional assignments that require students to write for "general audiences" into networked environments, then technology can work against them. It is perhaps clichéd to say so, but the Net is not a panacea. As writing teachers, we have to be prepared for the ways in which teaching on the Net will force us to change our assignment designs, our grading practices, our authority in the classroom, and the increased amount of time we will have to spend preparing to teach if we and our students are to benefit from teaching and writing on the Net.

Notes

1. Karis has also discussed this project in a 1994 paper, "Using Cases to Teach Electronic Communication and Intrafirm Politics," co-delivered with Stephen Doheny-Farina at the Annual Convention of the Conference on College Composition and Communication.

2. The file structure the students developed may be located via gopher at gopher.clemson.edu in the Academic Depts/Liberal Arts/International Studies directories.

3. At the time of writing, these software packages were available on NCTE's gopher server at ncte.clemson.edu in the Internet Resources: Mac Starter Kit folders.

4. At the time of writing, the URL for the pages the Webheads developed was http://marvin.clemson.edu/mapc/mapc.home.html.

5. The HTML SuperEdit software has been upgraded and, at the time of writing was called WebWeaver. These software packages were available via gopher at ncte.clemson.edu in the Internet Resources: Mac Starter Kit folder.

Works Cited

Balester, Valerie, Kay Halasek, and Nancy Peterson. "Sharing Authority: Collaborative Teaching in a Computer-Based Writing Course." *Computers and Composition* 9 (1992): 25–40.

Faigley, Lester. *Fragments of Rationality: Postmodernity and the Subject of Composition.* Pittsburgh: Pittsburgh University Press, 1992.

Gerrard, Lisa. "Computers and Compositionists: A View from the Floating Bottom." *Computers and Composition* 8 (1991): 5–15.

Haas, Christina. "Seeing It on the Screen Isn't Really Seeing It." *Critical Perspectives on Computers and Composition Instruction.* Ed. Gail Hawisher and Cynthia Selfe. New York: Teachers College Press, 1989. 16–29.

Hawisher, Gail. "Notes Toward a Pedagogy of E-Mail." Annual Convention of the Conference on College Composition and Communication, Nashville, 1994.

Howard, Tharon. "Mapping the Minefield of Electronic Ethics." *Telecommunications Is Not About Computers*. Ed. C. Edgar and S. Wood. New York: Teachers & Writers Collaborative (in press).

Kaplan, Nancy. "Ideology, Technology, and the Future of Writing Instruction." *Evolving Perspectives on Computers and Composition Studies: Questions for the 1990s*. Ed. Gail Hawisher and Cynthia Selfe. Urbana, IL: NCTE, 1991. 11–42.

Karis, William, and Stephen Doheny-Farina. "Using Cases to Teach Electronic Communication and Intrafirm Politics." Annual Convention of the Conference on College Composition and Communication, Nashville, 1994.

Lanham, Richard A. *The Electronic Word: Democracy, Technology, and the Arts*. Chicago: University of Chicago Press, 1993.

Laurel, Brenda. *Computers as Theatre*. Reading, MA: Addison-Wesley, 1993.

Selfe, Cynthia. "Politicizing the Educational Terrain of Electronic Mail." Annual Convention of the Conference on College Composition and Communication, Nashville, 1994.

Selfe, Cynthia, and Richard Selfe. "Politics of the Interface." *College Composition and Communication* 45 (1994): 480–504.

Sullivan, Patricia. "Taking Control of the Page." *Evolving Perspectives on Computers and Composition Studies: Questions for the 1990s*. Ed. Gail Hawisher and Cynthia Selfe. Urbana, IL: NCTE, 1991. 43–64.

IV Reflecting Dialogically

12 The Future of Dialogical Teaching: Overcoming the Challenges

Dawn Rodrigues
University of Texas at Brownsville

The contributing authors of *The Dialogic Classroom* provide readers with in-depth portraits of teaching and learning and inspire readers to build similar learning environments. But they do not address a key issue: Who will fund these computer environments in classrooms across the country? If circumstances do not change on most campuses, it is unlikely that many readers will be able to replicate the kinds of activities described in earlier chapters.

The projects described in *The Dialogic Classroom* illustrate exemplary uses of technology. They fit the definition of the ideal computer-equipped learning environments suggested by David Smallen, Director of Information Technology Services at Hamilton College, who has argued that the only use of technology worth funding is that which "heightens the opportunities for interactivity between students and teachers" (16). The learning experiences are also similar to those described in the Harvard Assessment Seminars report, for they center on "interactive classes" and "interactive relationships" in the student learning process (Light). In the language-rich classrooms described in this book, students have opportunities to learn more, and with more impact, than in traditional classrooms. Readers will no doubt want to replicate the projects and activities described in various chapters on their own campuses. But will that be possible?

Ideal learning environments are not usually cost-effective. Thus, the trend on most of our nation's campuses is to build labs, not classrooms. Robert C. Heterick Jr., the President of Educom, has recently pointed out that "relatively few campuses have classrooms appropriately equipped for 'high tech' teaching" (14). Discussing the national trend on campuses that runs directly counter to what one might assume after reading the essays in this collection, he points out that nearly all campuses have concentrated their energies and resources on creating "open laboratories" with personal computers and workstations, not computer-equipped classrooms (Heterick 5). We sometimes get the mistaken impression that the courses we read about in literature on computers in English studies always occur in computerized classrooms. This is not the case at institutions described in this collection, nor is it common elsewhere. At Colorado State University, for example, where many faculty have published accounts of their teaching in computer-intensive classes, only a small portion of the courses take place in the computer classrooms. The situation is similar at Michigan Technological University, where, except by special arrangement, classes do not take place in the computer labs described in journal articles. And in this collection, Michael Day's successful integration of mailing lists and newsgroups into technical writing courses, described in Chapter 8, took place in a classroom with only one computer. Campuses try to leverage the number of computers they have, making them serve the greatest number of students.

At a time when our nation's college and university administrators are under pressure to find cost-effective approaches to technology, we have to do more than ask our departments to provide computer classrooms for their own use. We must be prepared to justify our request for more computer-equipped classrooms, and we must be certain that our colleagues will be willing to put forth the effort it takes to learn how to teach in electronic spaces. Dialogical teaching is demanding; the results are not always obvious and the technology is expensive. Yet, if we believe that interactive, dialogical approaches to teaching with technology are critical for many students' success in college, we need to be willing to convince others on our campus of their value.

We need to persuade academic computer directors, other faculty in our departments, and academic administrators of the importance of dialogical teaching for all college students, but especially for those attending institutions where most classes are held in large lecture halls. We need to be prepared for resistance: Academic computer directors will be concerned about such issues as cost-effectiveness and staffing requirements; our faculty colleagues will require sufficient professional development and support; and academic administrators will want us to identify specific outcomes of instruction—gains in language and literacy skills or other kinds of growth—that support our claims that dialogical instruction is worth funding.

Most decision makers want to use the Information Superhighway to "beam" cheap education to everyone's telecomputers: "They think it's a great idea. A master teacher will lecture 10,000 learners! Economies of Scale!" (Ehrmann 13). Academic computer directors and other administrators such as vice presidents for technology often do not think about pedagogical implications affecting students. If computers can save an institution money and enhance the school's image, many administrators are happy. They are especially delighted if they can showcase "whiz-bang," cost-effective, dramatic uses of technology; they barely notice small projects such as those described in this book.

Contributors to a recent Educom publication repeatedly stress their commitment to linking the expansion of technology with productivity gains. Here are a few comments:

> We should be encouraged to design learning environments that provide sufficient efficiencies to permit us to operate within our budget constraints. Many of our new education models will feature attenuated contact between the teacher and the student in formal classroom settings. (Heterick 12)

> There is also still much to learn about the costs and benefits associated with bringing a group of people into the same place (classroom) at the same time vs. having them interact using computers, video, and telecommunications. Each institution, department, and faculty member must find the right balance in forming combinations of traditional practices and materials with new ones. (Heterick 67)

> We have yet to hear of an instance where the total costs . . . actually decline while maintaining the quality of learning. (Heterick 89)

Rather than encouraging faculty to teach in computer classrooms, academic computer directors more typically focus their efforts on massive software projects such as SYNERGY, a consortium of more than twenty-four colleges that use computer-directed instruction (CDI) to guide students step by step through various modules in a given course and to deliver the results via e-mail to students and faculty. Or they extol the benefits of distance learning projects such as those at Washington State University, where "real-time interactive video enables students and professors to both see and speak to one another" (Tucker 14). It is the size and scope of these projects that make them noteworthy approaches to technology. Small developmental writing classes such as Jeffrey Galin and Joan Latchaw's do not lend themselves to economies of scale. Tharon Howard is particularly frustrated by productivity arguments that are so common in computing journals: "I find it ironic that so many school administrators are motivated to shove technology into classrooms because they think it will make teachers more 'productive.' In my experience, planning a networked collaboration is a black hole that sucks up huge amounts of time and yet is never adequately filled" (214).

Unlike faculty, academic computing directors tend to value technology over pedagogy because their information derives primarily from academic computing journals and conferences. For example, the Case Studies section of a 1996 issue of *Syllabus* features a set of virtual classroom courses using the Web at Virginia Commonwealth University. Nowhere in the article is there any mention of how the Web is used in the classroom or how teachers might encourage students to exploit opportunities for interaction provided by the chat areas. Just because the course provides a space for interactivity does not mean that a teacher's pedagogy maximizes the potential of that interactivity.

Academic computing directors generally view computers as supplements to classroom instruction, not sites for teaching. The notion of "teaching" in a computer classroom is thus foreign to many academic computing directors and other administrators, who do *not* typically take it on themselves to foster what the American Association of Higher Education calls "deep change" or transformative change in pedagogy. As a result, only a limited number of computer classrooms are funded on a given campus.

Should academic computing directors be partners with faculty, helping them develop the kinds of teaching environments that their disciplines endorse? I think they should. But not everyone agrees. The Director of Information Technology Services at Hamilton College, for example, thinks that academic support staff have far too much work just keeping pace with technology installations and routine maintenance. He says faculty should look out for themselves:

> Evangelism in the name of technology is not possible! Software development and continuing support for discipline-specific software must be the responsibility of the faculty member. It is not an effective use of scarce resources to have the computing staff try to convince faculty to use computing technology to improve student learning. Leadership in this area must come from the faculty and senior academic administrators. (Smallen 59)

Even if we cannot get academic computing to provide much assistance, at least we need to enlist their cooperation. Can they be persuaded of the value of equipping classrooms with computers, if funding allows it? Perhaps. But academic computing administrators will need to be convinced that faculty are willing to both teach in these new classroom spaces and develop their technological expertise. The authors of this volume chose contributors such as Bruce Dobler and Harry Bloomberg in part because they offer technological and disciplinary expertise. Susanmarie Harrington and William Condon consulted with the psychology professors and, in doing so, integrated the technology with the pedagogy and research, as suggested by the title of this volume. Such faculty can address both academic and administrative issues and problems.

If academic computer staff are unwilling to do the professional development, then faculty who already have technological competence (like those mentioned above) may need to provide much of the professional development for their colleagues—that is, if their colleagues are interested in developing that expertise. Although faculty may be able to attend academic computing training sessions that focus on software (Powerpoint, Photoshop, or Pagemaker, for example), they rarely find on-campus workshops or seminars to help them design computer-intensive interactive instruction suitable for dialogic teaching. For that they must turn to books such as this one, national projects such as Epiphany, or training programs at national conferences in their disciplines.

However, faculty interested in pedagogically based interactive technologies are in the minority, another reason why few campuses have computer-equipped classrooms. Not all teachers are flexible; not all teachers can tolerate ambiguity; and not all teachers are as willing to risk failure as were the teachers in this collection. Dialogical teaching implies a major shift in pedagogy and will not appeal to all faculty, most of whom are more comfortable in lecture-based classes. When teachers do move to technology, they typically request training in the use of software that does not require them to change their ways of teaching. Trent Batson ponders the difficulty of helping faculty understand "what it means to teach and learn in an environment as radically different from the traditional classroom as a computer-networked writing classroom" (191) and notes that it is important for "writing teachers [to] find bridges from the familiar terrain of the current traditional classroom to carry them to this brave new world" (192). Yet, until faculty understand the potential of dialogical teaching, they cannot make educated judgments about whether or not they would want to explore its potential.

Faculty have to see technology as worth their time and effort. Unfortunately, many faculty will not be convinced. As David Smallen has noted, faculty are not willing to integrate new technologies into their teaching if the result is only a "marginal increase in student learning (over that achieved by traditional methods) and a [major] investment in time to learn to use the technology, integrate it with other course materials, [and] deal with problems related to the technology itself . . ." (54).

Helping Faculty Understand Dialogical Teaching

Even though many faculty resist pedagogical change, some are willing to take on the challenge of technology. We need to help them design their own computer-intensive interactive classrooms by explaining and demonstrating our pedagogy for them. We can develop pilot projects and invite colleagues into our classes. Then they can see models of dia-logical teaching in action. As a starting point, however, we need to be able to explain the terminology and its implications for instructional design.

A Definition of Dialogical Teaching

Although the term "dialogic classroom" as used in this book implies the presence of a computer, it would not have to. The term is comprehen-sive enough to account for a range of approaches to instruction, from classrooms without computers, to the "network pedagogy" classes de-scribed by Fred Kemp and Trent Batson that foreground online, virtual interaction (Chapters 7 and 10), to the workshop-based classroom of Howard's students or Dobler and Bloomberg's WebWeavers (Chapters 11 and 4), to the interactions surrounding the development of the hypertext software in Galin and Latchaw's and Dene Grigar's classes (Chapters 5 and 2). In these courses, students have regular opportuni-ties to rethink, reexamine, and reflect on their experiences.

Galin and Latchaw have explained how Bakhtinian theory provides a lens through which to understand the interactions and habits of mind they have named "dialogical" (Chapter 1). Faculty who are familiar with the work of Paulo Freire may also recognize some similarities between "liberatory pedagogy" and dialogical teaching. Ira Shor, who has adapted Freirian pedagogy for U.S. classrooms, explains liberatory classroom design: teachers sequence teaching activities so that students can move from a passive attitude toward learning to an active one. Shor writes that "the gradual emergence of a dialogue amongst peers, mediated by a commonly acknowledged problem[,]" is what we need to strive to create if we are trying to create a powerful environment for learning (Freire and Shor 36). According to this definition, many of the dialogical classrooms described in these chapters are also "liberatory."

By labeling what we do, we give teaching in computer-equipped class-rooms credibility; we also provide our colleagues with a way of seeing connections between seemingly disparate uses of technology in very different kinds of courses (e.g., Howard's or Day's technical writing projects and Grigar's students' work on Gertrude Stein's poetry). Being able to name and describe what we do can also help us communicate our needs to others and help them understand the differences between passive, lecture-based classes and interactive, reflective ones.

The term "dialogical classroom" provides a useful way for scholars in the field of computers and composition to describe a broad array of computer-based pedagogies. Discussions addressing issues, concerns, problems, and successes of such pedagogies are invaluable to teachers who often feel isolated and marginalized from other department members. Listservs such as the Alliance for Computers and Writing (ACW) are lifelines for many of us in the field. Queries on new conferencing software for collaborative learning, redefinitions of plagiarism (for Web-based projects), effective arguments for constructing educational MOOs, and electronic documentation usually receive instant feedback. Many scholar-teachers have come to rely on this dialogical community as a rich and essential resource.

The concept of "dialogical classrooms" can also help us construct linkages with professors in other disciplines across campus. At some institutions, history, art, chemistry, and engineering professors have developed strategies for teaching that follow the same approaches in this book. For example, Jack Wilson at Rensselaer Polytechnic Institute has designed "studio" engineering and science classes that encourage students to collaborate dialogically with one another; likewise, Barbara Olds and her colleagues at the Colorado School of Mines work collaboratively with engineering professors in classrooms that include both engineering software and writing tools. By forming alliances with faculty in other departments, we are more likely to be able to convince administrators of the value of computer-based teaching.

Some Features of Dialogical Instruction

Although each teacher in the classes described in this collection developed pedagogies appropriate to his or her own context, and although each teacher's version of dialogism is quite different from other teachers' approaches, there are some commonalties:

1. Dialogical teachers encourage students to work together as they re-think, re-examine, and reflect on their experiences.

    Dialogical classrooms are project oriented and often student centered. Instead of becoming more productive or time efficient, the goal for faculty who engage in interactive teaching with technology is to become more *effective* in new ways of teaching and new ways of reflecting on their teaching. Instead of focusing exclusively on content, the authors of these chapters believe teachers should encourage students to value the experience of learning and interacting continually with one another and with teachers as they learn how to negotiate problems and work on projects. Teachers design experiences that allow students to develop their own goals and determine their own courses of action. Dialogical classes tend to be small; but even large virtual classes can be dialogical if the curriculum is designed around groups of students working together on common projects.

2. Dialogical teachers continually and willingly rethink pedagogy through the lens of available technology.

Dialogical teachers are willing to design new approaches rather than merely adapt tried-and-true strategies for teaching. They are also ready to interrogate teaching practices and revise their instruction if technology makes more effective practices possible. The authors of the chapters in this collection describe dialogic learning experiences—with students and teachers learning from and with one another. They also imply rich inner dialogues between technology and pedagogy. Galin expected technology to change things, but even he did not anticipate that "The Quest offered . . . a way to interpret his own practice[s]" (55). Howard stresses the importance of adjusting pedagogy to fit available technology: "Different networking tools encourage different writing behaviors from students and require teachers to adjust their project designs accordingly" (238).

3. Dialogical teachers are action-researchers, continually learning from classroom interactions and adapting continually to the changing circumstances.

By observing his students' interactions with the online writing medium, Howard noticed "how much they depend[ed] on page design and formatting in their writing because they could not use it in e-mail" (213). Theresa Doerfler and Robert Davis explain that, until they began using the Confer software, it was difficult for them to imagine "how it might alter the teaching and the learning in our classrooms" (177). Only after they interacted with the software in the context of teaching could they see its possibilities. Only then could they recognize how students might work within a computer-mediated environment: As they explain, "the software gave the class and the conversation a collaborative, dialogic form. Our role as teachers was to revise our expectations—and those of our students—to suit the technologic capability" (187).

These features of dialogism can give faculty an overall sense of what they should expect. With the expectation of changing their teaching, faculty will be ready for the time-consuming but exciting task of envisioning their own classroom projects and developing the technical skills necessary to carry them out.

Assessing Technology Innovations

Conducting classroom research, which examines outcomes of interactive teaching projects like those described in this volume, is one way to convince academic affairs administrators to fund computer-equipped classrooms for dialogical instruction. Even though our courses may not be cost-effective in the traditional sense, if we can identify the specific "value" they add to students' college experiences, we may garner sufficient campuswide support for our efforts.

Unfortunately, most faculty in English departments who have developed considerable expertise in evaluating written composition have almost no experience evaluating classrooms for other purposes and goals. Rather than attempting to work in isolation, they might collaborate with institutional researchers or with colleagues in other disciplines in designing their research. As the authors of several chapters in this collection have demonstrated, when instructors integrate new technologies into their curriculum, teaching becomes a team effort between instructor, instructional designer, faculty across disciplines, and academic support staff. This set of shared responsibilities makes the task of assessing technology even harder. Some technology assessment specialists feel that new models of assessing technology must be found (Twigg, "Information Technology"). As Educom President Robert Heterick explains, "The highly quantitative, input-based assessment methodologies that have been introduced to date seem far too simplistic for this more complex model" (19).

We need to think dialogically as we design our research. What do we want to know? What are our claims? Instead of evaluating only through the lens of traditional disciplinary approaches to evaluation (such as portfolio assessment of writing or holistic assessment), we should let our questions and answers emerge as we experiment: What is going on in our classrooms that is worth assessing? Are students talking more with one another? What is the quality of that talk? Are students more likely to be bidimensional thinkers, more tolerant of one another's viewpoints as a result of being enrolled in dialogical courses? Do students learn how to collaborate more efficiently or effectively in these classrooms? Do students develop deeper understandings of literary texts when they collaborate on hypertext projects? Do students develop confidence as learners more readily than they do in large sections? Do students develop better facility as critical thinkers? We need to develop assessment instruments that capture the kinds of interactions leading to growth in language learning and thinking.

We should look to institutional research offices for assistance in designing evaluation tools. Institutional researchers know what kinds of data will convince legislators of the value of an institution's curriculum. For example, we might track retention of students in our classes. Or we might test whether the students who have taken small, dialogical classes do better in large, distance-learning courses than other students.

We have some evidence that information technology can be used effectively to enhance courses and that it can result in student learning. Robert Kozma and Jerome Johnston have noted that various Educom Award winners have found that information technology can serve as a catalyst for or enabler of teaching and learning, stressing that the key issue is making sure that technology resources are used as tools to support instruction and learning outcomes (30). We should, therefore, begin to document the important learning that goes on in courses such as those described in this collection. We need to demonstrate what components of these courses heighten students' desire to explore and examine meanings. We need to determine whether any compromise positions are worth pursuing, such as providing a few computers in many classrooms or using a computer classroom for only key components of a course.

Ultimately, we need to determine whether some of the benefits of small classroom teaching can be replicated in distance education courses. A recent study reported in the *Chronicle of Higher Education* has found that students in the virtual section of a course scored twenty points higher at the end of the term than students in the face-to-face classroom. The researcher is reasonably certain that it was the collaborative pedagogy, not the technology, that made a difference; students in the virtual course did more collaborating online than their counterparts did in the face-to-face classroom.

There may be a synergistic relationship between small, dialogic teaching and effective large-scale instruction: those faculty who gain experience designing interactive, face-to-face courses may, in the process, develop the skill to help with larger projects. Faculty who are the most effective in small, dialogical settings may be able to discover creative, yet cost-effective, ways of teaching large sections. Already, there are some indications that this is happening: many faculty who have been pioneers in the use of computers in writing classes are becoming leaders in online distance education, judging by self-reports of several computers and writing specialists on the Alliance for Computers and Writing Listserv (ACW-L) (March 1997).

What mix of face-to-face and virtual classrooms will we have in the future? Much depends on what we learn about "how and where . . . human interaction can be most effectively employed" (Massy and Zemsky 13). Even if distance learning can be designed to promote questioning and to encourage group collaboration, not all students can be expected to succeed in virtual courses. Small, interactive, face-to-face courses may certainly need to be provided as an alternative for students who need them.

Against a backdrop of technocentric reports about computer software and hardware, about massive projects connecting many students, the pedagogies described in this collection provide an important contrast to the mainstream ways of integrating technology into teaching. No one is suggesting that students will learn "more" in dialogical classrooms or courses—not even Grigar or Galin and Latchaw claim that. What the authors *do* claim is that students have opportunities to learn more powerfully in interactive, dialogical classes. If research confirms these claims, the future of education may lead to dialogical rather than one-way instruction.

Works Cited

Case Studies. *Syllabus* 9.3 (1995): 80–82.

Ehrmann, Stephen C. "New Technology, Old Trap." *Educom Review* 30.5 (1995): 41–44.

Freire, Paulo, and Ira Shor. *Dialogues on Transforming Education: A Pedagogy for Liberation.* New York: Macmillan, 1987.

Heterick, Robert C. *Reengineering Teaching and Learning in Higher Education: Sheltered Goves, Camelot, Windmills, and Malls.* CAUSE Professional Paper Series #10, Denver, 1995.

Kozma, Robert, and Jere Johnston. "The Technological Revolution Comes to the Classroom." *Change* 23.1 (1991): 10–30.

Light, Richard J. *Explorations with Students and Faculty about Teaching, Learning, and Student Life.* The Harvard Assessment Seminars, Second Report, 1992.

Massy, William F., and Robert Zemsky. "Using Information Technology to Enhance Academic Productivity." *Report from Educom National Roundtable Discussions, June 1995* (9 September 1998) <http://www.educom.edu/program/nlii/keydocs/massy.html>.

McClure, Polley Ann. "A Third Opinion from Camelot: 'Growing' Our Academic Productivity." In Heterick 116–21.

McCollum, Kelly. "In Test, Students Taught on Line Outdo Those Taught in Class." *The Chronicle of Higher Education,* 21 February 1997, A23.

Smallen, David L. "Reengineering of Student Learning? A Second Opinion from Camelot." In Heterick 58–61.

Tucker, Robert W. "Distance Programs: Models and Alternatives." *Syllabus* 9.3 (1995): 42–46.

Twigg, Carol A. "Navigating the Transition," *Educom Review* 29.5 (1994): 41–44. (9 September 1998) <http://www.educom.edu/web/pubs/review/reviewArticles/29516.html>.

———. "Information Technology<EM>Enabling Transformation." In Heterick, 97–107.

West, Thomas W., and Stephen L. Daigle. "Comprehensive Universities: Refocusing For the Next Century." In Heterick, 92.

Glossary

ASCII This acronym stands for American Standard Code for Information Interchange, a universal code of letters, numbers, and punctuation marks. This worldwide system allows thousands of word processing programs and many different kinds of computers to "read" each others' texts. However, documents sent in ASCII text lose some formatting features, such as bold, italics, and font size.

asynchronous communication The sharing of electronic information, verbal or textual, in which the sender and receiver are not communicating directly at the same time. E-mail and voice messaging are examples of asynchronous communication.

authoring The process of creating a document or application using an authoring program such as HyperCard, HyperStudio, Storyspace, Toolbook, or Authorware. These user-friendly, object-oriented programs allow developers to create sophisticated-looking programs without much programming experience. For example, novice users can build HyperCard stacks by adding prefabricated objects such as buttons, fields, and icons to new cards in a stack. Users can also import text, image, sound, and video with a minimum of training.

branch (branching structure) The path to a subset of information in a hypertext document. A branch might be programmed to help users explore one particular issue or concept. Taking a different "route" would allow users to follow another direction or area of exploration. For instance, in a Storyspace fiction, the reader might follow one path leading to a chain of novelistic events. However, clicking on a "hot link" might lead to a subtheme or alternate plot.

buttons Small graphical images that are scripted to serve navigational and other purposes within hypermedia documents or applications. Usually, the browser uses a computer mouse to set the cursor on a button before clicking the mouse to initiate the action.

card In HyperCard, a unit of information, which might include writing fields, buttons, or images, that is presented inside a rectangular frame that resembles an index card. Cards may be interlinked and usually appear in groups called *stacks*.

CD-ROM A read-only compact disc (CD) that stores up to one thousand megabytes of information, or about 714 times the information a standard high density floppy disk will hold.

CMC (computer-mediated communication) Communication forms that rely on networked computers for a medium to send and receive messages, text, or visual images. Some common examples of CMC for educational purposes are MOOs, conferencing and discussion software like CommonSpace, Daedalus Interchange, and Connect.

CommonSpace This networked writing software facilitates collaborative creation and revision of documents. Writers and educators working on different platforms, writing in various word processing programs, and corresponding from separate locations, can use this common workspace to post a document and generate side-by-side columns for feedback in the "margins." Authors can use these columns to evaluate and synthesize comments from multiple reviewers.

computer simulation A representation of at least some aspect of a real-life occurrence or situation on a computer. Computer simulations are often used in training or problem-solving applications.

Confer An asynchronous conferencing software that functions like an **asynchronous** threaded e-mail reader. Discussion threads are initiated by users, and each response within a thread is listed sequentially. Thus, the first message of the first thread would be archived as 1:1. The eighth message of the fourth thread would be archived as 4:8.

cyberspace A term coined by novelist William Gibson to describe virtual realities in his cyberpunk novels. This term now refers to networked computer environments, specifically the Internet.

Daedalus The Daedalus Integrated Writing Environment (DIWE) combines simple word processing, **synchronous** messaging, and writing heuristic and bibliography mechanisms with a menu-driven file management feature that allows students to turn in documents to a network and distribute them easily without fear of tampering or overwriting by other students. Like other network-based group-ware such as **Norton Connect** and **Aspects**, Daedalus software is best known for the writing environment that it supports, including its synchronous component, Interchange.

design A combination of features that result in the visual appearance and readability of a document, including layout, type style, graphics, and other visual features. In hypertext, design also involves the way text is interlinked and presented.

distance education Education as it is offered to students by remote systems, whether by computer network, satellite television, or other media.

download The process of transporting a file from a remote computer system to a personal computer. Often used in relation to receiving a file by FTP (file transfer protocol) from a computer linked to the Internet.

e-mail An electronic text messaging system operating on a computer network that allows a user to send, receive, and store messages.

ENFI (Electronic Networks For Interaction) is a real-time writing environment for the networked computer classroom, in which **synchronous** communication software allows teachers and students to explore, collaborate, and expand on ideas in class in writing. ENFI was pioneered by Trent Batson at Gallaudet University so that hearing-impaired students could have written discussions.

field A space for typing in text such as a file window in a word processing program. In programs such as HyperCard and Storyspace, the user places the cursor inside an area (field), clicks the mouse, and begins inputting text.

font A complete set of letters and numbers with a consistent style, size, and design. Common fonts are Geneva, Helvetica, and Courier.

FTP (file transfer protocol) A protocol which allows files (text and/or images) to be transferred electronically from one computer system or machine to another. For instance, a user can transmit information, such as an article or other lengthy document, from a networked user-account to his or her personal computer or vice versa. Most network systems utilize FTP software for users to upload and download files.

GIF (graphical image format) A compact image format established by the online service Compuserve for transferring images quickly over modem lines. It has become a standard image format on the World Wide Web.

gopher A database system that is menu-driven and is accessible via the Internet. Its popularity is waning as the World Wide Web replaces much of its function, but thousands of sites still exist.

gopher server A computer linked to the Internet that uses the gopher menu system to provide information to users at remote sites.

gopherspace The set of computers linked to the Internet that uses the gopher menu system.

graphical user interface (GUI) The common visual system that provides a bridge for the user between hardware and software. An example of a GUI would be the use of icons, windows, and other programmable objects for navigating the World Wide Web. Another aspect of a graphical user interface might be the use of pull-down menus.

hardware The physical components of a computer system. Hardware may include items such as the monitor, keyboard, printer, scanner, or any other device attached to the computer system.

heteroglossia Mikhail Bakhtin writes in "Discourse in the Novel" that the incorporation of heteroglossia and its stylistic utilization in the comic novel are represented by two features: (1) The "multiplicity of 'language,' voices from all walks of life" and (2) the incorporation of these languages and their concomitant socioideological belief systems which serve both to reflect authorial intentions and simultaneously to unmask and destroy these same belief systems (311).

hierarchical structure A design structure that places and orders information in terms of priority or importance. For instance, branching hypermedia and gopher spaces are generally arranged as hierarchical structures. Complex Web sites often provide multiple layers of subordinate nodes. In a program such as HyperCard, certain programming functions are "behind" others. One can create stacks, cards, backgrounds, buttons, and fields. Many cards may exist in a given stack, and several buttons and fields may exist on top of a single background within a card. Users can only work on attributes of a stack one layer at a time.

homepage A World Wide Web document that serves as a table of contents or indexing structure for a group of documents that may or may not be housed at the same site. The document is what the Web browser displays when a URL is accessed. Homepages are used to promote personal and professional interests, advertise products, and disseminate various kinds of information.

HTML (hypertext mark-up language) The ASCII text-based code used to format documents for the World Wide Web.

HyperCard A hypertext application for the Macintosh operating system that relies on the metaphor of a stack of index cards for the user interface. Sometimes called an information "toolkit," HyperCard can be used to collect, organize, and present information by building groups of cards, or stacks, which can be linked together. Thus, related information can be accessed immediately by a click of the mouse on a "hot link." Some HyperCard applications are used as tutorials or resource tools and may include text, images, and sound.

hypermedia A term used to describe the interlinking of textual information and other forms of media, such as audio, video, and photographic images. Many designers are using the multimedia capabilities of the World Wide Web. For instance, a teacher's syllaweb for a film course might include movie clips, graphic images of a vaudeville movie house, and sound bytes.

hypertext A term conceived and coined by Ted Nelson, who described it as natural language text with the computer capability for interactive branching. The branching occurs through electronic links among words and images in a database. The nonsequential nature of hypertext provides an openness and freedom highly valued by users who enjoy associational thinking and reading. The immediate linking from one referential point to another cannot occur through print text. Thus the experience of reading changes dramatically in such electronic formats.

    exploratory hypertext A term Michael Joyce defines as "delivery technology." Users may navigate freely along nodes and paths according to interest, in a sense exploring. Phrases such as "cruising the Net" or "exploring the Information Superhighway" suggest a kind of passivity, because users must browse through paths designated by designers and cannot alter the paths and nodes.

    constructive hypertext A term that signals a higher level of interactivity than with exploratory hypertexts. Users can develop their own hypertext webs or add to, delete, or significantly change initial information in a pre-existing hypertext by constructing new paths, links, and nodes.

icon A small graphic incorporating an easily understood symbol, like a tiny folder for storing information, to direct the user to a certain software function.

image map An image that has been programmed so that users can click on multiple regions with a mouse and access different hypertext nodes. Most image maps trace the cursor position within the image in pixels on the screen. When the user clicks the mouse button, the cursor coordinates of that spot on the image are matched against the preset regions to determine which node has been selected.

interface See **graphical user interface**

Internet A loose network of voluntarily maintained computers that began with four sites in 1969 called ARPAnet. The basic structure of the network allows different kinds of computers to be used, following a standardized transmission control protocol (TCP). Its flexibility allows many different types of client and server computers.

Internet Relay Chat (IRC) The equivalent on the Internet of large-scale conference calling. Messages typed in a chat "room" on an IRC channel are seen by all users connected to that channel.

JPEG image An image format created by the Joint Photographic Experts Group of the International Standards Organization (ISO), designed for compressing full-color or grayscale images. It is used mostly with photographs, and along with GIF, has become a standard for presenting images on the World Wide Web.

link The connection between two nodes of information in a hypertext document. When a user selects a link, the node is accessed.

listserv A program used to accept e-mail submissions from individual users that then distributes these messages directly to e-mail accounts of subscribers. The term is also used to refer to the automated mailing lists themselves.

menu A textual list or graphical representation of choices that may be selected by the user of a computer program or hypertext document.

MOO (multi-user dimension, object-oriented) A text-based virtual reality in which users interact in real time within a pseudophysical dimension: players talk in rooms, can move between rooms, interact with objects ranging from chairs to automated bartenders, and build their own spaces. MOOs are outgrowths of MUDs or multiple-user dungeons (see also **MUD**).

MPEG A compressed video imaging standard created by the Moving Pictures Experts Group, an International Standards Organization subcommittee. MPEG video clips are becoming more common on the World Wide Web as a way of presenting information.

MUD (multi-user dimension, domain, or dungeon) The precursor to MOOs, MUDs were originally designed as text-based virtual realities for real-time Dungeons and Dragons gaming over the Internet. Unlike MOOs, most MUDs allow only those who have acquired wizard status to add onto the system. MUD and MOO users can create characters for themselves (see also **MOO**).

multimedia A term used to reflect diverse platforms for presenting media. It suggests a mix of media information that may include written text, audio, video, and still pictures as ways of communicating meaning.

navigation The processes that users follow to move electronically through a hypertext document or application, or from page to page on the World Wide Web.

netnews This client software is used to access and manage Usenet newsgroups.

network A group of computers connected by wires that allows users to share information and peripheral hardware such as printers. Most networks use a central computer or a cluster of smaller machines as hosts to facilitate quick connections and file sharing.

Netscape A sophisticated World Wide Web browser, or GUI, that serves as a common interface for documents formatted in hypertext transfer protocol (HTTP), file transfer protocol (FTP), gopher searching, and Usenet News browsing (see also **Web browser**).

node Generally understood as a location of individual documents within a hypertext web (i.e., each individual page on the World Wide Web, a card in HyperCard, or a Storyspace box in Storyspace). Also, a computer that is linked to the Internet.

online A wide-ranging term for using computers connected to a network. It can apply to computers that are directly connected to local area networks (LANs) and/or the Internet and to computers connected to networks via modems.

operating system The first layer of software that a computer uses to perform basic functions such as disk operations and start-up.

path A sequence of related nodes that are linked by the author of a hypertext for users to follow, or the serendipitous progression of nodes that a user chooses to follow within a hypertext web or application.

platform A unique computer system such as IBM, UNIX, or Macintosh with proprietary hardware and system software on which other computer programs can run. Most software is platform-dependent. For instance, one may say "This version of WordPerfect was written for the Windows platform. There is another version for the Macintosh Power PC platform."

port A location in which data goes into and out of a computer. For instance, World Wide Web servers often "listen" on port 80. The term can also mean a place of physical connection on a computer for a data transfer cable.

program (or computer program) A set of codes that instructs a computer to perform specified tasks. Some programs such as HyperCard, Storyspace, and Toolbook provide an authoring (see **authoring**) environment so that teachers can develop sophisticated-looking, independent programs that are designed for their own course purposes.

real time Describes the experience of sharing information on a networked computer and receiving feedback immediately. For instance, in a real-time chat session, a person can talk to another individual at a remote site and receive immediate response, whereas in asynchronous communication such as the use of e-mail, the feedback is not immediate (see also **synchronous communications**).

remote site A computer serving files from a location other than the location to which a user is connected.

screen In addition to referring to the viewing surface of a computer monitor, the term often refers to the viewing area of a software program, such as the screens a person may scroll through when viewing a document on a word processor.

script A subroutine, or subset of programming code, that facilitates a specific operation of a piece of software. For example, every object within a HyperCard program is scripted in a language called HyperTalk. One script in The Borges Quest is eight single-spaced pages long. A simple HyperTalk script for a button that beeps when you click it looks like this:

```
on mouseUp
   beep
end mouseUp
```

software Applications or programs written to enable computers to perform complex tasks.

stacks A term used mainly in HyperCard to describe groups of cards that are organized in a specific hierarchy.

Storyspace A specialized hypertext program that allows the user to link on-the-fly Storyspace frames (which look like miniature boxes). These storyspaces can contain text, images, sound, and/or video files. The program is designed primarily for print manipulation that allows users to view their linked nodes from three different organizational perspectives. Some of the first hypertext novels were written in Storyspace.

synchronous communication Sharing of information in a real-time mode. Synchronous communication is analogous to holding a conversation with someone (see also **real time**).

Telnet Software used for accessing a remote location on the Internet from a local connection. Telnet uses a text-only protocol. One can, for example, connect to MOOs by using Telnet, or access a personal e-mail account that resides in California from a Telnet connection made in Israel.

UNIX A large-scale operating system designed by AT&T for networked computers. It is one of the most popular operating systems for running Internet file servers.

URL (universal resource locator) Also called an address, a URL is the standardized form for communicating the locations of files and Web sites on the Internet.

Usenet A system of newsgroups, primarily available via the Internet, that includes thousands of discussion areas, including academic topics of interest. The user may read and post articles.

videodisc Laser-imprinted multimedia storage system capable of storing large amounts of data on disc, similar to CD-ROM but of greater diameter.

virtual community A group of people with common interests who frequently interact in an online environment. Howard Rheingold, in his book *The Virtual Community*, discusses how support groups form around particular issues, such as parenting, medical conditions, and politics.

virtual reality An alternate reality to the physical world that exists only as electronically mediated experience (see also **MOOs** and **MUDs**).

virtual space An environment that is artificially created and accessed by networked computers, as opposed to space found in the physical world.

VMS (virtual memory system) A large-scale operating system developed for Digital Equipment Corporation's line of 32-bit computers. It facilitates networking and multitasking in much the same fashion as AT&T's UNIX operating system.

Web browser A software application that allows the user to access and view hypertext files on the World Wide Web. Netscape is the most commonly used Web browser.

Web site A set of related pages or hypermedia documents on the World Wide Web that resides in publicly accessible files connected to the Internet and can be accessed from remote computers.

Index

Abrams, M. H., 136
Academic computing directors, 246–47
Academic discourse, 94, 175
  providing access to, 100
ACW. *See* Alliance for Computers and
  Writing
Adobe Acrobat, 69
Adobe Photoshop, 71
AFS. *See* Andrew File System
Alliance for Computers and Writing, 249
  Internet address of, 147
American Sign Language, 134
American Standard Code for Information
  Interchange, 227
Anchors, 77
Andrew File System, 85
Annie John (Kincaid), 177
APIs. *See* Application Program Interfaces
Application Program Interfaces, 69
ARPAnet, 163 n 2
"Arts of the Contact Zone" (Pratt), 174,
  187
ASCII. *See* American Standard Code for
  Information Interchange
ASCII files, 228
Asynchronous communications, 15, 178
  student reactions to, 182–85
  See also E-mail
Authority, 203–4
  classroom, 135
  in networked class, 216–17

Bakhtin, Mikhail, ix, 192, 207, 248
  on heteroglossia, 65 n 1, 194–95
  theory of discourse, 4–5, 43, 197
Bakhtinian dialogics, 13–14
Balester, Valerie, 138
Barker, Thomas T., 94
Bartholomae, David, 8, 20 n 3, 136
Basic tags, 77
Basic Writing, 47, 56
Batson, Trent, 17, 134, 138, 146, 163 n 1,
  247, 248
BBEdit Lite, 73, 87

BBS. *See* Bulletin Board Services
Benenson, James, 218–220
Berger, John, 45
Berlin, James, 135
Black, Max, on metaphors, 14
Bloomberg, Harry, 67, 246, 248
"A Blue Coat" (Stein), 29, 41
Bolter, Jay David, 17–18, 21 n 9
Borges, Jorge Luis, 16, 44
Borges Quest, 16, 17, 43–65, 108–9
Bournellis, Cynthia, 145
"A Box" (Stein), 29, 35
Briggs, John, 126
Bruffee, Kenneth, 96, 135–37
Buber, Martin, 45
Bulletin Board Services, 164 n 2
Bump, Jerome, 137
Bush, Vannevar, 21 n 9
Butler, Wayne, 138

CAI. *See* Computer-assisted instruction
"A Carafe, That Is a Blind Glass" (Stein),
  29
Carter, Locke, 138
Centrifugal forces, 5
Centripetal forces, 5
Chabay, Ruth W., 94
  on writing assignments, 95–96
Chat, 140
Chronicle of Higher Education, 252
Ciampa, John, 20 n 1
Cinematography, grammar of, 90
Clarity, 112, 115, 116–20, 124, 126–27
Classroom, authority in, 135
Class-to-Class Design, networked
  classroom project, 217–21
CMC-based instruction, 139
  problems with, 147–49
  See also Networked classrooms
CMCs. *See* Computer-mediated communi-
  cations
Cognitive chunking, 96, 98
Cognitive issues, 6
Coherence, 120, 130

263

Editors

Jeffrey R. Galin (jgalin@wiley.csusb.edu) is assistant professor of English at California State University, San Bernardino, where he teaches all levels of computer-facilitated composition courses. He received his B.A. from Emory University, M.A. from the University of Alabama, and Ph.D. from the University of Pittsburgh. In addition to developing Web-based resources for teaching like MOOcentral and WWW for Newbies, he has presented numerous conference papers and workshops, has served on a range of outreach projects in rural Alabama and western Pennsylvania, and has spent the past seven years integrating technology into teaching. He is currently co-editing a volume of essays entitled *What Makes Teaching Good in the Late Age of Print* and is writing on issues of joint digital/print publication. Other areas of interest include the history of educational reform, literacy, and multicultural education, which are reflected in his dissertation research, *Sixty Years of Multicultural Education Unmasked: A Study of Discursive Strategies and Institutional Practices.*

Joan Latchaw (jlatchaw@cwis.unomaha.edu) is assistant professor at the University of Nebraska at Omaha, specializing in composition and rhetoric. She received her B.S. from the University of Minnesota, M.F.A. and M.A. from the University of Pittsburgh, and Ph.D. from the University of Pittsburgh. She has delivered papers and organized workshops and seminars on critical thinking, writing in the disciplines, and computers and writing. As director of Freshman Writing at Shepherd College, she reconceived the Basic Writing Program, which led to *Houses of Pain*, a student publication on rape and abuse. As director of first-year composition at North Dakota State University, Latchaw began incorporating technology into the classroom, developing computer-facilitated courses at all levels. She has recently co-authored with Jeff Galin a paper on intellectual property. Her article on criti-

271

cal thinking appeared in a recent issue of *Inquiry: Critical Thinking Across the Disciplines.* Other professional interests include graduate education, writing program administration, and poetry writing, her first love and entré into the field of English.

Contributors

Trent Batson (batsontr@shu.edu) is a faculty consultant at Seton Hall University in the Teaching, Learning, and Technology Center. He is the former director of Academic Technology and professor of English at Gallaudet University. His groundbreaking work with teaching writing using networked computers in 1985 was the prototype for the current "networked classroom" model of using computers to teach writing in universities. He directed the five-university ENFI Project from 1987 to 1990, work for which he received the 1989 EDUCOM/NCRIPTL award for best innovation in writing using computers; he has also twice been a finalist for the Computerworld Smithsonian Awards. In the early 1990s, he started, along with Fred Kemp and John O'Connor, the Alliance for Computers and Writing. In 1995, he was funded for the Epiphany Project, a forty-site project to create systematic support for writing faculty to integrate computers into their teaching, a project for which he shares leadership with his wife, Judy Williamson. He works with AAHE's national Teaching, Learning, and Technology Roundtables program and was one of the founding facilitators in this program. He has published and spoken widely on computers-and-writing issues.

Harry Bloomberg (hpb+@pitt.edu) is a software engineer for the Economics Department of the University of Pittsburgh. He is also an Internet consultant specializing in online commerce and Webmastering. Bloomberg has also worked in the defense industry designing mission-critical software for a variety of weapons systems. He holds a B.S. in electrical engineerng from the University of Pittsburgh and an M.S. in computer science from the University of Texas at Dallas. At Pitt, he has taught many noncredit courses that cover using the Internet and all levels of Internet software development. He was drawn to working with Bruce Dobler because it was an opportunity to bring advanced technology to a traditionally non-computer-oriented audience.

William Condon (bcondon@wsu.edu) is director of writing programs and associate professor of English at Washington State University, where he continues his research in portfolio-based writing assessment and computer-enhanced writing instruction. His latest projects include a textbook, *Writing the Information Superhighway*, with Wayne Butler; and a book-length study of college-level portfolio assessment, co-authored with Liz Hamp-Lyons.

Robert Davis (davisr@eou.edu) is assistant professor at Eastern Oregon University, where he coordinates the writing program. He and Mark Shadle have presented and written collaboratively on "Multi-Work": multi-vocal/genre/media/disciplinary/cultural texts and the pedagogical approaches that led to their creation. At Eastern Oregon, Davis is leading a team of faculty proposing a Multimedia Studies degree program. He is chair-elect of the Oregon Writing and English Advisory Committee and was co-chair of the 1997 Oregon Conference on Composition and Rhetoric. Davis received his M.A. and Ph.D. from the Ohio State University.

Michael Day (mday@silver.sdsmt.edu) is associate professor of English at South Dakota School of Mines and Technology, where he teaches composition, technical communications, and computers in society. He received a B.A. in English from Dartmouth College, an M.A. in English from the University of Wyoming, and a Ph.D. in rhetoric from the University of California, Berkeley. Day is the author of *Stylex*, a sentence revision software program, and several articles and chapters in the field of computers and writing. With Trent Batson, Day is the author of "The Network Based Writing Classroom: The ENFI Idea" in *Computer Mediated Communication and the Online Classroom*, volume 2, and with Rebecca Rickly and Eric Crump, he is the author of "Creating a Virtual Academic Community: Scholarship and Community in Wide Area Multiple User Synchronous Discussions" in *Computer Networking and Scholarship in the Twenty-first Century University*. He currently serves as chair of the National Council of Teachers of English Assembly on Computers in English, and co-chair of the Great Plains Alliance for Computers and Writing.

Bruce Dobler (bgd1+@pitt.edu) is the author of two "documentary" novels (*Icepick* and *The Last Rush North*) and an "as-told-to" memoir of a counterfeiter (*I Made It Myself*). He is also a freelance magazine writer. Dobler has been teaching a course in Web publishing at the University of Pittsburgh for three years, has offered public workshops on using the Internet for business, education, and personal enjoyment, and has worked as a consultant and online writer with a local Web provider.

Theresa Henley Doerfler (Tdoerfler@aol.com) received a Ph.D. in English from the Ohio State University. Her dissertation, *The Subject(s) of Diversity: Defining Electronic Discourse in Composition Classrooms*, is an ethnographic study of two computer-supported composition classes focused on multicultural issues. She was coordinator of Ohio State's Computers in Composition and Literature Program from 1994 to 1995.

Dene Grigar (dene@eaze.net) is assistant professor of English at Texas Woman's University, where she teaches composition in a networked computer lab, as well as upper-division literature courses focusing on Greek epic and modernist poetry. She is co-editing a collection entitled *New Worlds, New Words: Exploring Pathways for Writing about and in Electronic Environments*. She received an M.Ed. in curriculum and instruction from the University of Houston and an M.A. and a Ph.D. in humanities from the University of Texas at Dallas.

Susanmarie Harrington (sharrin@iupui.edu) is assistant professor of English and director of Placement and Assessment at Indiana University–Purdue University, Indianapolis, where she also chairs the department's Writing Coordinating Committee. She holds an M.A. and a Ph.D. from the University of Michigan. Her research interests include teaching with technology and writing assessment; she is currently at work on a series of articles about contemporary assessment theory and the role of reflection in placement testing. She teaches a range of writing courses, from basic writing to composition theory, as well as linguistic courses in language history and usage.

Gail Hawisher (hawisher@uiuc.edu), with Paul LeBlanc, Charles Moran, and Cynthia Selfe, is author of *Computers and the Teaching of Writing in Higher Education, 1979–1994: A History*. She is also co-editor of several books focusing on a range of theoretical, pedagogical, and research questions related to literacy and technology. With Cynthia Selfe, she edits *Computers and Composition: An International Journal for Teachers of Writing*. Their newest projects are a college reader entitled *Literacy, Technology, and Society: Confronting the Issues*, and a collection of essays entitled *Passions, Pedagogies, and 21st Century Technologies*. Her articles have appeared in *College English, College Composition and Com-*

munication, and *Written Communication,* among others. She is currently a member of the MLA Committee on Computers and Emerging Technologies and is assistant chair of the College Section of the National Council of Teachers of English.

Tharon W. Howard (tharon@hubcap.clemson.edu) is associate professor of English and teaches in the Master of Arts in Professional Communication program at Clemson University. Howard directs the Document Design Laboratory where—in addition to producing flyers, brochures, scholarly journals, and books for the College of Architecture, Arts, and the Humanities—he teaches MAPC graduate students to create and maintain digital publications on the Web and CD-ROM. Howard also directs the Clemson University Usability Testing Facility, where he conducts research aimed at improving and creating new interface and document designs in industry. He designed and directs Clemson's Multimedia Authoring Teaching and Research Facility, where faculty and graduate students in architecture, arts, and humanities learn to develop multimedia productions and have an opportunity to experiment with emerging instructional technologies. As the past chair of the Instructional Technology Committee for the National Council of Teachers of English and as co-director of the Carolinas Alliance for Computers and Writing, Howard has a commitment to the integration of instructional technologies into the classroom. He is the author of *A Rhetoric of Electronic Communities,* co-editor of *Electronic Networks: Crossing Boundaries, Creating Communities,* and has published articles in journals such as *Technical Communication, Technical Communication Quarterly,* and *Computers and Composition.*

Joan Huntley (joan-huntley@uiowa.edu) is project leader for the Instructional Technology Initiative, sponsored by Information Technology Services at the University of Iowa. She is also a special technology assistant to the Dean's Office at the College of Business. Most recently she was visiting professor at California State University at Monterey Bay, where, in addition to teaching in the Institute for Communication Science and Technology, she helped launch a new faculty development program. With a doctorate in instructional design, Huntley started Second Look Computing, an innovative new media development center for the University of Iowa campus. She has helped design projects in fields ranging from art history to pediatrics to anthropology. She has served on numerous review panels evaluating instructional software.

Fred Kemp (f.kemp@ttacs.ttu.edu) is associate professor of English at Texas Tech University, where he directs both First-Year Composition and Computer-Based Writing Instruction. He is a past member of the NCTE Instructional Technology Committee and past chair of the CCCC Computers in Composition Committee. He is co-director of the Alliance for Computers and Writing, for whom he manages a set of World Wide Web pages. Kemp is also founder and current president of The Daedalus Group, Inc., a company prominent in the development of educational software, and is co-author of DIWE, the "Daedalus Integrated Writing Environment" (1990 EDUCOM/ NCRIPTAL award winner for best writing software). The Internet e-mail discussion lists he has founded include Megabyte University (MBU-L), ACW-L, and WCENTER. He has written and presented extensively about computer-based writing pedagogies.

Dawn Rodrigues (drodrigues@utb1.utb.edu) has worked at several universities in the last decade, including Colorado State University, where she directed the Computer-Assisted Composition Lab, and Kennesaw State University, where she developed several graduate courses in computers and communications for the Master's program. At the University of Texas at Brownsville, she is teaching composition and technical writing courses and working on distance learning projects. She holds an M.A. and a Ph.D. in English, both from Kent State University in Kent, Ohio. Her publications include *Teaching Writing with a Word Processor* (with Raymond Rodrigues); *Computers in English and the Language Arts: The Challenge of Teacher Education* (with Cynthia Selfe); and several composition textbooks.

Cynthia L. Selfe (cyselfe@mtu.edu) is professor of Composition and Communication and chair of the Humanities Department at Michigan Technological University. A past chair of the Conference on College Composition and Communication, Selfe has served as co-editor of the *CCCC Bibliography on Composition and Rhetoric* (with Gail Hawisher) and has authored a number of journal articles and books on computer use in composition classrooms, including *Computer-Assisted Instruction in Composition: Create Your Own* and *Creating a Computer-Supported Writing Facility*. Selfe has also co-edited several collections of essays on computers, including *Literacy and Computers: The Complications of Teaching and Learning with Computers* (with Susan Hilligoss), *Evolving Perspectives on Computers in Composition Studies: Questions for the 1990s* (with Gail Hawisher), *Computers in English and*

Language Arts: The Challenge of Teacher Education (with Dawn Rodrigues and William Oates), *Critical Perspectives on Computers and Composition Instruction* (with Gail Hawisher), and *Computers and Writing: Theory, Research, and Practice* (with Deborah Holdstein).

In 1983, Selfe founded the journal *Computers and Composition* with Kate Kiefer; she continues to edit that journal with Gail Hawisher. In 1989, Selfe and Hawisher founded the Computers and Composition Press to support the publication of books on computers and their uses in English classrooms. Selfe is the winner of the 1996 EDUCOM Medal Award for innovation in educational technology use, the first woman and the first English teacher to be accorded that honor.

This book was typeset in Palatino by Electronic Imaging.
Typefaces used on the cover were Delphian and Stone Sans.
The book was printed by Versa Press.